Paul

1930

SELECTED ESSAYS
OF
J. B. BURY

Cambridge University Press
Fetter Lane, London
New York
Bombay, Calcutta, Madras
Toronto
Macmillan

Tokyo
Maruzen Company, Ltd

J. B. Bury

SELECTED ESSAYS

OF

J. B. BURY

Edited by

HAROLD TEMPERLEY

CAMBRIDGE
AT THE UNIVERSITY PRESS
1930

DEDICATED
TO
THE INTERNATIONAL CONGRESS OF
HISTORICAL STUDIES
MEETING IN CAMBRIDGE
28–30 APRIL 1930

TABLE OF CONTENTS

SELECTED ESSAYS OF J. B. BURY

FOREWORD

THE following ten essays illustrate some of the various phases of Professor Bury's thought. They have been recommended for publication by a number of historians, whose names, apart from those resident in Cambridge, are given on page xiii. The first five pieces offer for the first time within the limits of one volume a systematic survey of Bury's views on the general aims of history. If other justification for republication were needed it might be sought in the facts that only one out of all these essays is still in print, that some of them are not accessible even in well-known libraries, and that others are not known even to some scholars. The third essay, for example, which throws a most important light on Bury's historical ideas, was brought to my notice by Professor W. R. Sorley and was unknown to the compiler of Bury's Bibliography. Inquiry has shown that several other essays are very little known.

Some of these pieces, for example the fourth, sixth, seventh and eighth, make an appeal beyond the scholar to the general reader. And this is even more the case with the ninth essay on the Roman Emperors from Basil II to Isaac Komnênos. The period, so obscure to most readers, is one of much importance and more interest. In this early essay Bury shows a power of mordant wit and of characterisation less evident in his later work, and the portrait of Basil the Bulgar-slayer, the lives of Zôê and Theodôra, and the intrigues of Patriarchs and eunuchs afford ample scope for the exercise of such talents.

The essays are printed exactly as published. As they represent different periods of his historical career, there are differences in such matters as nomenclature, and also in treatment or interpretation of the facts or theories of history. In order that the reader may keep this point in mind, each essay or lecture has the date of publication or delivery attached to it. In the *Introduction* (*pp. xv–xxxii*) I have tried to sketch the chief stages in the evolution of his historical ideas.

This collection was originally designed to be issued simultaneously, or in connexion with the Bury Bibliography published by Mr Norman Baynes at the University Press in the autumn of 1929. Ultimately this project was not realised but the fact has enabled me to take full advantage of the erudite work of my predecessor.

I have to thank the Editors of the *Cambridge Medieval History*, the Editor of the *Quarterly*, the Editor of the *Morning Post*, Messrs Houghton Mifflin and the *Rationalist Press Association* for permission to reproduce some of the essays. These acknowledgements are made separately in the text.

The portrait of Professor Bury here given was taken late in 1913 or early in 1914. It was published in the *Cambridge Historical Journal*, vol. II, No. 1, of 1927, and is here reproduced by courtesy of the Editorial Committee.

H. T.

LIST OF HISTORIANS SIGNING THE RE-COMMENDATION TO THE CAMBRIDGE UNIVERSITY PRESS FOR THE PUBLICATION OF THE ESSAYS IN THIS VOLUME

Austria
A. Dopsch

Czecho-Slovakia
J. Šušta

France
M. Lhéritier

Germany
Karl Brandi

Hungary
Henrik Marczali

Italy
G. de Sanctis

Norway
Halvdan Koht

Poland
Bronislav Dembiński

Rumania
N. Jorga

United States
W. S. Ferguson
C. H. Haskins
Waldo Leland
Roger B. Merriman

ABBREVIATIONS, REFERENCES, ETC.

pp. where given in italics, these are references to pages in this work.

Baynes, i.e. N. H. Baynes. *A Bibliography of the Works of J. B. Bury, compiled with a Memoir.* Cambridge Univ. Press, 1929.

Notes where placed in square brackets with a star or stars [**] are by the Editor. All others are by Professor Bury himself.

INTRODUCTION

THE HISTORICAL IDEAS OF J. B. BURY

§ I

"History is a science, no less and no more". This famous sentence, emphasised in Bury's *Inaugural*,* has greatly obscured his thought to contemporaries. It at once produced a controversy and one into which Bury never really entered. He made no reply at the time to the campaign in the periodicals, and it was only after several years that he pointed out one obvious misinterpretation. He doubtless trusted that study of his other utterances would reveal his real ideas, and perhaps forgot that they were scattered in different publications. His works on the method and purpose of history have now been assembled, and the three first essays here printed seem to make the pattern on the carpet clear.

It was as a classical scholar that he first became acquainted with history. And as those who attended his lectures on the Use of Authorities will know, the consequences of this approach to the subject were momentous. For in classical times Clio was regarded as a Muse, and History therefore took her place as a branch of rhetoric. This view greatly distressed Bury and he gave several instances of its unfortunate result. Thus one classical writer would borrow the details of a battle from another, just because they happened to be picturesque and despite the fact that they related to a totally different period or event. He considered it one of the chief

[* *pp.* 4, 9, 19. It is not, I think, sufficiently considered by English readers that the word "science", as applied to history, has been adopted from the French where its meaning is not quite the same as in English.]

faults of the Renaissance, that its historians imitated the classical models in making history the instrument of rhetoric. It was the way of authors under Queen Elizabeth, who pilfered a scene or a character from an Italian drama to serve the purposes of an English one. The result might be magnificent, and might be art. It could not be history, and it showed the mischief of regarding history as a rhetorical art.

The first step forward was to cut history loose from rhetoric. For "so long as history was regarded as an art, the sanctions of truth and accuracy could not be severe" and "history is not a branch of literature". In writing thus (*pp.* 6, 9), Bury perhaps "strains the note", as he says Acton did. But it is easy to see why. A man with strong scientific instincts, beginning his studies with classical texts and orators, is apt to see history differently from one who begins it with state-papers and dry-as-dust historians. To the first rhetoric is a cloud, to the second a sunbeam. Bury's early vision was obscured by a purple haze of oratory, and he had to disperse it before truth could shine through. That is why he wished to put Clio in a laboratory, before allowing her to declaim in an Academy.

§ 2

The release of history from rhetoric was but the first step. Only one degree less evil than the rhetorical view of history were the various pragmatical conceptions associated with it. History was not a body of concrete maxims, supplying examples from which ordinary men could learn to be good and statesmen to be great. To learn morality or success from history was little better than to use it as an instrument of eloquence, and he regretfully records that Polybius and Thucydides, "the two greatest of the ancient historians", like Machiavelli, held that "the use of studying history was instruction in the art of politics" (*p.* 24). Another influence retarding the conception of history as a science was the weight of authority and church tradition. All these "political and ethical encumbrances" hindered the growth of a scientific method. Under the pressure of such circumstance even a scholar like Tillemont, whom Bury followed Gibbon in admiring, could do little. He could amass erudition and heap up incident, or produce "a collection of annals". But such works proceeded on no true system or plan. For "facts must be connected", and "I cannot imagine the slightest importance in facts or sequences of facts, unless they mean something in terms of reason". "Reason" could only be found in an author who pursued a method of selecting and analysing his facts according to some rational or scientific principle.

§ 3

Scientific method was foreshadowed by the rationalists like Gibbon and Voltaire, and established by technically trained investigators like Wolf, the critic of Homer, Niebuhr, the critic of Livy, and by Ranke, the founder of the modern school, basing its results on scientific dissection and reconstruction of authorities. But even Ranke, though a great Master, was not fully emancipated and was deeply influenced by two forces regarded by Bury as dangerous to a true conception of history. The first of these, nationalism, supplied a powerful motive for historical investigation and "quickened" the processes of study. Yet national and patriotic prejudice was a grave danger especially when, for purely political reasons, it stressed "inspiring and golden periods" at the expense of others historically more valuable and instructive. And from this "tendencious" nationalism Ranke was not wholly free.

A tendency to which Ranke was also prone was "the influence of philosophy and more particularly of the philosophy of history". On such philosophers Bury is rather severe. He regards Hegel, Comte and Krause as having constructed iron beds into which they forced living victims, or as founders of systems based on *à priori* conceptions without inductive value. He is likewise critical of all those, and they were not merely philosophers, "who so naively assume that the ideas which are within the horizon of *their* minds are the ultimate ideas to be sighted by man, the last ports to be visited in his voyage down the stream of time" (*p.* 50). He instances the thinker who regarded Christianity as the final religion, Prussia as the final state and his own Hegelianism as the final philosophy. He enforces these instances by asking how we can really believe that the present idea of freedom is the ultimate one, or that the present idea of nationality is "an end in itself or more than a phase in evolution" (*p.* 58). A generation later, when freedom is contracting into order and nationality expanding beyond the limits of country or of race, we can see the pregnant wisdom of this suggestion of 1904.

§ 4

Bury therefore held the position that the "doctrine of historical relativity applies no less to his [the historian's] own judgments than to other facts".* New facts might be discovered and new judgments delivered at any time, and he was himself the living illustration of the process. Between 1889 and 1923 he entirely remodelled his conceptions of the development of the later Roman Empire

[* *Ancient Greek Historians* (1909), p. 252.]

in the light of new materials and fresh interpretations. His judgments also altered with time. Thus a view of history that is purely unitary is shown in the first three essays here given, all written before 1909. By 1924 he certainly had begun to favour a pluralistic inter-pretation.* Again in 1904 he quoted Tacitus and Treitschke as useful examples of prejudice, but his letter of 1926 asserts that freedom from bias in history is not possible nor even desirable. For prejudices alone "engage the interest of the world" (*pp.* 70–1). He had thus reached a position the exact opposite of the Greek "who would have said that the judgment of a wise man at any time might be final or absolutely valid".** In his view a historian's judgment was of permanent interest only as an illustration of his epoch, and finality and impartiality were mistaken ideals.

§ 5

The chauvinistic influences of nationalism, the shadowy conceptions of philosophy, not only affected the im-partiality of Ranke, but diverted and muddied the course of historical investigation. And these influences tended to obscure the light already thrown by eigh-teenth-century philosophers like Turgot and Condorcet. For these men had developed the Idea of Progress, a conception which heralded the dawn of true history and led ultimately to its renovation. It was the first attempt to give a true unity and synthesis to history of the modern type, the first threading of beads on a string stout enough to resist pressure. The idea of progress certainly helped to link up the past with the present and to give a meaning and a name to modern history. For when

[* *Idea of Progress* (1924), p. 368, *note* to p. 302.]
[** *Ancient Greek Historians* (1909), p. 253.]

the improvement, and not the decadence, of the world became a dogma the past ages yielded in interest and importance to the present and still more to the future. Thus the idea of progress, though having no actual connexion with evolution, served a similar purpose in promoting the conception of the unity of history. But it was not until Darwin appeared on the scene that the victory was finally won. Evolution, in Bury's view, was the final determining influence in establishing the unity of history, in making it into a science, and in relating it to other sciences. Its supreme achievement was to realise that "our conception of the past" is "itself a factor in guiding and moulding our evolution and must become a factor of greater and increasing potency". This is "a new stage in the growth of the human mind" (*p.* 12).

§ 6

The transformation of history into a science meant the enlargement of its sphere and the extension of its influence to the furthest boundary of the earth. Ranke erred by confining history to politics, and Seeley by extending it only to political science. Bury would intrude it into every domain. For the temporary purpose of "isolating the phenomena" or for research, he might confine history to one aspect or to one period. But as all ages of history are of importance in the cosmic process, so all activities of man should be the province of the historian. He must look beyond governments to peoples, beyond laws to superstitions, beyond religions to folklore and the arts, he must study every intellectual, material and emotional aspect of human life and society. In his *Inaugural* Bury points to a passage in the *Antigone* as "the first amazed meditation of man" on what he had wrought (*p.* 11). One famous passage of this chorus suggests for a moment that political activities ranked high among the inventions of man.

καὶ φθέγμα καὶ ἀνεμόεν
φρόνημα καὶ ἀστυνόμους ὀργὰς ἐδιδάξατο.*

But a closer examination shows that even here the emphasis is on social rather than political inventiveness. In the whole passage there are some two or three lines devoted to the city state, and some fifty to man's mastery over beast and bird, earth, wind and sea and all other creative activities. Because of this very width of view "broad as ten thousand beeves" the passage exactly expresses Bury's view of the range of history.

§ 7

It is astonishing that Bury's *Inaugural* was interpreted by one distinguished critic as a pleading that Byzantine history was superior in importance to every other.** In fact he thought that history really became of decisive importance some fifty years after Byzantium and the Roman Empire perished together. It is even more extraordinary that the editor of Gibbon should hold that history began to be of real importance a few years from the date at which his master ceased writing it.

Those who knew Bury well, at Cambridge, could never have been in any doubt as to his preference for modern history. It was evident enough to anyone who heard his lectures on the Use of Authorities. It was

[* *Antigone*, lines 354–5. "Speech, wind-swift thought and all the moods that moved a State, hath he [man] taught himself". Jebb, *Antigone* [1888], p. 74 *note*, points out these are "feelings which lead men to organise *social* life, and to uphold the *social* order by their loyalty". Italics my own.]

[** Professor Carless Davis, *v. Baynes*, p. 112 and *note*.]

equally evident to anyone who was present at the History Board when the reform of the Historical Tripos was being discussed.* But, though the fact was certain, the reasons were not at first evident. Acton called modern history "the prize of all history", because he saw in it the improvement of the world under divine guidance and the ascending movement of man as the centuries quickened. Bury did not admit the existence of supernatural agency in history, or think it a demonstration of ethics, or even of progress. But he agreed with his great predecessor in regarding the study of modern times as "the most pressing of all".

Bury's reasons for his preference were intensely characteristic. He regarded modern history as the only period in which the records were abundant and certain, and therefore as the only period in which history could be set forth in its all-embracing range. You cannot portray an age in all its aspects unless you are "in direct relation with it". "The spiritual boundaries of the ancient and mediaeval worlds" were set too far back for us ever wholly to pass them, as his own long and sad experience had taught him. In the century and half between Theodosius and Justinian "no full account of a single battle is extant". And there were endless fragmentary inscriptions and untrustworthy chroniclers casting their fitful and broken lights upon dim emperors and shadowy events. It was not in such sources that you could read the minds and hearts of men. Only abundant records enable the historian to see with the eyes of contemporaries. "Sympathetic

[* Bury made a great effort to increase the amount of modern history studied in Part II of the Historical Tripos at Cambridge. He first proposed that two out of the five papers (excluding essay) in Part II should be devoted to Modern History Outlines. When the Board confined that study to one paper, Bury proposed that it should have double weight, i.e. receive twice the marks of any other paper.]

appreciation" is only possible to those near enough to understand the atmosphere, the passions, *les derniers frémissements* of an age. That was the only way to "see Shelley plain". It is the modern man's duty to posterity—above all—to study and to describe "the emancipatory movements of the sixteenth, seventeenth and eighteenth centuries". He states elsewhere that the "great movements of thought of the nineteenth century" are as remarkable and important as those of the sixteenth, and as "new and striking a departure as any to which our records go back". Because they give the true history of the freedom of the spirit, and because their records are fuller than any other, the last four centuries are superior in importance to all others.

§ 8

Bury viewed Darwin as having delivered history from its patriotic, philosophic, rhetorical and pragmatical obsessions. He believed the scientific method and "the dry light of science" to be essential to history. But he is very anxious to show that the analogy between history and other sciences must not be overemphasised. For instance he is at pains to draw a distinction between history and anthropology (*p.* 32 *note*). He is careful to demonstrate that human society is not an organism at least in the scientific sense (*p.* 28 *note*). He wrote that a man was not a historian if his "interest was primarily ethical". He rejected the idea of God as revealing himself in history or as altering its course, for that assumption postulated a *Deus ex machina*. And he did not, like some scientists, assume that energy or progress is a substitute for God. The idea of progress was a useful one but it was not strictly scientific nor identical with the Darwinian conceptions. "Evolution itself, it must be remembered, does not necessarily mean, as applied to Society, the movement of man to a desirable good. It is a neutral scientific conception, compatible either with optimism or pessimism. According to different estimates it may appear to be a cruel sentence or a guarantee of steady amelioration, and it has been actually interpreted in both ways".* Bury speaks indeed of the "countless stairs" man must ascend in the future, and believed perhaps that the movement would be upward. But his belief in the future was rather a hope than a conviction. And even if he had felt a conviction, he would not have maintained that it was scientifically defensible.

§ 9

Bury laid down that history was a science to be studied by scientific methods but he did not believe that it proceeded wholly along fixed lines and according to mathematical laws. As history never repeated itself the past history of man could not be exactly deduced, nor the future precisely predicted. The accidents of history were such as to disturb any calculations. Great men, and he instances Alexander, Frederic and Napoleon, in one sphere, St Paul, Plato or Spinoza in another, had power enough to disturb or divert the stream of history. Their exceptional brains might be explained as being due to scientific causes, but such explanations did not supply us with a calculus for the future. The great man is not only an accident, but an unforeseen and extremely disturbing accident. He is sufficient in himself to prevent even the special demesnes of economic and social history, "where generalisation is most fruitful", from

[* *Idea of Progress* (1920), pp. 335-6.]

being wholly subject to general laws. Even in these demesnes the great man can intrude his imperious and disturbing personality. "The heel of Achilles in all historical speculations of this class has been the role of the individual" (*p.* 41).

Not only does the great man himself affect history, but he is himself affected by the exceptional events and persons he may encounter. He is subject to an influence, at once obvious and attractive and apparently trivial. Bury speaks of "the shape of Cleopatra's nose" and "the pretty face of Anne Boleyn" as changing the currents of history. The first instance he owes, of course, to Pascal; the latter perhaps to Canning, who once convulsed the House of Commons by quoting the verse

> When Love could teach a monarch to be wise,
> And Gospel-light first dawned from Boleyn's eyes.

These two amusing examples are illustrations of that theory of "contingency" which bulks so large in Bury's later studies. He came finally to assert that general causes did not usually explain the great events of history. And he thus reached, by another road, a conclusion or lack of conclusion which is often held by great practical men. Few of these will admit that the causes of great events are simple or ascertainable, and some, like Frederic the Great, ascribe everything to chance. Those who are steeped in practical affairs know how blind an instrument of destiny even a great man may be.

§ 10

The best application of Bury's idea is to be found in his view of the causes of the fall of the Roman Empire. In his earliest study he adopted conventional explanations. In his latest (1923) he adopted the "contingency" theory throughout.* If there was any cause of the fall of the Roman Empire, it was that the German barbarians "peacefully penetrated" it, and finally took so many posts in the army that they rendered discipline impossible. "This was, of course, a consequence of the decline in military spirit, and of depopulation, in the old civilised Mediterranean countries".** But he asserts that "this policy need not have led to the dismemberment of the Empire" and that the barbarian infiltration is explained not by "any general considerations", but by "the actual events".***

It was the conflux of coincidences which proved decisive. The first contingent cause was the invasion of the Huns from Asia, a "historical surprise" and resulting from "events in Central Asia strictly independent of events in Europe".**** It was an "Asian mystery" how these Huns arose and poured into Europe. And to this first contingency was added a second, for the valiant Goths fled before them and poured into the Roman Empire. In their flight they met and defeated a Roman army and slew a Roman Emperor. This great defeat was mainly due to the contingent accident that the Roman Emperor was incompetent and rash. Theodosius, who succeeded Valens, set "the unfortunate precedent" of settling the Visigoths

[* I follow here the line of thought in my earlier (and anonymous) treatment of this subject in *Cambridge Historical Journal*, vol. II, No. 1 (1927), p. 162 *note*, and pp. 195, 196.

The *History of the Later Roman Empire*, vol. I, chap. III (1889), gives some general causes. An article in the *Quarterly*, 1920, vol. CXCII, follows a similar line (*v.* Appendix, *pp.* 231–42, for a part of this). The general causation is abandoned for the contingency theory in the *Later Roman Empire* (1923), vol. I, pp. 303–13. These views are explained more at length in *The Invasion of Europe by the Barbarians* (1928), *passim*. Baynes, pp. 74–6, should be consulted.]

[** *Later Roman Empire* (1923), I, 312.]
[*** *Later Roman Empire*, I, 311.]
[**** *v. infra*, *pp.* 62–3.]

—a new barbarian people—as a unit inside his borders. The fact that he died at the age of fifty was "a third contingency", for had he lived longer his great ability might have averted the evils of his blunder. But a fourth event, dependent on causes which had nothing to do with the condition of the Empire, was the mediocrity of his two sons who divided his Empire. The Eastern Arcadius was incompetent, and the Western Honorius was "feeble-minded". The final or fifth event was the fact that in the West poor Honorius was controlled by a German, Stilicho. His character is "a puzzle", and he admitted barbarians wholesale into the Roman Empire till he brought disaster on himself and it. When he died the mischief was done, Italy, Gaul and Spain were overrun by barbarians and "his Roman successors could not undo the results of events which need never have happened". It is thus that the true historian delicately poises his conclusion.

§ 11

In some respects Bury's mind was a hard one to read, for he possessed a humour which was not always appreciated. It would be a mistake for instance to lay stress on the famous remark that a historian did not do his duty unless he changed his mind every two years. No one indeed was more open to new influences, but one may conjecture that five or ten years would be actually more exact. And it was not only in remarks lightly dropped in conversation that he showed this archness. The famous published injunction to statesmen to "dare to be unjust" is a similar instance. The Saxon is not perhaps the fittest judge of such irony. But this side was not the only one which made it difficult to detect his real views. As he grew older it became a duty with him, so far as

possible, to avoid giving his personal impressions of a
historical problem. In his lectures on the Use of
Authorities he preferred telling you the way Ranke had
handled a problem of historical criticism to explaining
how he would handle it himself. On one occasion he
discoursed to the "Junior Historians" at Cambridge
on Lamprecht. He gave a most illuminating description
of that scholar's philosophy but left us at the end without
any clue as to his own judgment on its soundness. It
was not until I saw his written views (*v. p.* 39 *note*)
that it became evident that he regarded them with more
favour and sympathy than we had suspected. It was
not that he did not have strong views but that he feared
to disturb the judgment of others by expressing them.
He did not, for instance, believe in expressing moral
judgments when writing history, but he formed some
of his own none the less, as notably on religious
questions. Once when I was consulting him privately
about some points of German history, he told me he
thought that Frederic the Great's invasion of Silesia in
1740 was much more justifiable than most historians
had admitted. "After all", said he, "Austria had wiped
her boots on Prussia up till then".

§ 12

It is strange that it should have been ever thought that
Bury was opposed in principle to the literary art.
Several of the essays here printed, and particularly those
on the Byzantine Emperors, will sufficiently dispel this
illusion. In certain respects his sympathies were sin-
gularly drawn to works of imagination which were not
strictly historical. Thus he greatly admired some of the
works of the great Hungarian romancer Jokai, notably
A Christian but a Roman, and *Halil the Pedlar.* The last he

INTRODUCTION

once told me called up Constantinople for you as no
other book did and "made you feel as if you were there
and in the Arabian Nights". He was also much struck
by Eötvös—*The Village Notary*—as a picture of society
and life in early nineteenth-century Hungary. And in
the more legitimate historical field he was an admirer,
though not a disciple, of Treitschke and, as we see on
p. 18, he fully appreciated the literary flavour given by
prejudice or bias. He deprecated "the pernicious influence of rhetoric. One does not mean by that, the
cultivation of a clear, agreeable and rhythmical style;
one means the tendency to seek first of all and almost
at any cost what may be called rhetorical effects"
(*Ancient Greek Historians* [1909], p. 165). He thus insisted
that the discovery of truth was a scientific process, but
both admitted and desired an artistic presentation of the
results of research. It is difficult, however, to know
where one process ends and the other begins. Bury himself speaks of "sympathetic imagination" and "psychological imagination" as necessary to the interpretation
of the past. And this kind of sympathy or imagination
can hardly be purely scientific. Indeed there are undoubtedly cases in which the truth can only be ascertained by methods which are not purely scientific. For
instance the imagination of Maitland seems to discover
truth by methods at least as artistic as they are scientific.
There is in every way a reconciliation between the
opposed points of view due largely to the disappearance
of the old protagonists. The old scientific historians, who
regarded men as engines and progress as mechanical,
have disappeared taking with them the purely rhetorical historians of the old type. It is not necessary in
1930 to insist on the aspect of history as a science in the
way Bury did in 1903, for historians seem to be much
more agreed in their views than they were then. But

the circumstances under which Bury stated his doctrine, and the consequences which he deduced from it, will always remain of great typical importance.

§ 13

Science and Art have found a meeting ground in History to-day. But there remains a certain difference of emphasis between literary and scientific historians. The former tend primarily to generalisation and the latter to research. And the growth of Bury's historical ideas was undoubtedly from the one to the other. He is not afraid of certain generalisations even in his latest years. In 1919 he said that Byzantium produced "a succession of able and hard-working rulers such as cannot, I think, be paralleled in the annals of any other state during so long a period" (*p.* 122). In 1923 he said that a Byzantine army was *never* beaten except when its general was incompetent (*p.* 222). But he undoubtedly came to favour contingency at the expense of causation and to believe that many generalisations of to-day would become the fallacies of to-morrow. Holding this view of progress and the future, he was ready to think that the discovery of truth and the collection and interpretation of facts were the greatest service we can render to posterity. And it was for posterity and the future that he worked. From this point of view research, or the discovery of new truths or facts, was all important. He wished to revise the Historical Tripos at Cambridge not so as to make it an instrument of general education but as a means of promoting or training students for research.* To Bury that was the all-in-all. There was no project in his Cambridge career in which he took so

[* It is I think misleading to say (*v. Baynes*, p. 49) that Bury "had no admiration" for the Cambridge Tripos. If the view in the text is correct no History Honours Examination in any University would have satisfied

much interest as the foundation of the Cambridge Historical Society and the *Cambridge Historical Journal*. He was the first President of the Society, a member of the Editorial Board and a contributor to the *Journal*. The reason of his deep interest was that both were to be devoted to research. He told me more than once that the future of Cambridge historical study depended upon the development of these projects. And he said in his *Inaugural* that research is "the highest duty of Universities".

In the England of to-day it is unfortunately neither superfluous to insist on the importance of research in history nor to explain the value Bury attached to it. His wide outlook on historical development in other lands had taught him that history is too often a medium for patriotic propaganda. In such cases the historians work under difficulties we cannot conceive. They are sometimes the instruments of politicians, and are not always bold enough to tell the truth. He used to quote in his lectures how every Hungarian historian denies that the Rumans are descended from the Romans, every Rumanian historian asserts that they are. In Macedonia Serb historians reckon over a million Serbs, Bulgarians find not a single one in the country. In such cases only a fearless regard for truth based on research can emancipate men from prejudice.* And if we turn from East to West and seek light over the ocean we find that research in American history is the living example of

him as it would not sufficiently have promoted research. He certainly thought, as did everyone else, that the pre-1911 Tripos needed reform. But when it was reformed in 1911, he said in the Senate House, "I approve of a great many features of the new scheme", and he instanced the transfer of Special Periods to Part II as "an enormous gain". This Tripos is still in existence. Bury's interesting proposal about "set books" in connexion with examinations is well described by *Baynes*, p. 50, and was in fact again a suggestion for training researchers.]

[* *v.* especially *The Ancient Greek Historians* (1909), pp. 253–4.]

this. It has been shown almost wholly by the researches of American historians in the last thirty years that the Mother Country was by no means so tyrannical in its attitude as transpontine orators had asserted for a century. The knowledge thus acquired by scholarship is gradually penetrating to text-books in elementary schools in America. The result has been a definite softening of the old bitterness between England and America which, so far at least as educated leaders are concerned, will be permanent and lasting. There is no nobler victory achieved by research. The same methods are waiting to be adopted to a dozen other thorny problems. They have been applied to the origins of the World War of 1914, and are already producing appreciable results. It is not easy to see limits to the influence of well-directed research in assuaging national passions and in solving international problems. It is literally true to say that new forces may be set in motion by the historian from his study to-day just as they are released by the scientist from his laboratory. And it is some such thought as this which Bury had in mind, when he told us that "the study of history and the method of studying it are facts of ecumenical importance" and that "research might move the world". He was careful to add that results could not be immediate and that "short profits and quick returns" could not serve as a maxim for scholars. One day doubtless England will awake to this truth and will endow and encourage research on a scale comparable with that in some other countries in Europe. When this day dawns Bury's message will be understood and he will be seen in his true proportions as a historian.

HAROLD TEMPERLEY

I

GENERAL SCOPE AND METHOD OF HISTORY

1. THE SCIENCE OF HISTORY*

IN saying that I come before you to-day with no little
trepidation, I am not uttering a mere conventional
profession of diffidence. There are very real reasons
for misgiving. My predecessor told you how formidable
he found this chair, illuminated as it is by the lustre of
the distinguished historian whom he succeeded. But if
it was formidable then, how much more formidable is it
to-day! The terrors which it possessed for Lord Acton
have been enhanced for his successor.

In a home of historical studies where so much thought
is spent on their advancement, one can hardly hope to
say any new thing touching those general aspects of
history which most naturally invite attention in an inaugural lecture. It may be appropriate and useful now
and again to pay a sort of solemn tribute to the dignity
and authority of a great discipline or science, by reciting
some of her claims and her laws, or by reviewing the
measures of her dominion; and on this occasion, in this
place, it might perhaps seem to be enough to honour
the science of history in this formal way, sprinkling, as
it were, with dutiful hands some grains of incense on her
altar.

Yet even such a tribute might possess more than a
formal significance, if we remember how recently it is—
within three generations, three short generations—that
history began to forsake her old irresponsible ways and
prepared to enter into her kingdom. In the story of
the nineteenth century, which has witnessed such far-
reaching changes in the geography of thought and in
the apparatus of research, no small nor isolated place

[* Delivered in the Divinity School, Cambridge, on January 26, 1903.]

belongs to the transformation and expansion of history. That transformation, however, is not yet complete. Its principle is not yet universally or unreservedly acknowledged. It is rejected in many places, or ignored, or unrealised. Old envelopes still hang tenaciously round the renovated figure, and students of history are confused, embarrassed, and diverted by her old traditions and associations. It has not yet become superfluous to insist that history is a science, no less and no more; and some who admit it theoretically hesitate to enforce the consequences which it involves. It is therefore, I think, almost incumbent on a professor to define, at the very outset, his attitude to the transformation of the idea of history which is being gradually accomplished; and an inaugural address offers an opportunity which, if he feels strongly the importance of the question, he will not care to lose.

And moreover I venture to think that it may be useful and stimulating for those who are beginning historical studies to realise vividly and clearly that the transformation which those studies are undergoing is itself a great event in the history of the world—that we are ourselves in the very middle of it, that we are witnessing and may share in the accomplishment of a change which will have a vast influence on future cycles of the world. I wish that I had been enabled to realise this when I first began to study history. I think it is important for all historical students alike—not only for those who may be drawn to make history the special work of their lives, but also for those who study it as part of a liberal education—to be fully alive and awake to the revolution which is slowly and silently progressing. It seems especially desirable that those who are sensible of the importance of the change and sympathise with it should declare and emphasise it; just because it is less patent to the vision

4

and is more perplexed by ancient theories and traditions, than those kindred revolutions which have been effected simultaneously in other branches of knowledge. History has really been enthroned and ensphered among the sciences; but the particular nature of her influence, her time-honoured association with literature, and other circumstances, have acted as a sort of vague cloud, half concealing from men's eyes her new position in the heavens.

The proposition that before the beginning of the last century the study of history was not scientific may be sustained in spite of a few exceptions. The works of permanent value, such as those of Muratori, Ducange, Tillemont, were achieved by dint of most laborious and conscientious industry, which commands our highest admiration and warmest gratitude: but it must be admitted that their criticism was sporadic and capricious. It was the criticism of sheer learning. A few stand on a higher level in so far as they were really alive to the need of bringing reason and critical doubt to bear on the material, but the systematised method which distinguishes a science was beyond the vision of all, except a few like Mabillon. Erudition has now been supplemented by scientific method, and we owe the change to Germany. Among those who brought it about, the names of Niebuhr and Ranke are pre-eminent. But there is another name which historical students should be slow to forget, the name of one who, though not a historian but a philologist, nevertheless gave a powerful stimulus to the introduction of critical methods which are now universally applied. Six years before the eighteenth century closed a modest book appeared at Halle, of which it is perhaps hardly a grave exaggeration to say that it is one of half-a-dozen which in the last three hundred years have exercised most effective influence upon thought. The work I mean is Wolf's *Prolegomena to Homer*. It launched upon the world a new engine—*donum exitiale Minervae*—which was soon to menace the walls of many a secure citadel. It gave historians the idea of a systematic and minute method of analysing their sources, which soon developed into the microscopic criticism, now recognised as indispensable.

All truths (to modify a saying of Plato) require the most exact methods; and closely connected with the introduction of a new method was the elevation of the standard of truth. The idea of a scrupulously exact conformity to facts was fixed, refined, and canonised; and the critical method was one of the means to secure it. There was indeed no historian since the beginning of things who did not profess that his sole aim was to present to his readers untainted and unpainted truth. But the axiom was loosely understood and interpreted, and the notion of truth was elastic. It might be difficult to assign to Puritanism and Rationalism and other causes their respective parts in crystallising that strict discrimination of the true and the false which is now so familiar to us that we can hardly understand insensibility to the distinction. It would be a most fruitful investigation to trace from the earliest ages the history of public opinion in regard to the meaning of falsehood and the obligation of veracity. About twenty years ago a German made a contribution to the subject by examining the evidence for the twelfth, thirteenth, and fourteenth centuries, and he showed how different were the views which men held then as to truth-telling and lying from those which are held to-day. Moreover, so long as history was regarded as an art, the sanctions of truth and accuracy could not be severe. The historians of ancient Rome display what historiography can become when it is associated with rhetoric. Though we may point to

6

individual writers who had a high ideal of accuracy at various ages, it was not till the scientific period began that laxity in representing facts came to be branded as criminal. Nowhere perhaps can we see the new spirit so self-conscious as in some of the letters of Niebuhr.

But a stricter standard of truth and new methods for the purpose of ascertaining truth were not enough to detach history from her old moorings. A new transfiguring conception of her scope and limits was needed, if she was to become an independent science. Such a conception was waiting to intervene, but I may lead up to it by calling to your recollection how history was affected by the political changes of Europe.

It was a strange and fortunate coincidence that the scientific movement in Germany should have begun simultaneously with another movement which gave a strong impetus to historical studies throughout Europe and enlisted men's emotions in their favour. The saying that the name of hope is remembrance* was vividly illustrated, on a vast scale, by the spirit of resurgent nationality which you know has governed, as one of the most puissant forces, the political course of the last century, and is still unexhausted. When the peoples, inspired by the national idea, were stirred to mould their destinies anew, and, looking back with longing to the more distant past, based upon it their claims for independence or for unity, history was one of the most effective weapons in their armouries; and consequently a powerful motive was supplied for historical investigation. The inevitable result was the production of some crude uncritical histories, written with national prejudice and political purpose, redeemed by the genuine pulse of national aspiration. But in Germany the two movements met. Scientific method controlled, while the

[* Madame de Staël.]

7

national spirit quickened, the work of historical research. One of the grave dangers was the temptation to fix the eyes exclusively on the inspiring and golden periods of the past, and it is significant to find Dahlmann, as early as 1812, warning against such a tendency, and laying down that the statesman who studies national history should study the whole story of his forefathers, the whole development of his people, and not merely chosen parts.

But the point which concerns us now is that the national movements of Europe not only raised history into prominence and gave a great impulse to its study, but also partially disclosed where the true practical importance of history lies. When men sought the key of their national development not in the immediate but in the remoter past, they had implicitly recognised in some measure the principles of unity and continuity. That recognition was a step towards the higher, more comprehensive, and scientific estimation of history's practical significance, which is only now beginning to be understood.

Just let me remind you what used to be thought in old days as to the utility of history. The two greatest of the ancient historians, Thucydides and Polybius, held that it might be a guide for conduct, as containing examples and warnings for statesmen; and it was generally regarded in Greece and at Rome as a storehouse of concrete instances to illustrate political and ethical maxims. Cicero called history in this sense *magistra vitae*, and Dionysius designated it "Philosophy by examples". And this view, which ascribed to it at best the function of teaching statesmen by analogy, at worst the duty of moral edification, prevailed generally till the last century. Of course it contained a truth which we should now express in a different form by saying that history supplies the material for political and social science. This is a very important function; but, if it were the only function, if the practical import of history lay merely in furnishing examples of causes and effects, then history, in respect of practical utility, would be no more than the handmaid of social science.

And here I may interpolate a parenthesis, which even at this hour may not be quite superfluous. I may remind you that history is not a branch of literature. The facts of history, like the facts of geology or astronomy, can supply material for literary art; for manifest reasons they lend themselves to artistic representation far more readily than those of the natural sciences; but to clothe the story of a human society in a literary dress is no more the part of a historian as a historian, than it is the part of an astronomer as an astronomer to present in an artistic shape the story of the stars. Take, for example, the greatest living historian. The reputation of Mommsen as a man of letters depends on his Roman History; but his greatness as a historian is to be sought far less in that dazzling work than in the *Corpus* and the *Staatsrecht* and the *Chronicles*.

This, by way of parenthesis; and now to resume. A right notion of the bearing of history on affairs, both for the statesman and for the citizen, could not be formed or formulated until men had grasped the idea of human development. This is the great transforming conception, which enables history to define her scope. The idea was first started by Leibnitz, but, though it had some exponents in the interval, it did not rise to be a governing force in human thought till the nineteenth century, when it appears as the true solvent of the anti-historical doctrines which French thinkers and the French Revolution had arrayed against the compulsion of the past. At the same time, it has brought history into line with other sciences, and, potentially at least, has delivered her from the political and ethical encumbrances which continued to impede her after the introduction of scientific methods. For notwithstanding those new engines of research, she remained much less, and much more, than a science in Germany, as is illustrated by the very existence of all those bewildering currents and cross-currents, tendencies and countertendencies, those various schools of doctrine, in which Lord Acton was so deeply skilled. The famous saying of Ranke—"Ich will nur sagen wie es eigentlich gewesen ist"—was widely applauded, but it was little accepted in the sense of a warning against transgressing the province of facts; it is a text which must still be preached, and when it has been fully taken to heart, though there be many schools of political philosophy, there will no longer be divers schools of history.

The world is not yet alive to the full importance of the transformation of history (as part of a wider transformation) which is being brought about by the doctrine of development. It is always difficult for those who are in immediate proximity to realise the decisive steps in intellectual or spiritual progress when those steps are slow and gradual; but we need not hesitate to say that the last century is not only as important an era as the fifth century B.C. in the annals of historical study, but marks, like it, a stage in the growth of man's self-consciousness. There is no passage, perhaps, in the works of the Greek tragedians so instructive for the historical student as that song in the *Antigone* of Sophocles, in which we seem to surprise the first amazed meditation of man when it was borne in upon him by a sudden startling illumination, how strange it is that he should be what he is and should have wrought all that he has wrought—should have

wrought out, among other things, the city-state. He had
suddenly, as it were, waked up to realise that he himself
was the wonder of the world. Οὐδὲν δεινότερον πέλει.*
That intense expression of a new detached wondering
interest in man, as an object of curiosity, gives us the
clue to the inspiration of Herodotus and the birth of
history. More than two thousand years later human
self-consciousness has taken another step, and the "sons
of flesh" have grasped the notion of their upward development through immense cycles of time. This idea
has recreated history. Girded with new strength she has
definitely come out from among her old associates,
moral philosophy and rhetoric; she has come out into a
place of liberty; and has begun to enter into closer relations with the sciences which deal objectively with the
facts of the universe.**

The older view, which we may call the politico-
ethical theory, naturally led to eclecticism. Certain
periods and episodes, which seemed especially rich in
moral and political lessons, were picked out as preeminently and exclusively important, and everything
else was regarded as more or less the province of anti-
quarianism. This eclectic and exclusive view is not
extinct, and can appeal to recent authority. It is
remarkable that one of the most eminent English historians of the latter half of the last century, whose own
scientific work was a model for all students, should have
measured out the domain of history with the compasses
of political or ethical wisdom, and should have pro-
tested as lately as 1877 against the principle of unity and
continuity. That inconsistency is an illustration of the
tenacity with which men cling to predilections that are

[* Sophocles, *Antigone*, lines 331–75.]
[** For a further development of this argument *v. p.* 12 and note on
b. 51.]

incongruous with the whole meaning of their own life-work.* But it is another great Oxford historian to whom perhaps more than to any other teacher we owe it that the Unity of History is now a commonplace in Britain. It must indeed be carried beyond the limits within which he enforced it, but to have affirmed and illustrated that principle was not the least useful of Mr Freeman's valuable services to the story of Europe. In no field, I may add, have the recognition of continuity and the repudiation of eclecticism been more notable or more fruitful than in a field in which I happen to be specially interested, the history of the Eastern Roman empire, the foster-mother of Russia.

The principle of continuity and the higher principle of development lead to the practical consequence that it is of vital importance for citizens to have a true knowledge of the past and to see it in a dry light, in order that their influence on the present and future may be exerted in right directions. For, as a matter of fact, the attitude of men to the past has at all times been a factor in forming their political opinions and determining the course of events. It would be an instructive task to isolate this influence and trace it from its most rudimentary form in primitive times, when the actions of tribes were stimulated by historical memories, through later ages in which policies were dictated or confirmed by historical judgments and conceptions. But the clear realisation of the fact that our conception of the past is itself a distinct factor in guiding and moulding our evolution, and must become a factor of greater and increasing potency, marks a new stage in the growth of the human mind. And it supplies us with the true theory of the practical importance of history.

[* The reference is to Stubbs, Lecture of 15 May 1877, printed in *Mediaeval and Modern History*, Oxford, 1886, *v.* esp. pp. 83-7.]

It seems inevitable that, as this truth is more fully and widely though slowly realised, the place which history occupies in national education will grow larger and larger. It is therefore of supreme moment that the history which is taught should be true; and that can be attained only through the discovery, collection, classification, and interpretation of facts—through scientific research. The furtherance of research, which is the highest duty of Universities, requires ways and means. Public money is spent on the printing and calendaring of our own national records; but we ought not to be satisfied with that. Every little people in Europe devotes sums it can far less well afford to the investigation of its particular history. We want a much larger recognition of the necessity of historical research; a recognition that it is a matter of public concern to promote the scientific study of any branch of history that any student is anxious to pursue. Some statesmen would acknowledge this; but in a democratic state they are hampered by the views of unenlightened taxpayers. The wealthy private benefactors who have come forward to help Universities, especially in America, are deplorably shortsighted; they think too much of direct results and immediate returns; they are unable to realise that research and the accumulated work of specialists may move the world. In the meantime, the Universities themselves have much to do; they have to recognise more fully and clearly and practically and preach more loudly and assiduously that the advancement of research in history, as in other sciences, is not a luxury, subsidiary though desirable, but is a pressing need, a matter of inestimable concern to the nation and the world.

It must also be remembered that a science cannot safely be controlled or guided by a subjective interest.

This brings me to the question of perspective in ecumenical history. From the subjective point of view, for
our own contemporary needs, it may be held that certain
centuries of human development are of a unique and
predominant importance, and possess, for purposes of
present utility, a direct value which cannot be claimed
for remoter ages. But we should not forget that this
point of view if legitimate and necessary, in one sense,
is subjective, and unscientific. It involves a false perspective. The reason is not merely the brevity of the
modern age in comparison with the antecedent history
of man; it is a larger consideration than that.

In his inaugural lecture at Oxford sixty years ago,[1]
Arnold propounded as his conviction the view that
what we call the modern age coincides with "the last
step" in the story of man. "It appears", he said, "to
bear marks of the fulness of time, as if there would be no
future history beyond it". He based this view on the
ground that one race had followed another in the torch-
bearing progress of civilisation, and that after the Teuton
and the Slav, who are already on the scene, there exists
on earth no new race fitted to come forward and succeed
to the inheritance of the ages. This argument rests on
unproven assumptions as to the vital powers and capaci-
ties of races, and as to the importance of the ethnical
factor in man's development. The truth is that at all
times men have found a difficulty in picturing how the
world could march onward ages and ages after their
own extinction. And this difficulty has prejudiced their
views. We may guess that if it had been put to a king of
Egypt or Babylonia 6000 years ago, he would have said
that his own age represented the fulness of days. The
data to which Arnold appealed are insufficient even to
establish a presumption. The only data which deserve

[1] 1841.

to be considered are the data furnished by cosmic science. And science tells us that—apart from the incalculable chances of catastrophes—man has still myriads and myriads of years to live on this planet under physical conditions which need not hinder his development or impair his energies. That is a period of which his whole recorded history of six or seven thousand years is a small fraction.

The dark imminence of this unknown future in front of us, like a vague wall of mist, every instant receding, with all its indiscernible contents of world-wide change, soundless revolutions, silent reformations, undreamed ideas, new religions, must not be neglected, if we would grasp the unity of history in its highest sense. For though we are unable to divine what things indefinite time may evolve, though we cannot look forward with the eyes of

"the prophetic soul
Of the wide world brooding on things to come",

yet the unapparent future has a claim to make itself felt as an idea controlling our perspective. It commands us not to regard the series of what *we* call ancient and medieval history as leading up to the modern age and the twentieth century; it bids us consider the whole sequence up to the present moment as probably no more than the beginning of a social and psychical develop-ment, whereof the end is withdrawn from our view by countless millenniums to come. All the epochs of the past are only a few of the front carriages, and probably the least wonderful, in the van of an interminable pro-cession.

This, I submit, is a controlling idea for determining objectively our historical perspective. We must see our petty periods *sub specie perennitatis*. Under this aspect the modern age falls into line with its predecessors and loses its obtrusive prominence. Do not say that this view sets us on too dizzy a height. On the contrary, it is a supreme confession of the limitations of our knowledge. It is simply a limiting and controlling conception; but it makes all the difference in the adjustment of our mental balance for the appreciation of values—like the symbol of an unknown quantity in the denominator of a fraction. It teaches us that history ceases to be scientific, and passes from the objective to the subjective point of view, if she does not distribute her attention, so far as the sources allow, to all periods of history. It cannot perhaps be too often reiterated that a University, in the exercise and administration of learning, has always to consider that more comprehensive and general utility which consists in the training of men to contemplate life and the world from the highest, that is the scientifically truest point of view, in the justest perspective that can be attained. If one were asked to define in a word the end of higher education, I do not know whether one could find a much better definition than this: the training of the mind to look at experience objectively, without immediate relation to one's own time and place. And so, if we recognise the relative importance of the modern period for our own contemporary needs, we must hold that the best preparation for interpreting it truly, for investigating its movements, for deducing its practical lessons, is to be brought up in a school where its place is estimated in scales in which the weight of contemporary interest is not thrown.

Beyond its value as a limiting controlling conception, the idea of the future development of man has also a positive importance. It furnishes in fact the justification of much of the laborious historical work that has been done and is being done to-day. The gathering of

materials bearing upon minute local events, the colla-
tion of MSS. and the registry of their small variations,
the patient drudgery in archives of states and munici-
palities, all the microscopic research that is carried on
by armies of toiling students—it may seem like the bearing of mortar and bricks to the site of a building which
has hardly been begun, of whose plan the labourers
know but little. This work, the hewing of wood and the
drawing of water, has to be done in faith—in the faith
that a complete assemblage of the smallest facts of
human history will tell in the end. The labour is performed for posterity—for remote posterity; and when,
with intelligible scepticism, someone asks the use of the
accumulation of statistics, the publication of trivial records, the labour expended on minute criticism, the true
answer is: "That is not so much our business as the
business of future generations. We are heaping up
material and arranging it, according to the best methods
we know; if we draw what conclusions we can for the
satisfaction of our own generation, we never forget that
our work is to be used by future ages. It is intended for
those who follow us rather than for ourselves, and much
less for our grandchildren than for generations very remote". For a long time to come one of the chief services
that research can perform is to help to build, firm and
solid, some of the countless stairs by which men of distant ages may mount to a height unattainable by us and
have a vision of history which we cannot win, standing
on our lower slope.

But if we have to regard the historical labours of man,
for many a century to come, as the ministrations of a
novitiate, it does not follow that we should confine
ourselves to the collection and classification of materials,
the technical criticism of them, and the examination of
special problems; it does not follow that the constructive

works of history which each age produces and will continue to produce according to its lights may not have a permanent value. It may be said that like the serpents of the Egyptian enchanters they are perpetually swallowed up by those of the more potent magicians of the next generation; but—apart from the fact that they contribute themselves to the power of the enchantment which overcomes them—it is also true that though they may lose their relative value, they abide as milestones of human progress; they belong to the documents which mirror the form and feature of their age, and may be part of the most valuable material at the disposal of posterity. If we possessed all the sources which Tacitus used for his sketch of the early imperial period, his *Annals* would lose its value in one sense, but it would remain to the furthest verge of time a monument of the highest significance, in its treatment, its method and its outlook, for the history of the age in which he lived. When the ultimate history of Germany in the nineteenth century comes to be written, it will differ widely from Treitschke's work, but that brilliant book can never cease to be a characteristic document of its epoch.

The remarks which I have ventured to offer are simply deductions from the great principle of development in time, which has given a deep and intense meaning to the famous aphorism of Hippocrates, that Science is long, a maxim so cold and so inspiring. The humblest student of history may feel assured that he is not working only for his own time; he may feel that he has an interest to consult and a cause to advance beyond the interest and cause of his own age. And this does not apply only to those who are engaged in research. It applies also to those who are studying history without any intention of adding to knowledge. Every individual who is deeply impressed with the fact that man's grasp of his past development helps to determine his future development, and who studies history as a science not as a branch of literature, will contribute to form a national conscience that true history is of supreme importance, that the only way to true history lies through scientific research, and that in promoting and prosecuting such research we are not indulging in a luxury but doing a thoroughly practical work and performing a great duty to posterity.

One of the features of the renovation of the study of history has been the growth of a larger view of its dominion. Hitherto I have been dwelling upon its longitudinal aspect as a sequence in time, but a word may be said about its latitude. The exclusive idea of political history, *Staatengeschichte*, to which Ranke held so firmly, has been gradually yielding to a more comprehensive definition which embraces as its material all records, whatever their nature may be, of the material and spiritual development, of the culture and the works, of man in society, from the stone age onwards. It may be said that the wider view descends from Herodotus, the narrower from Thucydides. The growth of the larger conception was favoured by the national movements which vindicated the idea of the people as distinct from the idea of the state; but its final victory is assured by the application of the principle of development and the "historical method" to all the manifestations of human activity—social institutions, law, trade, the industrial and the fine arts, religion, philosophy, folklore, literature. Thus history has acquired a much ampler and more comprehensive meaning, along with a deeper insight into the constant interaction and reciprocity among all the various manifestations of human brain-power and human emotion. Of course in actual practice labour is divided; political history and the histories of the various parts of civilisation can and must be separately treated;

but it makes a vital difference that we should be alive to the interconnexion, that no department should be isolated, that we should maintain an intimate association among the historical sciences, that we should frame an ideal—an ideal not the less useful because it is impracticable—of a true history of a nation or a true history of the world in which every form of social life and every manifestation of intellectual development should be set forth in its relation to the rest, in its significance for growth or decline.

Cambridge has officially recognised this wider view of history by the name and constitution of the body which administers historical studies—the "Board of Historical and Archaeological Studies". If that branch of historical research which we call archaeology bears a distinct name and occupies its distinct place, it is simply because the investigation of the historical records with which it deals requires a special training of faculties of observation not called into play in the study of written documents. But it must not be forgotten that the special historian whom we call an archaeologist needs a general training in history and a grasp of historical perspective as much as any other historical specialist. It must be borne in mind that this, as well as his special scientific training, is needed to differentiate the archaeologist from the antiquarian of the prescientific Oldbuck type, who in the first place has no wide outlook on history, and secondly cannot distinguish between legitimate profitable hypotheses and guesses which are quite from the purpose. Such antiquarians have not yet disappeared. It is significant that two brilliant historians, to both of whom the study of history in this country is deeply indebted, built perilous superstructures in regard to the English Conquest upon speculations which were only superior specimens of the prescientific type. It is earnestly to be wished that the history schools of the Universities may turn out a new kind of critical antiquarians in Britain who instead of molesting their local monuments with batteries of irrelevant erudition and fanciful speculation, with volleys of crude etymologies, will help to further our knowledge of British history, coming with a suitable equipment to the arduous, important and attractive task of fixing, grouping, and interpreting the endless fragments of historical wreckage which lie scattered in these islands. I venture to insist with some emphasis on this, because there are few fields where more work is to be done or where labourers are more needed than the Celtic civilisations of Western Europe. In tracing from its origins the course of western history in the Middle Ages, we are pulled up on the threshold by the uncertainties and obscurities which brood over the Celtic world. And for the purpose of prosecuting that most difficult of all inquiries, the ethnical problem, the part played by race in the development of peoples and the effects of race blendings, it must be remembered that the Celtic world commands one of the chief portals of ingress into that mysterious prae-Aryan foreworld, from which it may well be that we modern Europeans have inherited far more than we dream. For pursuing these studies it is manifest that scholars in the British islands are in a particularly favourable position.

Most beginners set to work at the study which attracts them, and follow the lines that have been constructed for them, without any clear apprehension or conviction of the greater issues involved. That apprehension only comes to them afterwards, if indeed it ever comes. It has seemed to me that it might not be amiss if historical students, instead of merely taking the justification of their subject for granted, were brought at the outset to consider its significance and position from the highest point of view—if they were stimulated to apprehend vividly that the study of history and the method of studying it are facts of ecumenical importance. In attempting to illustrate this—very inadequately in the small compass of an introductory address—I have sought to indicate the close interconnexion between the elevation of history to the position of a science and the recognition of the true nature of its practical significance as being itself a factor in evolution.

I may conclude by repeating that, just as he will have the best prospect of being a successful investigator of any group of nature's secrets who has had his mental attitude determined by a large grasp of cosmic problems, even so the historical student should learn to realise the human story *sub specie perennitatis*; and that, if, year by year, history is to become a more and more powerful force for stripping the bandages of error from the eyes of men, for shaping public opinion and advancing the cause of intellectual and political liberty, she will best prepare her disciples for the performance of that task, not by considering the immediate utility of next week or next year or next century, not by accommodating her ideal or limiting her range, but by remembering always that, though she may supply material for literary art or philosophical speculation, she is herself simply a science, no less and no more.

2. DARWINISM AND HISTORY*

1. Evolution, and the principles associated with the Darwinian theory, could not fail to exert a considerable influence on the studies connected with the history of civilised man. The speculations which are known as "philosophy of history", as well as the sciences of anthropology, ethnography, and sociology (sciences which though they stand on their own feet are for the historian auxiliary), have been deeply affected by these principles. Historiographers, indeed, have with few exceptions made little attempt to apply them; but the growth of historical study in the nineteenth century has been determined and characterised by the same general principle which has underlain the simultaneous developments of the study of nature, namely the *genetic* idea. The "historical" conception of nature, which has produced the history of the solar system, the story of the earth, the genealogies of telluric organisms, and has revolutionised natural science, belongs to the same order of thought as the conception of human history as a continuous, genetic, causal process—a conception which has revolutionised historical research and made it scientific. Before proceeding to consider the application of evolutional principles, it will be pertinent to notice the rise of this new view.

2. With the Greeks and Romans history had been either a descriptive record or had been written in practical interests. The most eminent of the ancient historians were pragmatical; that is, they regarded history as an instructress in statesmanship, or in the art of war,

[* Reprinted from *Darwinism and Modern Science*, ed. A. C. Seward, Cambridge University Press (1909), pp. 529-42.]

or in morals. Their records reached back such a short way, their experience was so brief, that they never attained to the conception of continuous process, or realised the significance of time; and they never viewed the history of human societies as a phenomenon to be investigated for its own sake. In the middle ages there was still less chance of the emergence of the ideas of progress and development. Such notions were excluded by the fundamental doctrines of the dominant religion which bounded and bound men's minds. As the course of history was held to be determined from hour to hour by the arbitrary will of an extra-cosmic person, there could be no self-contained causal development, only a dispensation imposed from without. And as it was believed that the world was within no great distance from the end of this dispensation, there was no motive to take much interest in understanding the temporal, which was to be only temporary.

The intellectual movements of the fifteenth and sixteenth centuries prepared the way for a new conception, but it did not emerge immediately. The historians of the Renaissance period simply reverted to the ancient pragmatical view. For Machiavelli, exactly as for Thucydides and Polybius, the use of studying history was instruction in the art of politics. The Renaissance itself was the appearance of a new culture, different from anything that had gone before; but at the time men were not conscious of this; they saw clearly that the traditions of classical antiquity had been lost for a long period, and they were seeking to revive them, but otherwise they did not perceive that the world had moved, and that their own spirit, culture, and conditions were entirely unlike those of the thirteenth century. It was hardly till the seventeenth century that the presence of a new age, as different from the middle ages as from the ages of Greece and Rome, was fully realised. It was then that the triple division of ancient, medieval, and modern was first applied to the history of western civilisation. Whatever objections may be urged against this division, which has now become almost a category of thought, it marks a most significant advance in man's view of his own past. He has become conscious of the immense changes in civilisation which have come about slowly in the course of time, and history confronts him with a new aspect. He has to explain how those changes have been produced, how the transformations were effected. The appearance of this problem was almost simultaneous with the rise of rationalism, and the great historians and thinkers of the eighteenth century, such as Montesquieu, Voltaire, Gibbon, attempted to explain the movement of civilisation by purely natural causes. These brilliant writers prepared the way for the genetic history of the following century. But in the spirit of the *Aufklärung*, that eighteenth-century Enlightenment to which they belonged, they were concerned to judge all phenomena before the tribunal of reason; and the apotheosis of "reason" tended to foster a certain superior *a priori* attitude, which was not favourable to objective treatment and was incompatible with a "historical sense". Moreover the traditions of pragmatical historiography had by no means disappeared.

3. In the first quarter of the nineteenth century the meaning of genetic history was fully realised. "Genetic" perhaps is as good a word as can be found for the conception which in this century was applied to so many branches of knowledge in the spheres both of nature and of mind. It does not commit us to the doctrine proper of evolution, nor yet to any teleological hypothesis such as is implied in "progress". For history it meant that the present condition of the human race is simply and

strictly the result of a causal series (or set of causal series)—a continuous succession of changes, where each state arises causally out of the preceding; and that the business of historians is to trace this genetic process, to explain each change, and ultimately to grasp the complete development of the life of humanity. Three influential writers, who appeared at this stage and helped to initiate a new period of research, may specially be mentioned. Ranke in 1824 definitely repudiated the pragmatical view which ascribes to history the duties of an instructress, and with no less decision renounced the function, assumed by the historians of the *Aufklärung*, to judge the past; it was his business, he said, merely to show how things really happened. Niebuhr was already working in the same spirit and did more than any other writer to establish the principle that historical transactions must be related to the ideas and conditions of their age. Savigny about the same time founded the "historical school" of law. He sought to show that law was not the creation of an enlightened will, but grew out of custom and was developed by a series of adaptations and rejections, thus applying the conception of evolution. He helped to diffuse the notion that all the institutions of a society or a nation are as closely inter-connected as the parts of a living organism.

4. The conception of the history of man as a causal development meant the elevation of historical inquiry to the dignity of a science. Just as the study of bees cannot become scientific so long as the student's interest in them is only to procure honey or to derive moral lessons from the labours of "the little busy bee", so the history of human societies cannot become the object of pure scientific investigation so long as man estimates its value in pragmatical scales. Nor can it become a science until it is conceived as lying entirely within a sphere in

which the law of cause and effect has unreserved and unrestricted dominion. On the other hand, once history is envisaged as a causal process, which contains within itself the explanation of the development of man from his primitive state to the point which he has reached, such a process necessarily becomes the object of scientific investigation and the interest in it is scientific curiosity.

At the same time, the instruments were sharpened and refined. Here Wolf, a philologist with historical instinct, was a pioneer. His *Prolegomena to Homer* (1795) announced new modes of attack. Historical investigation was soon transformed by the elaboration of new methods.

5. "Progress" involves a judgment of value, which is not involved in the conception of history as a genetic process. It is also an idea distinct from that of evolution. Nevertheless it is closely related to the ideas which revolutionised history at the beginning of the last century; it swam into men's ken simultaneously; and it helped effectively to establish the notion of history as a continuous process and to emphasise the significance of time. Passing over earlier anticipations, I may point to a *Discours* of Turgot (1750), where history is presented as a process in which "the total mass of the human race" "marches continually though sometimes slowly to an ever increasing perfection". That is a clear statement of the conception which Turgot's friend Condorcet elaborated in the famous work, published in 1795,* *Esquisse d'un tableau historique des progrès de l'esprit humain*. This work first treated with explicit fulness the idea to which a leading role was to fall in the ideology of the nineteenth century. Condorcet's book reflects the triumphs of the *Tiers état*, whose growing importance had also inspired Turgot; it was the political

[* Written in 1793 in prison before he took poison.]

changes in the eighteenth century which led to the doctrine, emphatically formulated by Condorcet, that the masses are the most important element in the historical process. I dwell on this because, though Condorcet had no idea of evolution, the predominant importance of the masses was the assumption which made it possible to apply evolutional principles to history. And it enabled Condorcet himself to maintain that the history of civilisation, a progress still far from being complete, was a development conditioned by general laws.

6. The assimilation of society to an organism, which was a governing notion in the school of Savigny, and the conception of progress, combined to produce the idea of an organic development, in which the historian has to determine the central principle or leading character. This is illustrated by the apotheosis of democracy in Tocqueville's *Démocratie en Amérique*, where the theory is maintained that "the gradual and progressive development of equality is at once the past and the future of the history of men". The same two principles are combined in the doctrine of Spencer (who held that society is an organism, though he also contemplated its being what he calls a "super-organic aggregate"),[1] that social evolution is a progressive change from militarism to industrialism.

7. The idea of development assumed another form in the speculations of German idealism. Hegel conceived the successive periods of history as corresponding to the

[1] A society presents suggestive analogies with an organism, but it certainly is not an organism, and sociologists who draw inferences from the assumption of its organic nature must fall into error. A vital organism and a society are radically distinguished by the fact that the individual components of the former, namely the cells, are morphologically as well as functionally differentiated, whereas the individuals which compose a society are morphologically homogeneous and only functionally differentiated. The resemblances and the differences are worked out in E. de Majewski's striking book, *La Science de la Civilisation*, Paris, 1908.

ascending phases or ideas in the self-evolution of his Absolute Being. His *Lectures on the Philosophy of History* were published in 1837 after his death. His philosophy had a considerable effect, direct and indirect, on the treatment of history by historians, and although he was superficial and unscientific himself in dealing with historical phenomena, he contributed much towards making the idea of historical development familiar. Ranke was influenced, if not by Hegel himself, at least by the Idealistic philosophies of which Hegel's was the greatest. He was inclined to conceive the stages in the process of history as marked by incarnations, as it were, of ideas, and sometimes speaks as if the ideas were independent forces, with hands and feet. But while Hegel determined his ideas by *a priori* logic, Ranke obtained his by induction—by a strict investigation of the phenomena; so that he was scientific in his method and work, and was influenced by Hegelian prepossessions only in the kind of significance which he was disposed to ascribe to his results. It is to be noted that the theory of Hegel implied a judgment of value; the movement was a progress towards perfection.

8. In France, Comte approached the subject from a different side, and exercised, outside Germany, a far wider influence than Hegel. The 4th volume of his *Cours de philosophie positive*, which appeared in 1839, created sociology and treated history as a part of this new science, namely as "social dynamics". Comte sought the key for unfolding historical development, in what he called the social-psychological point of view, and he worked out the two ideas which had been enunciated by Condorcet: that the historian's attention should be directed not, as hitherto, principally to eminent individuals, but to the collective behaviour of the masses, as being the most important element in the

29

process; and that, as in nature, so in history, there are general laws, necessary and constant, which condition the development. The two points are intimately connected, for it is only when the masses are moved into the foreground that regularity, uniformity, and law can be conceived as applicable. To determine the social-psychological laws which have controlled the development is, according to Comte, the task of sociologists and historians.

9. The hypothesis of general laws operative in history was carried further in a book which appeared in England twenty years later and exercised an influence in Europe far beyond its intrinsic merit, Buckle's *History of Civilisation in England* (1857–61). Buckle owed much to Comte, and followed him, or rather outdid him, in regarding intellect as the most important factor conditioning the upward development of man, so that progress, according to him, consisted in the victory of the intellectual over the moral laws.

10. The tendency of Comte and Buckle to assimilate history to the sciences of nature by reducing it to general "laws", derived stimulus and plausibility from the vista offered by the study of statistics, in which the Belgian Quetelet, whose book *Sur l'homme* appeared in 1835, discerned endless possibilities. The astonishing uniformities which statistical inquiry disclosed led to the belief that it was only a question of collecting a sufficient amount of statistical material, to enable us to predict how a given social group will act in a particular case. Bourdeau, a disciple of this school, looks forward to the time when historical science will become entirely quantitative. The actions of prominent individuals, which are generally considered to have altered or determined the course of things, are obviously not amenable to statistical computation or explicable by general laws. Thinkers like

Buckle sought to minimise their importance or explain them away.

11. These indications may suffice to show that the new efforts to interpret history which marked the first half of the nineteenth century were governed by conceptions closely related to those which were current in the field of natural science and which resulted in the doctrine of evolution. The genetic principle, progressive development, general laws, the significance of time, the conception of society as an organic aggregate, the metaphysical theory of history as the self-evolution of spirit—all these ideas show that historical inquiry had been advancing independently on somewhat parallel lines to the sciences of nature. It was necessary to bring this out in order to appreciate the influence of Darwinism.

12. In the course of the dozen years which elapsed between the appearances of *The Origin of Species** (observe that the first volume of Buckle's work was published just two years before) and of *The Descent of Man* (1871), the hypothesis of Lamarck that man is the co-descendant with other species of some lower extinct form was admitted to have been raised to the rank of an established fact by most thinkers whose brains were not working under the constraint of theological authority.

One important effect of the discovery of this fact (I am not speaking now of the Darwinian explanation) was to assign to history a definite place in the coordinated whole of knowledge, and relate it more closely to other sciences. It had indeed a defined logical place in systems such as Hegel's and Comte's; but Darwinism certified its standing convincingly and without more ado. The prevailing doctrine that man was created *ex abrupto* had placed history in an isolated position, disconnected

[* 1859.]

with the sciences of nature. Anthropology, which deals with the animal *anthropos*, now comes into line with zoology, and brings it into relation with history.[1] Man's condition at the present day is the result of a series of transformations, going back to the most primitive phase of society, which is the ideal (unattainable) beginning of history. But that beginning had emerged without any breach of continuity from a development which carries us back to a quadrimane ancestor, still further back (according to Darwin's conjecture) to a marine animal of the ascidian type, and then through remoter periods to the lowest form of organism. It is essential in this theory that though links have been lost there was no break in the gradual development; and this conception of a continuous progress in the evolution of life, resulting in the appearance of uncivilised Anthropos, helped to reinforce, and increase a belief in, the conception of the history of civilised Anthropos as itself also a continuous progressive development.

13. Thus the diffusion of the Darwinian theory of the origin of man, by emphasising the idea of continuity and breaking down the barriers between the human and animal kingdoms, has had an important effect in establishing the position of history among the sciences which deal with telluric development. The perspective of history is merged in a larger perspective of development. As one of the objects of biology is to find the exact steps

---

[1] It is to be observed that history is (not only different in scope but) not coextensive with anthropology *in time*. For it deals only with the development of man in societies, whereas anthropology includes in its definition the proto-anthropic period when *anthropos* was still non-social, whether he lived in herds like the chimpanzee, or alone like the male ourang-outang. (It has been well shown by Majewski that congregations —herds, flocks, packs, etc.—of animals are not *societies*; the characteristic of a society is differentiation of function. Bee hives, ant hills, may be called quasi-societies; but in their case the classes which perform distinct functions are morphologically different.)

in the genealogy of man from the lowest organic form, so the scope of history is to determine the stages in the unique causal series from the most rudimentary to the present state of human civilisation.

It is to be observed that the interest in historical research implied by this conception need not be that of Comte. In the Positive Philosophy history is part of sociology; the interest in it is to discover the sociological laws. In the view of which I have just spoken, history is permitted to be an end in itself; the reconstruction of the genetic process is an independent interest. For the purpose of the reconstruction, sociology, as well as physical geography, biology, psychology, is necessary; the sociologist and the historian play into each other's hands; but the object of the former is to establish generalisations; the aim of the latter is to trace in detail a singular causal sequence.

14. The success of the evolutional theory helped to discredit the assumption or at least the invocation of transcendent causes. Philosophically of course it is compatible with theism, but historians have for the most part desisted from invoking the naive conception of a "god in history" to explain historical movements. A historian may be a theist; but, so far as his work is concerned, this particular belief is otiose. Otherwise indeed (as was remarked above) history could not be a science; for with a *deus ex machina* who can be brought on the stage to solve difficulties scientific treatment is a farce. The transcendent element had appeared in a more subtle form through the influence of German philosophy. I noticed how Ranke is prone to refer to ideas as if they were transcendent existences manifesting themselves in the successive movements of history. It is intelligible to speak of certain ideas as controlling, in a given period— for instance, the idea of nationality; but from the scientific

point of view, such ideas have no existence outside the minds of individuals and are purely psychical forces; and a historical "idea", if it does not exist in this form, is merely a way of expressing a synthesis of the historian himself.

15. From the more general influence of Darwinism on the place of history in the system of human knowledge, we may turn to the influence of the principles and methods by which Darwin explained development. It had been recognised even by ancient writers (such as Aristotle and Polybius) that physical circumstances (geography, climate) were factors conditioning the character and history of a race or society. In the sixteenth century Bodin emphasised these factors, and many subsequent writers took them into account. The investigations of Darwin, which brought them into the foreground, naturally promoted attempts to discover in them the chief key to the growth of civilisation. Comte had expressly denounced the notion that the biological methods of Lamarck could be applied to social man. Buckle had taken account of natural influences, but had relegated them to a secondary plane, compared with psychological factors. But the Darwinian theory made it tempting to explain the development of civilisation in terms of "adaptation to environment", "struggle for existence", "natural selection", "survival of the fittest", etc.[1]

The operation of these principles cannot be denied. Man is still an animal, subject to zoological as well as mechanical laws. The dark influence of heredity continues to be effective; and psychical development had [has?] begun in lower organic forms—perhaps with life itself.

---

[1] Recently O. Seeck has applied these principles to the decline of Graeco-Roman civilisation in his *Untergang der antiken Welt*, 2 vols., Berlin, 1895, 1901.

The organic and the social struggles for existence are manifestations of the same principle. Environment and climatic influence must be called in to explain not only the differentiation of the great racial sections of humanity, but also the varieties within these sub-species and, it may be, the assimilation of distinct varieties. Ritter's *Anthropogeography* has opened a useful line of research. But on the other hand, it is urged that, in explaining the course of history, these principles do not take us very far, and that it is chiefly for the primitive ultra-pre-historic period that they can account for human development. It may be said that, so far as concerns the actions and movements of men which are the subject of recorded history, physical environment has ceased to act mechanically, and in order to affect their actions must affect their wills first; and that this psychical character of the causal relations substantially alters the problem. The development of human societies, it may be argued, derives a completely new character from the dominance of the conscious psychical element, creating as it does new conditions (inventions, social institutions, etc.) which limit and counteract the operation of natural selection, and control and modify the influence of physical environment. Most thinkers agree now tha the chief clews to the growth of civilisation must be sought in the psychological sphere. Imitation, for instance, is a principle which is probably more significant for the explanation of human development than natural selection. Darwin himself was conscious that his principles had only a very restricted application in this sphere, as is evident from his cautious and tentative remarks in the 5th chapter of his *Descent of Man*. He applied natural selection to the growth of the intellectual faculties and of the fundamental social instincts, and also to the differentiation of the great races or "sub-species" (Caucasian, African, etc.) which differ in anthropological character.[1]

16. But if it is admitted that the governing factors which concern the student of social development are of the psychical order, the preliminary success of natural science in explaining organic evolution by general principles encouraged sociologists to hope that social evolution could be explained on general principles also. The idea of Condorcet, Buckle, and others, that history could be assimilated to the natural sciences was powerfully reinforced, and the notion that the actual historical process, and every social movement involved in it, can be accounted for by sociological generalisations, so-called "laws", is still entertained by many, in one form or another. Dissentients from this view do not deny that the generalisations at which the sociologist arrives by the comparative method, by the analysis of social factors, and by psychological deduction may be an aid to the historian; but they deny that such uniformities are laws or contain an explanation of the phenomena. They can point to the element of chance coincidence. This element must have played a part in the events of organic evolution, but it has probably in a larger measure helped to determine events in social evolution. The collision of two unconnected sequences may be fraught with great results. The sudden death of a leader or a marriage without issue, to take simple cases, has again and again led to permanent political consequences. More em-

[1] Darwinian formulae may be suggestive by way of analogy. For instance, it is characteristic of social advance that a multitude of inventions, schemes and plans are framed which are never carried out, similar to, or designed for the same end as, an invention or plan which is actually adopted because it has chanced to suit better the particular conditions of the hour (just as the works accomplished by an individual statesman, artist or savant are usually only a residue of the numerous projects conceived by his brain). This process in which so much abortive production occurs is analogous to elimination by natural selection.

phasis is laid on the decisive actions of individuals, which cannot be reduced under generalisations and which deflect the course of events. If the significance of the individual will had been exaggerated to the neglect of the collective activity of the social aggregate before Condorcet, his doctrine tended to eliminate as unimportant the roles of prominent men, and by means of this elimination it was possible to found sociology. But it may be urged that it is patent on the face of history that its course has constantly been shaped and modified by the wills of individuals,[1] which are by no means always the expression of the collective will; and that the appearance of such personalities at the given moments is not a necessary outcome of the conditions and cannot be deduced. Nor is there any proof that, if such and such an individual had not been born, some one else would have arisen to do what he did. In some cases there is no reason to think that what happened need ever have come to pass. In other cases, it seems evident that the actual change was inevitable, but in default of the man who initiated and guided it, it might have been postponed, and, postponed or not, might have borne a different cachet. I may illustrate by an instance which has just come under my notice. Modern painting was founded by Giotto, and the Italian expedition of Charles VIII, near the close of the sixteenth century, introduced into France the fashion of imitating Italian painters. But for Giotto and Charles VIII, French painting might have been very different. It may be said that "if Giotto had not appeared, some other great initiator would have played a role analogous to his, and that without Charles VIII

---

[1] We can ignore here the metaphysical question of freewill and determinism. For the character of the individual's brain depends in any case on ante-natal accidents and coincidences, and so it may be said that the role of individuals ultimately depends on chance—the accidental coincidence of independent sequences.

there would have been the commerce with Italy, which in the long run would have sufficed to place France in relation with Italian artists. But the equivalent of Giotto might have been deferred for a century and probably would have been different; and commercial relations would have required ages to produce the *rayonnement imitatif* of Italian art in France, which the expedition of the royal adventurer provoked in a few years".[1] Instances furnished by political history are simply endless. Can we conjecture how events would have moved if the son of Philip of Macedon had been an incompetent? The aggressive action of Prussia which astonished Europe in 1740 determined the subsequent history of Germany; but that action was anything but inevitable; it depended entirely on the personality of Frederic the Great.

Hence it may be argued that the action of individual wills is a determining and disturbing factor, too significant and effective to allow history to be grasped by sociological formulae. The types and general forms of development which the sociologist attempts to disengage can only assist the historian in understanding the actual course of events. It is in the special domains of economic history and *Kulturgeschichte* which have come to the front in modern times that generalisation is most fruitful, but even in these it may be contended that it furnishes only partial explanations.

17. The truth is that Darwinism itself offers the best illustration of the insufficiency of general laws to account for historical development. The part played by coincidence, and the part played by individuals—limited by, and related to, general social conditions—render it impossible to deduce the course of the past history of man

---

[1] I have taken this example from G. Tarde's *La logique sociale*[2] (p. 403), Paris, 1904, where it is used for quite a different purpose.

or to predict the future. But it is just the same with organic development. Darwin (or any other zoologist) could not deduce the actual course of evolution from general principles. Given an organism and its environment, he could not show that it must evolve into a more complex organism of a definite predetermined type; knowing what it has evolved into, he could attempt to discover and assign the determining causes. General principles do not account for a particular sequence; they embody necessary conditions; but there is a chapter of accidents too. It is the same in the case of history.

18. Among the evolutionary attempts to subsume the course of history under general syntheses, perhaps the most important is that of Lamprecht, whose "kultur-historische Methode", which he has deduced from and applied to German history, exhibits the (indirect) influence of the Comtist school.* It is based upon psychology, which, in his view, holds among the sciences of mind (*Geisteswissenschaften*) the same place (that of a *Grundwissenschaft*) which mechanics holds among the sciences of nature. History, by the same comparison, corresponds to biology, and, according to him, it can only become scientific if it is reduced to general concepts (*Begriffe*). Historical movements and events are of a psychical character, and Lamprecht conceives a given phase of civilisation as "a collective psychical condition (*seelischer Gesamtzustand*)" controlling the period, "a diapason which penetrates all psychical phenomena and thereby all historical events of the time".[1] He has worked out a series of such phases, "ages of changing

---

[* Bury delivered an address on Lamprecht and his method to the *Junior Historians* (a club of the younger Historical Fellows) at Cambridge 2 March 1911. His attitude was then descriptive and so judicial that none of those present guessed even the limited adhesion to his views which he here exhibits.]

[1] *Die kulturhistorische Methode*, Berlin, 1900, p. 26.

psychical diapason", in his *Deutsche Geschichte*, with the aim of showing that all the feelings and actions of each age can be explained by the diapason; and has attempted to prove that these diapasons are exhibited in other social developments, and are consequently not singular but typical. He maintains further that these ages succeed each other in a definite order; the principle being that the collective psychical development begins with the homogeneity of all the individual members of a society and, through heightened psychical activity, advances in the form of a continually increasing differentiation of the individuals (this is akin to the Spencerian formula). This process, evolving psychical freedom from psychical constraint, exhibits a series of psychical phenomena which define successive periods of civilisation. The process depends on two simple principles, that no idea can disappear without leaving behind it an effect or influence, and that all psychical life, whether in a person or a society, means change, the acquisition of new mental contents. It follows that the new have to come to terms with the old, and this leads to a synthesis which determines the character of a new age. Hence the ages of civilisation are defined as the "highest concepts for subsuming without exception all psychical phenomena of the development of human societies, that is, of all historical events".[1] Lamprecht deduces the idea of a special historical science, which might be called "historical ethnology", dealing with the ages of civilisation, and bearing the same relation to (descriptive or narrative) history as ethnology to ethnography. Such a science obviously corresponds to Comte's social dynamics, and the comparative method, on which Comte laid so much emphasis, is the principal instrument of Lamprecht.

[1] Lamprecht, *Die kulturhistorische Methode*, Berlin, 1900, pp. 28, 29.

19. I have dwelt on the fundamental ideas of Lamprecht, because they are not yet widely known in England, and because his system is the ablest product of the sociological school of historians. It carries the more weight as its author himself is a historical specialist, and his historical syntheses deserve the most careful consideration. But there is much in the process of development which on such assumptions is not explained, especially the initiative of individuals. Historical development does not proceed in a right line, without the choice of diverging. Again and again, several roads are open to it, of which it chooses one—why? On Lamprecht's method, we may be able to assign the conditions which limit the psychical activity of men at a particular stage of evolution, but within those limits the individual has so many options, such a wide room for moving, that the definition of those conditions, the "psychical diapasons", is only part of the explanation of the particular development. The heel of Achilles in all historical speculations of this class has been the role of the individual.

The increasing prominence of economic history has tended to encourage the view that history can be explained in terms of general concepts or types. Marx and his school based their theory of human development on the conditions of production, by which, according to them, all social movements and historical changes are entirely controlled. The leading part which economic factors play in Lamprecht's system is significant, illustrating the fact that economic changes admit most readily this kind of treatment, because they have been less subject to direction or interference by individual pioneers.

Perhaps it may be thought that the conception of *social environment* (essentially psychical), on which Lamprecht's "psychical diapasons" depend, is the most valuable and fertile conception that the historian owes to the suggestion of the science of biology—the conception of all particular historical actions and movements as (1) related to and conditioned by the social environment, and (2) gradually bringing about a transformation of that environment. But no given transformation can be proved to be necessary (predetermined). And types of development do not represent laws; their meaning and value lie in the help they may give to the historian, in investigating a certain period of civilisation, to enable him to discover the interrelations among the diverse features which it presents. They are, as some one has said, an instrument of heuretic method.

20. The men engaged in special historical researches —which have been pursued unremittingly for a century past, according to scientific methods of investigating evidence (initiated by Wolf, Niebuhr, Ranke)—have for the most part worked on the assumptions of genetic history or at least followed in the footsteps of those who fully grasped the genetic point of view. But their aim has been to collect and sift evidence, and determine particular facts; comparatively few have given serious thought to the lines of research and the speculations which have been considered in this paper. They have been reasonably shy of compromising their work by applying theories which are still much debated and immature. But historiography cannot permanently evade the questions raised by these theories. One may venture to say that no historical change or transformation will be fully understood until it is explained how social environment acted on the individual components of the society (both immediately and by heredity), and how the individuals reacted upon their environment. The problem is psychical, but it is analogous to the main problem of the biologist.

3. THE PLACE OF MODERN HISTORY IN THE PERSPECTIVE OF KNOWLEDGE*

To define the position which the history of the last four hundred years occupies as an object of study, or to signalise its particular importance as a field of intellectual activity, requires a preliminary consideration of the place which history in general holds in the domain of human knowledge. And this consideration cannot be confined to purely political history. For political history is only an abstraction—an abstraction which is useful and necessary both practically and theoretically, but is unable to serve as the basis of a philosophical theory. Political development in the chronicle of a society, or set of societies, is correlated with other developments which are not political; the concrete history of a society is the collective history of all its various activities, all the manifestations of its intellectual, emotional, and material life. We isolate these manifestations for the purpose of analysis, as the physiologist can concentrate his attention on a single organ apart from the rest of the body; but we must not forget that political history out of relation to the whole social development of which it is a part is not less unmeaning than the heart detached from the body.

The inevitable and perfectly justifiable habit of tracing political development by itself, and making political events chronological landmarks, led to an unfortunate restriction of the use of the word *history*, which, when used without qualification, is commonly taken to

[* Delivered at the Congress of Arts and Sciences, St Louis, U.S.A. (1904), and published in vol. II of the transactions. Houghton Mifflin, Boston and New York (1906), pp. 142-52.]

mean political history, and not history in the larger concrete sense which I have just defined. This ambiguity furnishes an explanation and excuse for the view that history is subservient to political science, and that the only or main value of historical study consists in its auxiliary services to the study of political science. This doctrine was propagated, for instance, by Seeley, and gained some adhesion in England. Now if we detach the growth of political institutions and the sequence of political events from all the other social phenomena, and call this abstraction history, then I think Seeley's theory would have considerable justification. History, in such a sense, would have very little worth or meaning beyond its use as supplying material for the inductions of political science, the importance of which I should be the last to dispute. But if the political sequence is grasped as only one part of the larger development which constitutes history in the fuller sense, then it is clear that the study of political history has its sufficient title and justification by virtue of its relation to that larger development which includes it, and that it is not merely the handmaid of political science. Political science depends upon its data, and, in return, illuminates it; but does not confer its title-deeds.

But a larger and more formidable wave, threatening the liberty of history, has still to be encountered. It may be argued that the relation of dependence holds good, though it must be stated in a different and more scientific form. It may be said: Political science is a branch of social science, just as political history is a part of general history; and the object of studying general history is simply and solely to collect and furnish material for sociological science. Thus the former theory reappears, subsumed under a higher principle. The study of history generally is subordinate to sociology; and it follows that the study of political history especially is subordinate to that branch of sociology which we call political science. The difference, and it is a very important difference, is that, on this theory, political history is no longer isolated; its relations of coordination and interdependence with the other sides of social development would be recognised and emphasised. But the study of general history, including political, would be dependent on, and ancillary to, a study ulterior to itself.

Now this theory seems to run counter to an axiom which has been frequently enunciated and accepted as self-evident in recent times, namely, that history should be studied for its own sake. It is one of the remarkable ideas which first emerged explicitly into consciousness in the last century that the unique series of the phenomena of human development is worthy to be studied for itself, without any ulterior purpose, without any obligation to serve ethical or theological, or any practical ends. This principle of "history for its own sake" might be described as the motto or watchword of the great movement of historical research which has gone on increasing in volume and power since the beginning of the last century. But has this principle a theoretical justification, or is it only an expedient but indefensible fiction instinctively adopted? Is the postulate of "history for its own sake" simply a regulative idea which we find it convenient to accept because experience teaches us that independence is the only basis on which any study can be pursued satisfactorily and scientifically; and while we accord history this status, for reasons of expedience, is it yet true that the ultimate and only value of the study lies in its potential services to another discipline, such as sociology?

It seems to me that our decision of this question must fall out according to the view we take of the relation of man's historical development to the whole of reality. We are brought face to face with a philosophical problem. Our apprehension of history and our reason for studying it must be ultimately determined by the view we entertain of the *moles et machina mundi* as a whole. Naturalism will imply a wholly different view from idealism. In considering the place of history in the kingdom of knowledge, it is thus impossible to avoid referring to the questions with which the so-called philosophy of history is concerned.

If human development can be entirely explained on the general lines of a system such as Saint-Simon's or Comte's or Spencer's, then I think we must conclude that the place of history, within the frame of such a system, is subordinate to sociology and anthropology. There is no separate or independent precinct in which she can preside supreme. But on an idealistic interpretation of knowledge, it is otherwise. History then assumes a different meaning from that of a higher zoology, and is not merely a continuation of the process of evolution in nature. If thought is not the result, but the presupposition, of the process of nature, it follows that history, in which thought is the characteristic and guiding force, belongs to a different order of ideas from the kingdom of nature and demands a different interpretation. Here the philosophy of history comes in. The very phrase is a flag over debated ground. It means the investigation of the rational principles which, it is assumed, are disclosed in the historical process due to the cooperation and interaction of human minds under terrestrial conditions. If the philosophy of history is not illusory, history means a disclosure of spiritual reality in the fullest way in which it is cognisable to us in these particular conditions. And, on the other hand, the possibility of an interpretation of history as a move-

ment of reason, disclosing its nature in terrestrial circumstances, seems the only hypothesis on which the
postulate of "history for its own sake" can be justified
as valid.

This fundamental problem belongs to philosophy and
lies outside the scope of discussion. All that can be done
for the present occasion is to assume the validity of that
kind of interpretation which is generally called the
philosophy of history, and, starting with this postulate,
to show the particular significance of modern history.
Perhaps it may be said that such interpretation is quite
a separate branch of speculation, distinct from history
itself, and not necessarily the concern of an historical
student. That is a view which should be dismissed, for
it reduces history to a collection of annals. Facts must
be collected, and connected, before they can be interpreted; but I cannot imagine the slightest theoretical importance in a collection of facts or sequences
of facts, unless they mean something in terms of reason,
unless we can hope to determine their vital connection
in the whole system of reality. This is the fundamental
truth underlying Macaulay's rather drastic remark that
"facts are the [mere] dross of history".*

It is to be observed that the idea of history as a self-
centred study for its own sake arose without any consciousness of further implications, without any overt
reference to philosophical theory or the systematisation
of knowledge. It appeared as an axiom which at once
recommended itself as part of the general revolutionary
tendency of every branch of knowledge to emancipate
itself from external control and manage its own con-

[* Essay on *History* (1828) in *Miscellaneous Works*. Macaulay's meaning
becomes clearer if the quotation is continued: "Facts are the mere dross
of history. It is from the abstract truth which interpenetrates them,
and lies among them like gold in the ore, that the mass derives its whole
value".]

cerns. While this idea was gaining ground, a large number of interpretations or "philosophies" of history were launched upon the world, from Germany, France, England, and elsewhere. They were nearly all constructed by philosophers, not by historians; they were consequently conditioned by the nature of the various philosophical systems from which they were generated; and they did a great deal to bring the general idea of a philosophy of history into discredit and create the suspicion that such an idea is illusory. I observe with interest that this Congress, in the Department of Philosophy, assigns a section to the Philosophy of Religion but not to the Philosophy of History. I feel, therefore, the less compunction, that my argument compels me to make some remarks about it here.

I need hardly remind you that the radical defect of all these philosophical reconstructions of history is that the framework is always made *a priori*, with the help of a superficial induction. The principles of development are superimposed upon the phenomena, instead of being given by the phenomena; and the authors of the schemes had no thorough or penetrative knowledge of the facts which they undertook to explain. Bossuet boldly built his theory of universal history on the hardly disguised axiom that mankind was created for the sake of the Church; but nearly all the speculative theories of historical development framed in the nineteenth century, though less crudely subjective, fall into the same kind of fallacy.

Two of the most notable attempts to trace the rational element in the general movement of humanity were those of Hegel and Krause. They are both splendid failures, Hegel's more manifestly so. They are both marked by an insufficient knowledge of facts and details, but in imposing his *a priori* framework Hegel is far more mercilessly Procrustean than Krause. It was the modern period which suffered most painfully through Hegel's attempt to screw history into his iron bed. His scheme implies that the modern period represents the completion of historical development, is part of the last act in the drama of the human spirit. This implication is preposterous. What we know about the future is that man has an indefinite time in front of him, and it is absurd to suppose that in the course of that time new phases of thought will not be realised, though it is quite impossible for us to predetermine them. This error alone is sufficient to cast suspicion on the whole edifice. For the stages of history, as a revelation of spirit, correspond *ex hypothesi* to the dialectical stages in the logical evolution of the idea; and if Hegel fixes the terminus of the historical evolution at a point immeasurably distant from the true term, it evidently follows that the correspondences which he has established for the preceding stages with stages in the logical evolution must be wholly or partly wrong, and his interpretation breaks down. The keys are in the wrong locks.

Krause's system, which has had considerable influence in Belgium, avoids the absurdity of not allowing for progress in the future—a consideration which there was no excuse for ignoring, since it had been recognised and emphasised by Condorcet. He divides the whole of human history, including that which is yet to come, into three great periods—the ages of unity, of variety, and of harmony—and pronounces that mankind is now in the third and last stage of the second period. This theory, you perceive, has an advantage over Hegel's in that it gives the indefinite future something to do. But, although this Procrustes is more merciful, the Procrustean principle is the same; there is an *a priori* system into which human development has to be constrained.

I am not concerned here to criticise the method on which
Krause proceeds; I only want to illustrate by two
notable examples, that of Hegel who ignores the future,
and that of Krause who presumes to draw its horoscope,
how the philosophy of history has moved on false lines,
through the illusion that it could construct the development of reason in history from any other source than
history itself. By the one example we are taught that,
in attempting to interpret history, we must remember
there is no such thing as finality within measurable
distance:

His ego nec metas rerum nec tempora pono;

while the other example warns us that in considering the
past it is idle to seek to explain it by any synthesis involv-
ing speculations on the inscrutable content of the future.

It is, indeed, curious to note how the authors of the
numerous attempts to present a philosophical construction of history, which appeared during the nineteenth
century, assume, so naively, that their own interpretations are final, and that the ideas which are within the
horizon of *their* minds are the ultimate ideas to be
sighted by man, the last ports to be visited in his voyage
down the stream of time. It is strange how this childish
delusion, this spell of the present, has blinded the pro-
foundest thinkers. Hegel thought that the final form of
political constitution was something closely resembling
the Prussian state, that the final religion is Christianity,
that the final philosophy is his own. This was logical in
his case, because it was part of his view that the plenitude of time has come; yet we can have very little doubt
that this doctrine was prompted psychologically by
what I have called the spell of the present. But even
those who were able, in phrase at least, to transcend the
present and look forward to indefinite progress, speak

and argue nevertheless as if the ideas which are now accessible and within the range of our vision could never be transcended in the course of the progress which they admit. The absurdity of this view is illustrated by reflecting that the ideas with which these writers conjured —such as *humanity*, *liberty*, *progress*, in the pregnant meanings which those words now possess—were beyond men's horizon a few centuries before. We must face the fact that our syntheses and interpretations can have only a relative value, and that the still latent ideas which must emerge in the process of the further development of man will introduce new and higher controlling conceptions for the interpretation of the past.*

I have pointed out the common error into which philosophies of history have fallen, through not perceiving that in order to lay bare the spiritual process which history represents, we must go to history itself without any *a priori* assumptions or predetermined systems. All that philosophy can do is to assure us that historical experience is a disclosure of the inner nature of spiritual reality. This disclosure is furnished by history and history alone. It follows that it is the historian and not the philosopher who must discover the diamond net; or the philosopher must become an historian if he would do so.

But not only is it necessary to abandon unreservedly the Procrustean principle; the method of approach must also be changed. This is the point to which it has been my particular object to lead up. The interpreter of the movement of history must proceed backward, not forward; he must *start from the modern period*. For a thorough, fully articulated knowledge of the phenomena is essential —not the superficial acquaintance with which specu-

[* *v. supra, pp.* 11–12. This principle, which he calls that of "historical relativity", is still further developed in the *Ancient Greek Historians*, Macmillan (1909), pp. 250–1, and n., 252–3.]

4-2

lators like Hegel worked; and such a knowledge is only attainable for the modern period, because here only are the requisite records preserved. Here only can one hope to surprise the secrets of the historical process and achieve a full analysis of the complex movement. The records of ancient and medieval history are starred with lacunae; we are ignorant of whole groups of phenomena, or have but a slight knowledge of other groups; and what we do know must often be seen in false perspective and receive undue attention on account of the adjacent obscurities. We can survey and attempt syntheses; but syntheses without fully articulated knowledge are no more than vague shots in the direction of a dimly seen object. And the only syntheses possible in such conditions are insignificant generalities, bloodless abstract conceptions, like the ἀμενηνὰ κάρηνα of Homer's world of shades. The interpretation of history that shall be more than a collection of plausible labels must grasp the vital process, perceive the breath and motion, detect the undercurrents, trace the windings, discern the fore-shadowings, see the ideas travelling underground, dis-cover how the spiritual forces are poised and aimed, de-termine how the motives conspire and interact. And it is only for the history of the last three or four hundred years that we possess material for investigating this com-plicated process.

And it is for the development of the nineteenth century that our position in some respects is most favour-able. It is commonly said that recent history cannot be profitably studied, on the ground that we are too near to the events to be able to treat them objectively and see them in the right perspective. Admitting the truth of the objection, recognising fully that recent events are seen by us "foreshortened in the tract of time", we must nevertheless remember that there is a compensation in proximity which it is disastrous to ignore. For those who are near have opportunities of tracing the hidden moral and intellectual work of an age which subsequent generations cannot reach, because they are not in direct relation. De Tocqueville said: "What contemporaries know better than posterity is the mental movement, the general passions and feelings of the time, whereof they still feel the last shuddering motions (*les derniers frémissements*) in their minds or in their hearts". If this is so, it is one of the most pressing duties to posterity that men in each generation should devote themselves to the scientific study of recent history from this point of view.

We may go further, and declare that, in this light, modern history as a whole possesses a claim on us now, which does not belong either to antiquity or to the Middle Ages. We have ourselves passed so completely beyond the spiritual boundaries of the ancient and medieval worlds that we can hardly suppose that we possess any greater capacity for a sympathetic apprehension of them than our descendants will possess a thousand years hence. Whereas, on the other hand, we may fairly assume that we are in a much better position than such remote posterity for sympathetic appreciation of the movements—the emancipatory movements—of the sixteenth, seventeenth, and eighteenth centuries. It therefore devolves upon us before we have drifted too far away to do what may be done to transmit to future generations the means of appreciating and comprehending. In this sense the study of what we call modern history is the most pressing of all.

But I have permitted myself to digress from the argument. I was concerned to show that our only chance of tracing the movement and grasping the principles of universal history is to start with the study of the modern age where our material is relatively full, and proceed regressively. One great mistake of those who have attempted philosophies of history has been that they began at the other end—not at the beginning, but at whatever point their knowledge happened to reach back to, perhaps in China, perhaps in the Garden of Eden—and were consequently obliged to adopt a difficult and precarious synthetic method. Precarious, because in passing on from one stage to another there is no guarantee, owing to our fragmentary material, that we have knowledge of all that is significant, and therefore the synthesis which expresses the transition to a higher stage may be vitiated by incompleteness. We may be acquainted only with some of the forces which determine the sequel, and, if we proceed as though we had all those forces in our hands, our conception of the sequel will be inadequate.

On the analytic method, on the contrary, we start from a definite terminus, namely the present—contingent indeed, but not arbitrary, since it is the only possible limit for the given investigator—and in the first stage we have all the material, so that it is the fault of the investigation and not the result of accident if the analysis is not exhaustive. The problem then is, having grasped the movement of the ideas and spiritual forces which have revealed themselves in the modern period, to trace, regressively, the processes out of which they evolved, with the help of our records. This, at least, is the ideal to which the interpreter would try to approximate. That, with fragmentary records, the whole historical movement can ever be traced by methods of inference, I do not indeed believe; but assuredly it is only in the period where the records exist that we can first detect the secret of the process or begin to discern the figure on the carpet.

But the question will be asked: Can we define absolutely the position of the modern period in the secular perspective of history? The field of what we call "modern history" has a roughly marked natural boundary at the point where it starts, towards the end of the fifteenth century. We may say this without any prejudice to the doctrine of continuity. But the phrase is used to cover all post-medieval history, and therefore the hither limit is always shifting. For while it is usual to mark off the last thirty or forty years as "contemporary history", as years pass on the beginning of "contemporary history" moves forward, and the end of the modern as distinguished from the contemporary period moves forward too. The question arises whether this conventional nomenclature is any longer appropriate, whether all post-medieval history can be scientifically classified as a period, with the same right and meaning as the Middle Ages. "Ancient History" is of course a merely conventional and convenient, unscientific term; is this true of "Modern History" also? It may be thought that the answer is affirmative. It may seem probable that the changes which began at the end of the eighteenth century, the great movements of thought which have thrilled the nineteenth century, the implications of the far-reaching vistas of knowledge which have been opened, mark as new and striking a departure as any to which our records go back, and constitute a *Neuzeit* in the fullest sense of the word; that in the nineteenth as in the sixteenth century man entered into a new domain of ideas; that of the nineteenth as much as of the sixteenth are we justified in saying

Ab integro saeclorum nascitur ordo.

If so, our nomenclature should be altered. The three centuries after Columbus should be called by some other name, such as post-medieval, and "modern" should be appropriated to the period ushered in by the French Revolution and the formation of the American Commonwealth, until in turn a new period shall claim a name which can never be permanently attached. It would follow that in the Historical Department at this Congress, there should be another section; the nineteenth century, the more modern modern period, should have a section to itself. In Germany, a distinction of this kind has been adopted. The sixteenth, seventeenth, and eighteenth centuries are described as *die neuere Zeit*; while the nineteenth is distinguished as *die neueste Zeit*.

Among the notes which form the stamp and signature of this *neueste Zeit* is the new historical interest, if I may say so, which has become prevalent in the world and is itself an historical fact of supreme importance. It is expressed not only in the enormous amount of research that has been done, but in the axiom of "history for its own sake", and also in the attempts to create a philosophy of history. It is a new force set free, which will have its own place in the complex of the driving forces of the world. It is to be taken along with the equally recent development of a consciousness of our relations to future generations, which is practically reflected in a growing sense of duty to posterity. Both facts taken together, the interest in human experience and the interest in human destiny, represent a new sense of the solidarity of humanity, linking past ages and ages to come. In other words, the human mind has begun to rise above the immediate horizon of the circumstances and interests of the present generation, and to realise seriously, not as a mere object of learned curiosity, the significance of the past and the potentialities of the future. The most familiar of words, *past* and *future*, have become pregnant with significance; they are charged with all the implications of a new perspective.

It is clear that this new sense is inconsistent with the affirmation of Arnold and Seeley that contemporary is superior to preceding history by all the superiority of an end to the means. This doctrine expresses the attitude of the old unregenerate spirit. The theoretical truth which it contains is simply this, that contemporary history represents a more advanced stage than any preceding it, or, in other words, there is a real evolution. But for the same reason it is itself inferior to the development which will succeed it; and if past history is to be described as a means, contemporary history must be equally described as a means, on the same ground. Theoretically, therefore, this teleological argument has no application; it would not become relevant till the end of the process has been reached. But what Arnold and Seeley probably had most in mind was the importance of comprehending the past for the sake of comprehending the present for practical purposes. (This is now so fully understood and recognised that I have not thought it necessary to dwell on it to-day. It is now generally acknowledged, by those whose opinion need be considered, that the practical value of history consists not, as used to be thought, in lessons and examples, but in the fact that it explains the present, and that without it the present, in which we have to act, would be incomprehensible. It is modern history, of course, that is here chiefly concerned. Lord Acton said: "Modern history touches us so nearly, it is so deep a question of life and death, that we are bound to find our own way through it, and to owe our insight to ourselves".* I venture to think that Lord Acton, in this characteristic statement, rather strains the note; but the statement concerns, you observe, the practical not the theoretical value of the subject.)

[* *Inaugural* (1895) in *Modern History*, Macmillan (1906), p. 28.]

To attempt to define absolutely the significance of modern or recent history in the order of development would be to fall into an error like that for which I criticised Hegel and Krause and others who thought to draw forth Leviathan with a hook. It is much if it can be established, as I think it can, that with the nineteenth century the curtain has risen on a new act in the drama. But we can be more confident in asserting negatives. The ideas and forces which have driven man through the last four hundred years and are driving him now, are not the last words or dooms in the progress of reason. The idea of freedom which the modern world has struggled to realise has been deemed by many the *ultima linea rerum*; but it is difficult to see how or why it should be final, in the sense of not being superseded by the appearance of higher ideas which its realisation shall have enabled to emerge. Or again, it is unreasonable to suppose that the idea of nationality which has recently played and still plays a great role, is an end in itself or more than a phase in evolution. We must acquiesce in our incompetence to form any scientific judgment as to the value or position of this stage in the total development.

To state briefly the main thesis of this paper. The answer to the question, "What is the position of modern history in the domain of universal knowledge?" depends in the first instance on our view of the fundamental philosophical question at issue between idealism and naturalism. If we are believers in naturalism, then all history, including modern history, has its sole theoretical value in the function of providing material for the investigation of sociological laws. It must accept a position such as Comte assigns to it. But if we are idealists, if we hold that thought is a presupposition of physical existence and not a function of matter, then history as a disclosure of the evolution of thought has an independent realm of its own and demands a distinct interpretation, to prepare for which is the aim of historical research. The segment of history which we call modern, from the sixteenth century onward, occupies a peculiar place, because here, partly in consequence of the invention of printing, our materials begin to be adequate for a complete analysis. This gives us the theoretical significance of the modern period as an object of study; it is the field in which we may hope to charm from human history the secret of its rational movement, detect its logic, and win a glimpse of a fragment of the pattern on a carpet, of which probably much the greater part is still unwoven.*

[* This seems the natural end of the lecture but the following paragraph was added (Ed.):

"This Congress is suggestive in many ways, suggestive especially of the distance the world has travelled since 1804 or since 1854. There will be many more of its kind; but this is unique as the first. It is not very bold to predict that historians of the distant future, in tracing the growth of cooperation and tendencies to a federation of human effort, which are one of the transformative influences now affecting mankind, will record this Congress in which we are here met together as a significant point in this particular stage of man's progress toward his unknown destiny".]

4. CLEOPATRA'S NOSE*

The course of history appears in very different lights to those who view human movements and events as a logical development, and to those who view them as due to the play of chance except so far as they are the result of the conscious will and purpose of men. The first view has been generally held in the form of the theory of Providence, an external power guiding human societies and ordering human events according to a deliberate plan. It has also been held in subtler forms, of which we may take as representative Hegel's conception of history as spirit realising itself in time by a process which corresponds to the logical process of thought. The second view has been expressed in the famous dictum that the course of the world's history depends on accidents like the shape of Cleopatra's nose.

The principle known as the law of causation does not affect the problem. It is probably true that every phenomenon is the consequent of antecedent causes, and that no phenomenon contains any element which is not determined by a sequence of causes and effects. In any case it is a hypothesis which we are obliged to assume if the world is not to become a chaos and science to commit suicide. For as the function of science is to explain phenomena, and explanation means the assignment of causes, it is clear that, if a phenomenon containing lawless elements may occur, scientific research is hopeless.

This principle is compatible with either of these two views of history. According to the first view, cause and effect can be regarded as the machinery by which Providence executes its plan, or through which thought

[* Reprinted from the *R.P.A. Annual*, 1916, pp. 16–23.]

manifests itself in time. And it is consistent with the second view, provided we give a proper meaning to chance. It would be inconsistent if we conceive chance as the intrusion of a lawless element; but our use of the word does not really imply this, as a little reflection will show.

I visit Paris. I meet an American friend, whom I had not seen for years, in the Rue de la Paix. We were mutually ignorant of each other's presence in Paris, and we describe our meeting as a happy chance. My visit to Paris and my walking in the Rue de la Paix at a particular hour were the result of a sequence of causes and effects. His visit to Paris and his presence in the same street at the same hour followed upon another sequence of causes and effects. The collision, as we may say, of these two independent chains made what we call the chance of our meeting.

Now, it may be said that in the case of every stranger whom I passed in the street there was a similar collision. Yes, but all these were collisions of no value, because they had no consequences. The meeting with my friend had consequences—emotions of surprise and pleasure for both, conversation, the arrangement perhaps of a future meeting, etc. A chance may therefore be defined as *the valuable collision of two or more independent chains of causes*—"valuable" meaning that it is attended with more or less important consequences. It is obvious that daily life, and therefore history, is full of such chances. Few things can happen, even carefully prepared plans can seldom be carried out, without the intrusion of this element, to however small an extent. But there are endless cases where chance appears to occur on a large scale in history, and to modify or determine its course. A few examples may be chosen to illustrate various types of historical contingency.

In the early years of the war between the Athenians and Peloponnesians, in the fifth century B.C., a plague broke out in Athens which devastated the population and affected the course of the war, causing among other effects the death of the Athenian statesman Pericles. The appearance of the microbes which caused the plague had its own definite chain of causes, but this sequence had nothing to do with the sequence of events which led to the war. The microbe had no interest in the war. The political effects of the plague were a contingency.

The shape of Cleopatra's nose was rightly conditioned by the causal sequence of her heredity. This sequence had nothing to do with the causes which produced the situation of the Roman world and the political position of Antony when he fell a victim to her charms. The collision of the two sequences modified the course of history.

In the fourth century A.D. a man of exceptional discernment, who regarded on the one hand the internal condition of the Roman Empire, and on the other Central Europe seething with populous and rapacious German tribes, driven by the urgency of the food question to seek new abodes and attracted by the rich provinces of Rome, might easily have foretold that the Germans were destined to enter and occupy large portions of Roman territory. The German dismemberment of the Empire may be said to have lain in the logic of the situation. The prediction would have been true. But before the last quarter of the century the prophet could not have foretold how the process of the dismemberment would be determined by an event which had nothing to do in its origin with the European situation. This contingent event, which we may describe as a historical surprise, was the invasion of the Huns. The irruption of the Huns into Europe was the result of a series of political events in Central Asia which was strictly independent of events in Europe. The disarrangement of the Germanic world by the descent of the nomads altered at many points the natural development of events in Europe, with which it had no causal connection.

In A.D. 1740 a memorable step was taken in the expansion of Prussia by the conquest of Silesia. It may be said that the expansion of Prussia lay in the logic of events. This may be true, and in any case we will suppose it to be true. But the moment and method of this decisive step in aggrandisement were determined by three facts, which were independent of the needs of Prussia and her relation to Austria. Frederic William I died early in the year. This was the first fact. The second was the character of his successor, Frederic the Great. The third was the death of the Emperor Charles VI in October, which opened the question of the "Austrian succession", and gave Frederic the political opportunity for using the mailed fist. These facts were conditions of the Prussian attack on Silesia, and each of them was determined by a rigorous sequence of cause and effect. But each of these sequences was entirely independent of the others. The chain of causes which led to the death of the Prussian King had nothing to do with that which led to the death of the Emperor, and neither had any connection with the causes which conditioned the character of Frederic the Great. The Silesian war was thus due to the coincidence of three contingencies.

The American War of Independence may furnish another illustration. It may be said that the separation of the colonies from Great Britain must inevitably have occurred. This is a proposition on which it would be rash to dogmatise. But granting it for the sake of argument, there can yet be no doubt that if George II had been still reigning when the difficulties arose, or if George III had been a man of different character, the differences between the colonies and the mother country would have been amicably composed. If the independence of the colonies was inevitable, it would have come about at a later time and in another way. The American War, one of the most far-reaching events of modern history, was determined by the contingency of the personal character and political ideas of George III, which were the result of a chain of causes, unconnected with the relation between the interests of the colonies and those of England.

Exceptional military genius is a contingency (such as that of Alexander the Great or Napoleon) which may divert the paths of history on a colossal scale. Napoleon's supremacy in France was linked by a logical chain with the French Revolution, but conditioned by his genius for war. The possibility of his hegemony in Europe was entirely determined by his military talent.

The triumph of Christianity early in the fourth century was also due to chance as above defined. However satisfied you may be that its ultimate triumph was assured in view of the progress which it had already made, and the origin of its propagation, the circumstances of its position in A.D. 300 pointed to the probability that for a couple of centuries to come it must abide, at best, in the position of the tolerated cult of a minority. The audacity of Constantine the Great in exalting Christianity to the dominant place cannot be sufficiently emphasised. A revolution defiant of the wishes of the vast majority has never in the world's history been accomplished on so large a scale. The estimates which have been attempted of the number of Christians in the Empire in the time of Constantine vary from one-twentieth to one-sixth of the whole population. If we estimate the population at one hundred millions, it seems certain that there were at least ten million, but not more than seventeen or eighteen million, Christians. Of course, these figures were the merest approximations, but they are amply sufficient for the present purpose. It is obviously due to the contingency of Constantine's personal characteristics, not to any manifest strength or equity in Christian claims, that the cult of a small minority was raised to the supreme place. If in the struggle for power a monarch of another mould than Constantine had emerged the final victor, Christianity would, doubtless, have obtained toleration, but not privilege. And it is hardly likely that, unassisted by the stimulus which privileged position and power of persecuting gave to proselytising, the Church would in less than 150 or 200 years have embraced such a majority of the population that it could have imposed upon the State its recognition as the exclusive religion. It is needless to point out what great differences this would have made in the course of universal history.

The element of contingency seems to enter into the history of the development of thought as well as into the course of external events. The logical relationship of Platonism to the philosophy of Socrates is clear, but it depended on the character of Plato's brain, which was a contingency. If Plato had died in infancy, there is no reason to suppose that the Platonic ideas would have been conceived in the form in which he conceived them. Other different systems, such as those of Aristippus and Eucleides, each depending on the contingency of the individual author's brain, were also logical developments of the Socratic teaching. In the same way Cartesianism, it is easy to see, may lead logically to the system of Spinoza. But the advance on this particular line might not have been made if Spinoza had not lived.

Apply this to the origin of Christianity. In this case we have the collision, in the brain of Paul of Tarsus, of conceptions and methods of reasoning derived from Greek sources with the traditions of the life, death, and teaching of Jesus, which he learnt in Judæa. The Pauline doctrines, from which fully-fledged Christianity was developed, were thus the fortuitous union of two different sequences, and it might easily be shown that further elaborations of Christian dogma, in many cases, depended on contingencies. A universal religion, based on the union of Oriental mysticism with Greek dialectic, was doubtless inevitable. It may also be maintained that the life and teaching of Jesus were a germ so strong in vitality that it must have developed into a universal religion. It is, nevertheless, clear that if the Galilean traditions had been manipulated by a man whose brain was differently constituted from that of Paul, and whose training had been on other lines, Christianity and history would have been incalculably different.

The course of history seems, then, to be marked at every stage by contingencies, some of greater, some of smaller import. In some cases they produce a situation to which the antecedent situation does not logically lead. In others they determine the form and means of the realisation of a logical tendency. This conclusion is theoretically compatible with either of the two hypotheses which I mentioned at the beginning of this paper. On the theory of Providence, history becomes an epic like the *Æneid*, in which all the contingencies are pre-arranged to work together towards a foregone conclusion, with this difference—that the conclusion is not known. The storm which drives Æneas and his companions to the Libyan shores is not an accident; it is devised by Juno. All the incidents which appear to the actors effects of entirely disconnected causes are, through the operation of divine agency, displayed as parts of one woven chain.

On the theory that history is a process by which thought realises itself externally in time, contingencies must be explained, if it is an explanation, by the metaphysical conception that contingency is a logical category, and therefore must be an element in the process. But I need not dwell on either the theological or the metaphysical hypothesis, each of which is improbable, and both of which for other reasons many of my readers will consider impossible. What I wish to suggest here is the view that a systematic study of contingencies is a necessary preliminary to any speculations which aim at historical synthesis.

Perhaps I may further illustrate this subject by dividing contingencies into pure and mixed. This division is not strictly scientific, but is convenient. If Napoleon at an early stage in his career had been killed by a meteorite, that would have been the purest of pure contingencies. The fall of the meteorite on a particular spot at a particular moment was the effect of a rigid causal sequence, and the presence of Napoleon at the same moment on the same spot was also rigidly determined. The meteorite was completely disinterested in his death. If his death had been caused by an earthquake or by disease, the contingency would have been of the same order, and the consequences the same. Both these hypotheses suggest that pure contingencies might be arranged in gradation according to frequency or probability. Death by a meteorite is clearly an outside chance. Death by an earthquake is a chance less remote. Death from disease is a possibility with which one has always to reckon. But suppose Napoleon had been killed by the hand of an assassin who detested his policy. This would not be a pure contingency. For the assassin was interested in

5-2

Napoleon's death, and the causal sequence which led him to commit the act would have been connected with the causal sequence which rendered the great man's death historically important. It can, however, easily be shown by analysis that a mixed contingency contains some purely contingent elements which can be separated.*

The problem of contingencies which meets us in the development of human societies, though it must be studied separately and is profoundly modified by human purposes, is similar to that which meets us in the evolution of nature. The appearance of the various botanical and animal species which exist and have existed seems to have depended on accidents. There was nothing in the logic of life that made the existence of an oak or of a hippopotamus inevitable. Nor can it be proved that there was anything that made the existence of *anthropos* inevitable. At the remote threshold of history we seem to find a primordial contingency—the origin of man. And we may conjecture that the origin, formation, and primitive development of human societies, which are inaccessible to our knowledge, depended chiefly on contingencies. But this soon ceased to be the case. The experience and knowledge of man became more and more important, until finally this became the predominant factor in social evolution. It is to this that the historical process owes its logic, so far as it is logical. When we speak of a logical situation at a given moment in history we mean this complex factor. The logical consequences may be facilitated or upset, accelerated or retarded, by contingencies; and it is this which makes history so interesting and so baffling.

[* Cf. a similar reference to Napoleon and a careful examination of the general relation of contingency to determinism in the *Idea of Progress*, Macmillan (1920), pp. 303–4.]

One synthesis may perhaps be risked. A survey of history seems to suggest that as time goes on contingencies will become less important in human evolution and chance have less power over the course of events. This tendency of social development to become more and more logical is due not only to the increase of experience and of men's knowledge of the conditions under which they live, and to their larger command over nature, but also in recent times to the growth of democratic societies, the consequences being that the destinies of societies are moulded less and less by single individuals. And the growth of knowledge itself is less casual and occasional; although the element of contingency is not eliminated, the march of science is continuous, systematic, and imperturbable. It appears probable that as time advances the fates of nations will become more and more independent of accidents, whether more or less serious than the pretty face of Anne Boleyn or the shape of Cleopatra's nose.

5. A LETTER ON THE WRITING OF HISTORY

PROFESSOR BURY *on* PERSONAL BIAS*

To the Editor of the *Morning Post*

SIR,

In reference to your article on "The Writing of History", it seems to me that it would be necessary first to elucidate two or three fundamental questions. For instance, Is history a sequence of contingencies, and can our knowledge of events of the past claim to be much more than a *fable convenue*? But to go into either of these problems is impossible here, it would need too much space and lead too far, but there is another fundamental question about which I will venture to make a brief observation.

It seems to be always assumed as self-evident and universally admitted that impartiality and freedom from bias are indispensable qualifications in every Historian's ideal of how history should be written. Here I totally disagree, I do not think that freedom from bias is possible, and I do not think it is desirable. Whoever writes completely free from bias will produce a colourless and dull work.

Bishop Stubbs, our great authority on the early constitutional history of England, has remarked somewhere, if my memory does not betray me, "That it seems as if

[* Reprinted from the *Morning Post* of November 30, 1926, and here reproduced by courtesy of the Editor.]

history could not be written without a certain spite;* and it is a fact that the most effective histories have usually been partial and biassed, like those of Tacitus, Gibbon, Macaulay, and Mommsen, to take familiar examples. Is there any event or any transaction worth investigating or writing about on which the writer can fail to have a definite bias if the subject really engages his interest? And it will be admitted that otherwise he cannot hope to produce anything that will engage the interest of the world.

No history can be instructive if the personality of the writer is entirely suppressed; it will be dead and colourless and inhuman, however faultless it may be in detail, however carefully the rules of historical method may be applied.

J. B. BURY.

Rome.

[* It is here that the inverted commas should stop. The quotation is not verbal but seems to be based on the following passage: Lecture V of Stubbs' *Mediaeval and Modern History*, 1887, p. 124, "It seems as if... no one has the spirit to undertake it [such work] unless he is stirred by something stronger than the desire of being useful, the desire of ventilating some party view or destroying the character of some partisan opposed to him". This note is taken from my anonymous contribution to the *Cambridge Historical Journal*, vol. II, No. 2 [1927], p. 196 n.]

II

FREEDOM OF THOUGHT, ETC.

6. THE TRIAL OF SOCRATES*

IN the history of toleration and in the history of Rationalism the episode of the trial and death of Socrates occupies a prominent place. The main facts are familiar, thanks to Plato, whose *Apology of Socrates* may be assumed to be known to all who are likely to read this paper. There is no doubt about the general nature of the accusations; there is no doubt about the death; and perhaps most people who have read the Platonic dialogues which are concerned with the subject are aware that the extreme penalty could have been escaped if Socrates had chosen to live. But there are probably many who have never realised that the trial has not its face-value, and that the true motive of the prosecution was not hatred of Rationalism.

Socrates was brought to trial in 399 B.C., when he was seventy years old, on a charge of irreligion and of corrupting young men of Athens by his conversations, and it is surprising on the face of it that such a charge should have been brought against him in his old age, considering that all his life, and it was not a short one, he had been well known as a man of unorthodox views, who did not conceal them, and had been suffered to pursue his way with impunity. In his old age he had done nothing that was new or startling or likely to scandalise the conventional public more than it had been constantly scandalised before by the same bad man. If his teaching was dangerous, it had been just as dangerous in the past, for years and years. Why was it decided at this moment

[* Reprinted from *R.P.A. Annual*, 1926, pp. 17–26. This Essay should be compared with the treatment in *History of Freedom of Thought* (Williams and Norgate, 1914), pp. 30–6.]

to indict him? It is difficult to believe that the motive
of those who brought him into court was simply to
punish a prominent and loquacious Rationalist.

There had been several trials for irreligion or blasphemy at Athens during the preceding half-century.
We are sadly ill-informed about them; but I think that
in the cases we know of there is always reason to suspect
another motive than sincere concern for the interests of
religious orthodoxy. A brief survey of them will not be
out of place; they belong to the annals of the history of
Rationalism. The earliest and best-known case is that of
Anaxagoras, the Ionic philosopher, who lived at Athens,
and was intimate with Pericles. There is no doubt that
his accusers were bitter enemies of the statesman, and
that their real object was not to suppress the scientific
doctrines of the philosopher, but to hurt and embarrass
Pericles. They found themselves, however, in a difficulty. Anaxagoras seems to have done nothing that
could bring him under the Athenian laws against impiety. Unfortunately we do not know the precise terms
of those laws. One of them seems to have made it an
offence not to observe the usual practices which were
enjoined by the State religion. This law was one which
Anaxagoras did not apparently contravene. Conforming
to the established religious observances of a city was a
thing that never seems to have troubled a tolerant
ancient Freethinker. It was therefore necessary to introduce a new law which would entrap Anaxagoras.
Accordingly, a certain man named Diopeithes persuaded
the Assembly to pass a decree authorising any one to im-
peach a person who did not conform to the religion of
the city, or who taught doctrines about things in the sky.
The teaching of astronomy was thus proscribed. As
Anaxagoras denied that the sun and moon were deities
and asserted that the sun was a hot mass of metal, he

was exposed to an attack under this decree. Pericles could do no more than help him to escape from Athens. We are told that the charge of irreligion was supported by another accusation of having intrigued treacherously with Persia.

At a later time another indirect attack was made on Pericles by accusing his talented mistress, Aspasia, of irreligion; but we are not informed on what conduct the accusation was founded. In her case, too, the charge of impiety was bolstered up by another charge of a different kind. It was alleged that she entertained ladies at her house to introduce them to Pericles for improper purposes. Pericles went into court to defend her; and his eloquence and passionate pleading availed to secure her acquittal.

Some years after this Diagoras of Melos—another foreigner—was brought to trial, on the ground that he had said blasphemous things about some foreign deities and rites which were acknowledged by the city. He had the reputation of being an Atheist. We do not know what happened to him, but it is not probable that he was put to death; his execution could hardly have escaped being recorded. It may have been much about the same time that the leading democratic politician, Cleon, prosecuted the poet Euripides, but the action failed. Few documents of that time would be more interesting than an account of this trial, of which we first learned only a few years ago from a short life of the poet discovered in an Egyptian papyrus. It is natural to suppose that Cleon was much less concerned with bold unorthodox things Euripides said in his plays than with criticisms on some of his own political actions. There was no one who would have been more indignant than the humane poet at the proposal of Cleon to put to death the whole population of Mitylene.

Another case of a blasphemy trial has been recorded; but, though it is a rather famous one, it is doubtful whether it ever occurred. It is the case of Protagoras. But there are chronological difficulties which have led Mr Burnet[1] to suspect the truth of the story, and I am inclined to agree with him. We thus reach the important conclusion that, notwithstanding the prevalence of orthodox views and prejudices at Athens, there is no clear evidence of a policy of pure and simple persecution of freethought as such. When for some other reason it was desired to suppress somebody, a charge of unorthodoxy was a facile means to excite the prejudices of the average citizens who served in the jury courts.

Whatever the true object of the prosecution and trial of Socrates, it was ostensibly a trial for irreligion, and it was staged as such in due form.

The man who came forward as the accuser was one who was well known for his irreproachably orthodox opinions, just the man who would carry weight with jurors as a sincere champion of the gods. His name was Meletus. In that same year he brought another action for impiety, and a portion of his speech on that occasion has survived, which lets us see what a fanatical person he was. In modern summaries of the trial it is commonly stated that there were two other accusers. This is certainly inaccurate. There was only one accuser—Meletus; two others were prominently concerned in the trial, Anytus and Lycon, as opponents of Socrates. These two acted as *synēgoroi*, or advocates for the prosecution. Lycon seems to have been almost a lay figure; he was an orator, and if he had not been associated with this trial his name would not have been remembered. Anytus was one of the most influential politicians of the day, and there can be no doubt that but for him Socrates would

[1] *Greek Philosophy*, I, pp. 111–12.

not have been brought into court, and that it was at his instigation that Meletus was put up to prosecute—a congenial role, which he must have been only too glad to undertake. This is recognised in the *Apology* of Plato when Socrates speaks of his foes as "Anytus and his friends"—not, as we should expect, "Meletus and his friends".

In 423 B.C. the notoriety of Socrates and his followers reached a culminating point, when Aristophanes produced his *Clouds*, in which he was lampooned for his scientific studies and speculations. About the same time other comic poets were also introducing Socrates on the stage. It can hardly be questioned that his theories were just as offensive to orthodoxy as those of Anaxagoras. Yet no one had cared to take any public action against him, and throughout the Peloponnesian War he talked and taught with impunity, attracting to his society young men of the richer classes who had leisure for philosophical conversation. From politics he held strictly aloof; he had never attached himself to any political leader or joined any political group; and he was let alone, though some of his companions proved afterwards that they were not loyal democrats. In the troubles which followed the fall of the Athenian Empire, through the defeat at Ægospotami (405 B.C.), he was involved in a political incident against his will. The democracy was overthrown, and the oligarchy of the Thirty Tyrants seized the power. Two of these—Critias, the most important of them, and Plato's uncle Charmides—had been friends of Socrates. They knew that he was by no means an admirer of democracy, and they calculated that they could count on his support. They found they were mistaken. Nothing could justify in his eyes their despotism and defiance of law. Probably he criticised them openly, and freedom of speech could not be tolerated by this unscrupulous government. We hear that Critias warned him that he must abandon his habit of conversing with the young men who were attached to him. After this they determined to implicate him in the responsibility for one of their illegal acts. They had decided to put to death a democrat, Leo of Salamis, who had committed no crime and had not been legally tried and condemned. The tyrants ordered several persons, of whom Socrates was one, to arrest him. Socrates made no reply to the command, but simply went home. He would, no doubt, have been executed himself for his contumacious disobedience if the oligarchy had not fallen at this juncture.

It might have been thought that this incident would have been enough to make him a *persona grata* with the democracy, however unpopular he might have been before, and serve to cancel suspicions that he was disloyal; that at the least he would have been as fully tolerated by the new democracy as he had been by the old. But the Athenians were too intelligent to imagine that his views about democracy had changed. They understood that his protest against the execution of Leo of Salamis was not made because Leo was a democrat, but because the act was tyrannous and illegal. For some time the restored democracy did not feel itself very secure, and one can understand that it appeared to some to be dangerous to have his polite but effective tongue at large criticising democracy in general with the utmost urbanity.

Anytus, a man who was honest and sincere and highly reputed, was of this opinion, and came to the conclusion that Socrates must be silenced or got rid of in some way. No political charge was possible, and Socrates had not broken the law. The only weapon that could be used was the prejudice against his religious heresies. And for warfare of that kind Meletus was obviously the right man.

There were, however, rather awkward difficulties which hampered the prosecution. One of the most statesmanlike acts of the restored democracy was the amnesty which gave immunity to all citizens for anything they had done before the year 403; and no one was more earnest about observing this act loyally and strictly than Anytus. This precluded the prosecution from bringing up against Socrates his compromising intimacies with Alcibiades or any of the enemies of the democracy. In the second place, there had been a thoroughgoing revision of the laws, and one result of this was that no decrees which had been passed before 403 B.C. retained their validity, so that no one could now be indicted under the decree of Diopeithes which had been levelled against Anaxagoras. The vagueness of the accusation which it was agreed to formulate indicates the embarrassment. It ran thus: Socrates is guilty of not worshipping the gods whom the city worship, and of introducing religious novelties. He is guilty also of corrupting the young men.

This is well attested as the literal text of the charge. Plato and Xenophon agree, and there is a confirmatory record which seems to have been derived from the official document preserved in the archives of the King Archon before whom the action was originally filed.[1]

It seems legitimate to infer that the Laws of Solon, which remained valid, contained an enactment which made religious observances compulsory and another which made "corrupting" the young a legal offence. But it is a puzzle what the religious novelties were that Socrates was alleged to have introduced. This is left vague; there is even a difficulty about the precise

---

[1] See Diogenes Laertius, II, 40.

meaning of the Greek phrase (*kaina daimonia*) which is generally translated "strange divinities", but which, according to Mr Burnet, means "strange religious observances".

We do not possess the speech of the accuser Meletus; it could have been preserved only if he had chosen to publish it himself, and perhaps he was not very proud of the performance. The sources for the trial are Plato's *Apology* and two works of Xenophon—the *Apology*, a brochure on the subject of the way in which Socrates defended himself, containing what professes to be a brief abstract of what he said; and the *Memorabilia* of Socrates, in which much the same ground is traversed. Xenophon was not present at the trial; he was in the East with the Ten Thousand; on his return to Athens he obtained his information at secondhand, especially from Hermogenes, who had been one of the companions of Socrates.

Plato was in court and heard the whole proceedings. How close his *Apology* is to the original speech of Socrates is a question on which different views have been held, and which, as Mr Jowett said, admits of no precise solution. It is certain that Plato's work is not a report in anything like our sense of the word. When an orator published a speech he had delivered, he revised and improved its literary form, and there can be no doubt that Plato took pains to make his master's defence a work of art. But how far did he permit himself to go in taking liberties with what Socrates had said? Keeping to the general tenor of the argument, did he add to it or did he omit? For one thing, it seems improbable that the prisoner, after sentence had been passed, would have been allowed to address a portion of the jury on the subject of death, as Plato makes him do. We can hardly help believing that this last section of the speech was an addition of Plato, designed to make the whole trial look like a beautiful work of art. And if this is admitted, the general considerations which have led some of the best and most recent critics to regard Plato's *Apology* as a trustworthy and generally accurate version of what Socrates actually said cannot be taken as conclusive. There may have been additions to or enlargements of his argument. And then what about omissions?

Now, Socrates had a complete answer to the first charge in the indictment, that he did not worship the gods of the city or observe its religious observances—a simple denial, supported by witnesses, that the accusation was true; and it is almost incredible that he should not have said so. In Plato he says nothing of the kind. But in Xenophon's *Apology* he says so emphatically: "I should like to know on what grounds Meletus asserts that I do not worship the gods worshipped by the city, for at public festivals I am seen sacrificing at the public altars, and Meletus could have seen me, if he wished". It is hard to believe that Socrates could have omitted to make this simple direct statement of fact, and I have no hesitation in accepting this from Xenophon and in regarding it as a point which Plato has omitted.

Another remarkable difference between the two defences is the treatment of the charge of introducing religious novelties. In Plato's defence this is referred to only for the purpose of showing that it is inconsistent with the allegation that he did not acknowledge the gods, and no hint is given of the precise meaning of *kaina daimonia*. Meletus, however, was absolutely bound to explain its meaning in order to justify the accusation. In Xenophon's defence, on the other hand, it is explained as meaning that Socrates professed to hear a divine voice which warned him what to do. Socrates did not deny it, but replied that to be warned by an inner voice was not to introduce a new religious practice; an inner voice is in exactly the same category as the voice of an oracle, or omens from birds, or the prophecies of seers. He added that he sometimes communicated to friends the counsels of the gods conveyed by this inner voice, and that none of them had ever proved false. At this point, Xenophon records, there were interruptions on the part of the judges, of whom some were incredulous and others envied him for his access to greater gods than they had access to themselves. Then Xenophon says Socrates told the story of the oracle which Apollo gave at Delphi to his companion Chærephon, which Plato introduces in a different connection and a different and much more impressive form. I cannot resist the conclusion that here again Plato has omitted a part of the original speech.

The other charge of corrupting the young men is dealt with very slightly in Plato's *Apology*, and what Socrates says there leads one to suppose that Meletus had dwelt merely or mainly on the corruption consisting in communicating the irreligious views of which the defendant was accused in the first clauses of the indictment. This brings us to another problem: Does Plato's *Apology* supply a complete account of the trial? It seems clear that what Socrates says is a reply only to the speech of Meletus, and that the advocates Anytus and Lycon have not yet spoken in his support. It is natural to infer that they spoke after Socrates. Socrates did not employ advocates; if he had, they would have replied to Anytus and Lycon. The evidence points to the conclusion that it was arranged that Meletus should deal with the charges of irreligion, and that Anytus should develop the charge of corrupting the young men.

To justify and explain this conclusion I must refer to

a polemical work which appeared at Athens subsequently to the death of Socrates. Between the years 394 and 390 B.C. an attack upon Socrates was published by a sophist named Polycrates. It has been plausibly conjectured[1] that the motive of this attack was to furnish a counterblast to Plato's *Gorgias*, which may have appeared in 394 B.C. or soon after, and contains a very unfavourable criticism of Themistocles and Cimon, Thucydides and Pericles, the leading statesmen of the old Athenian democracy, who were the *dii minores* of men like Anytus. Plato puts this criticism in the mouth of Socrates; but it is probable that the Platonic Socrates says much more severe things than the actual Socrates ever said. The work of Polycrates was put in the shape of a prosecuting speech, pretending to be the speech Anytus delivered in the trial of 399 B.C. It is not preserved, but we virtually know its tenor. For it imposed in later times on readers as being what it feigned to be; and among others it imposed on the rhetorician Libanius, nearly 800 years later (in the second half of the fourth century A.D.), and he conceived the not unhappy idea of composing a reply to it as a rhetorical exercise. This reply is preserved among his declamations, and the German philologist L. Dindorf made the discovery that it was a reply to the work of Polycrates. Every one now recognises that this is true. And as Libanius takes the fictitious speech of Anytus, point by point, the lost work of Polycrates can be reconstructed.

This lost work has, I think, some importance for the actual trial of Socrates, at which Polycrates may or may not have been present. His attack dwelled entirely on the charge of corrupting the young, and was put into the mouth of Anytus. This may be taken to support the conjecture made above, that this part of the charge was

[1] By Mr U. von Wilamowitz-Möllendorff.

left to Anytus, while the religious side was handled by Meletus. Polycrates would have been likely so far to keep to fact.

It may also be noticed that Libanius takes the same view of the proceedings of the trial that has just been suggested. After Meletus, Anytus comes forward with an ill-natured speech, and then Lycon reviles the accused. "Are we, the friends of Socrates, to listen to the evil speaking of these two and sit dumb? I will confront Anytus", says the orator of Libanius. This shows that he imagined Meletus to have been answered by Socrates before Anytus spoke.

The Anytus of Polycrates was not restricted, as the Anytus of history was, by considerations of the amnesty. He was quite free to paint a lurid picture of the tyranny of Critias and his associates, and to attribute their evil doings to the malign influence of Socrates. He could recite with rhetorical indignation the iniquities and levities of Alcibiades and his treachery to Athens, and represent his whole discreditable career as a fruit of the corrupting discourses of the philosopher. It seems pretty certain that Polycrates would have included in his arraignment the evidence that was actually brought forward at the trial as to the corrupting character of the conversations of Socrates, and therefore his attack may contain material which may give us information about that part of the trial of which Plato tells us nothing.

Among such borrowings from the actual speech of Anytus comes first the charge of attacking the classical poets, especially Homer, Hesiod, Theognis, and Pindar (Libanius, chap. 62 *sqq.*). Socrates, no doubt, did constantly criticise passages in the poets and censure their sentiments, and a clever advocate could easily make out a case which would carry weight with a prejudiced public, that he taught disrespect and irreverence for the inspired teachers of wisdom and virtue. The absurdity of such an obscurantist attitude is very judiciously exposed by Libanius.

Another point which Anytus might have introduced into his denunciation is that Socrates hated democracy as a form of government, and constantly ridiculed it (Libanius, chap. 54 *sqq.*)—a charge which he could probably have made good without touching on any forbidden ground. It seems also extremely likely that another point urged by Anytus to substantiate the charge of corrupting the young men was the habit of Socrates to find fault with Athenian institutions and customs (Libanius, chap. 80 *sqq.*). Evidence for all this could easily have been collected and produced in court. Another insinuation which Anytus may have possibly made is that Socrates induced or encouraged people to spend an ideal life and neglect their business (Libanius, chap. 127) for the sake of unprofitable speculations. I thus suggest that the whole portion of the work of Polycrates corresponding to chapters 54–135 of the reply of Libanius may have reproduced the tenor of what Anytus actually said in court, and, if so, it had probably much more weight with the judges than the flag of orthodoxy waved by Meletus.

On one point all those who heard the speech of Socrates at his trial seem to have been agreed, so we are told by Xenophon (*Apology*, 1), and that was the lofty superior tone he adopted towards his judges. His companions were surprised at it, as it was manifestly foolish in a man who was being tried for his life to adopt an attitude which those on whom the verdict depended would regard as insolent bravado. Hence some of them drew the conclusion that he preferred death to life, as a way of avoiding the pains and weaknesses of old age, being determined to seal his own doom, and to avert the undesirable issue of an acquittal.

This theory strikes one as fantastic. Socrates was barely seventy years old. He had an unusually strong constitution, and was in good health. If he had to die, he, like any other philosophically minded person, might have considered the avoidance of old age a mitigation of a premature fate; but to act deliberately for the purpose of ensuring such a fate would have been as morbid as to commit suicide. And that is contrary to all our ideas of the character of Socrates.

There is really no need of any explanation of the tone of superiority which characterises the speech, as reported by Plato. It is the natural expression of his deep conviction of the reasonableness and rightness of his own life and conduct, and he saw no cause for condescending from it in order to conciliate. The verdict of Guilty did not mean that he must die. The majority of the votes which condemned him was not enormous, and there is hardly a doubt that, if he had proposed banishment as his punishment, that would have been accepted by the court instead of death, which had been proposed by the prosecution. This is most probably the result which Anytus expected, and would have preferred. Socrates declined to do this; he proposed a derisory fine, which the court would not accept. The Judges, therefore, being obliged to choose between the penalties proposed by the accuser and the accused, in accordance with the curious law governing cases of this kind in which there was no legally prescribed penalty, were forced to pass the sentence of death.

I can find no evidence that Socrates wished to die. But, and this is quite a different thing, he wished to live only on his own terms. After his condemnation he had the choice between two alternatives: death or exile. It was a hedonistic calculation, and he states quite distinctly in Plato's *Apology* why exile seems to him the less tolerable of the two:

If I say exile, I must indeed be blinded by the love of life if I am so irrational as to expect that, when you who are my own citizens cannot endure my discourses and words, and have found them so grievous and odious that you would fain have done with them, others are likely to endure me. No, indeed, men of Athens, that is not very likely. And what a life should I lead, at my age, wandering from city to city, living in everchanging exile, and always being driven out! For I am quite sure that into whatever place I go, as there as here, the young men will come and listen to me; and if I drive them away, their elders will drive me out at their desire; and if I let them come, their fathers and friends will drive me out for their sakes.[1]

The peculiar interest of the end of Socrates lies in the fact that it was a rational choice between two fates—between death, of which neither he nor any one else knew the nature or meaning, and banishment, of which he had calculated the probable pains and miseries. He was clear-sighted and strong-minded enough not to allow reason to be defeated by the natural instinct of clinging to life at any cost.

He goes on then to the crucial point:

Some one will say: Yes, Socrates, but cannot you hold your tongue, and then you may go into a foreign city, and no one will interfere with you? Now I have a great difficulty in making you understand my answer to this. For if I tell you that to do as you say would be a disobedience to the God, and therefore that I cannot hold my tongue, you will not believe that I am serious; and if I say again that the greatest good of man is daily to converse about virtue and all that concerning which you hear me examining myself and others, and that the life which is unexamined is not worth living, you are still less likely to believe me.

[1] I have borrowed the translation of Jowett.

If Socrates could have resigned himself to giving up the excitement of "conversing daily about virtue", he might have avoided the trial altogether. He could have gone to Anytus and given an undertaking to abandon his habit of holding conversations which were so disagreeable to the democrats. There can be no doubt that his promise would have been accepted and the prosecution dropped. But he would risk death rather than consent to what would make life worthless for him. He would live only upon his own terms. He cannot fitly be called a martyr, except in the wide, vague sense in which that word is often applied to any victim of intolerance. If he bore witness to any cause, it was to the cause of freedom of speech.

7. FREEDOM OF SPEECH AND THE CENSORSHIP*

Misgivings have been felt during the present War at the policy of the Government in yielding to the alleged necessity of placing restrictions on the free expression of opinion. I am not thinking of the people, comparatively few, who have personally suffered from the censorship, but of others who, though far from wishing to publish anything that could embarrass the Government in the conduct of the War, have been unable to help feeling something like dismay at coercive measures that seemed to defy and menace the principles which Mill's classical essay *On Liberty* were supposed to have definitely established. Misgivings of this kind have been expressed from time to time, and must be entertained by many who have not expressed them—misgivings as to the defensibility of a censorship of opinion in any circumstances whatever. Is this coercion justified by the reasons, *primâ facie* cogent, which prompted it; by the desirability of suppressing speech and discussion which might weaken, however little, our efforts in the struggle or those of our Allies, or encourage, however little, the efforts of our enemies, or play, however slightly, into their hands? If we have to admit that some coercion is unavoidable in our present situation, is the general doctrine laid down by Mill, and widely accepted as almost axiomatic, in jeopardy? Can a theoretical principle be sound if its adherents, under the stress of harsh facts, are driven to admit exceptions, or to resort to new interpretations?

The importance of the doctrine that perfect liberty of

[* *R.P.A. Annual*, 1919, pp. 16–19.]

discussion is a fundamental condition of social progress was recently impressed upon the Working Men's Club and Institute Union in the presidential address delivered last May by Mr J. J. Dent, who kindly sent me a copy of his thoughtful discourse. He quoted some remarks of mine, among which was this:

The considerations of permanent utility on which it [the doctrine in question] rests must outweigh any calculation of present advantage which, from time to time, might be thought to demand its violation.*

In writing these words in the days before the Flood—it was 1912—I thought as little of a situation such as that which now confronts the allied countries as Mill did when he wrote his essay in the middle of the nineteenth century. Does this statement require modification? When common-sense declares that restrictions on the publication of opinions at such a crisis as this are necessary, is common-sense mistaken, or can the doctrine of freedom be reconciled to it, without losing its general validity?

The political theory which is developed in Mill's essay, and lies behind most of his arguments, was widely held in Victorian England as self-evidently true. It coincides in general spirit with the doctrines of Bentham and Spencer. In Europe, outside England, it never prevailed. Government is regarded as an evil, unfortunately indispensable, and its legitimate functions are contracted to the narrowest possible limits. This view, which inspired the old Liberalism, has been discredited by later criticism. It rests on assumptions concerning the nature of society and the social relations of the individual which do not sustain a penetrating scrutiny, and probably no political thinker would now accept it as a true theory of the functions of the State.

[* *History of Freedom of Thought* (Williams and Norgate, 1914), p. 239.]

Yet, even when the rightful action of the State is reduced to Mill's minimum, the principle which he lays down as entitled to govern absolutely the dealings of society with the individual might be held to cover the present case. The principle is that

The sole end for which mankind are warranted, individually or collectively, in interfering with the liberty of action of any of their number is self-protection. That the only purpose for which power can be rightfully exercised over any member of a civilised community, against his will, is to prevent harm to others.

This principle would clearly entitle a Government to apply compulsion if it is convinced that the publication of certain opinions would cause the risk of prolonging a war or of weakening the defence of the society against its enemies, as this risk means the risk of causing harm to others.[1]

But, it will be said, while a Government has indisputably a right to take legal measures to prevent harm to others, is it not unwisdom and contrary in the long run to social utility to limit that complete freedom of speech which is a fundamental condition of progress so important that it ought to prevail over all considerations of immediate expediency? Granting that the publication of certain opinions is in present circumstances distinctly undesirable, that it may tend to jeopardise our victory, yet, from a higher point of view, the maintenance of free speech is of such radical and permanent importance that to curtail it is as unjustifiable as it would be, say, to reduce a population temporarily to a

---

[1] Such a coercion is a milder exercise of the rights of society than conscription, for which Mill implicitly supplies the justification in chap. IV when he says that the individual is bound to bear his share "of the labours and sacrifices incurred for defending the society or its members from injury and molestation".

condition of slavery for the sake of ensuring victory in an admittedly good cause.

An answer to this might be attempted by reverting to the reasons which establish freedom of discussion as an overmastering principle. They are developed in chap. II, the most valuable part of Mill's essay, because it is not compromised by the precariousness of his political theory. It would be too long to reproduce or even condense his arguments here, but their upshot is that perfect freedom of discussion is the only means of attaining such certainty as a fallible being may attain.

The beliefs which we have most warrant for have no safeguard to rest on, but a standing invitation to the whole world to prove them unfounded. If the challenge is not accepted, or is accepted and the attempt fails, we are far enough from certainty still; but we have done the best that the existing state of human reason admits of; we have neglected nothing that could give the truth the chance of reaching us.

Hence the supreme social utility of unstifled discussion. There is a debatable subject, and the free expression of opinions is the means of ventilating it and approaching the truth. To silence any opinion is an injury to society, is (to use Mill's words) "robbing the human race". But observe what the assumption is. The sphere in which truth is to emerge by unrestricted freedom of speech is the sphere of argumentative debate; it is not the sphere of arms. If, for instance, the issue between the Entente and the Central Powers were being fought with word and pen, and not on the battlefield, it would be criminal in any of the Entente Governments to silence the voices of minorities among their own people who supported the views of the Central Powers. But when the debate is being conducted on the battlefield the issue is removed from the sphere of argument, where alone prevail the conditions in which the free expression of opinion can be of supreme social utility. It may, therefore, be argued that in these circumstances the principle ceases to be unreservedly valid so far as the questions are concerned which have been committed to the arbitration of Mars.

This answer is not altogether satisfactory. Especially, it does not meet the point that the principle whose suspension it would justify has such universal validity that it is wrong to over-ride it for the sake of any immediate particular utility. A truer answer is that every social principle is subject to the general limiting rule that it must not endanger its own existence. In circumstances where its operation means its possible destruction a self-contradiction emerges; and in such a case we are not really true to it if we risk its permanent interests by adhering to it absolutely. *Fiat justitia, ruat caelum* is a maxim which would lose its validity in a case where the catastrophe involved the disappearance of justice itself. Apply this to the present situation. The large majority of our society see in the War a defence of freedom against tyranny; we are convinced that our enemies threaten the cause of liberty throughout the world. If the unreserved maintenance of the particular liberty of discussion endangers in any way the triumph of a cause which includes itself, that is a self-contradiction which can be reasonably overcome only by sacrificing the lesser to the greater, the temporary to the permanent. War offers an analogous case. If a society devoted to the idea of universal peace and abhorring physical violence as a supreme evil encounters a situation in which resort to physical violence is the only means of rescuing the world from an order founded on physical violence, it must transgress its principle in order to save it. The principle ceases to be valid at the point at which its operation would be suicidal.

95

If we agree that all general principles of conduct are limited by the more general principle that they must not frustrate or destroy themselves, the statement quoted from myself at the beginning of this paper is not compromised by the admission that a certain censorship of opinion is necessary during the present War.

III

BYZANTINE HISTORY

8. THE CONSTITUTION OF THE LATER ROMAN EMPIRE*

THE forms of government which are commonly classified as absolute monarchies have not received the same attention or been so carefully analysed as those forms which are known as republics and constitutional monarchies. There is a considerable literature on absolute monarchy considered theoretically, in connexion with the question of Divine Right, but the actual examples which history offers of this kind of government have not been the subject of a detailed comparative study. Montesquieu, for instance, treats them indiscriminately as despotisms. Probably the reason lies in the apparent simplicity of a constitution, by which the supreme power is exclusively vested in one man. When we say that the monarch's will is supreme, we may seem to say all there is to be said. The Later Roman Empire is an example of absolute monarchy, and I propose to show that so far as it is concerned there is a good deal more to be said.

The term absolute monarchy is applied in contradistinction to limited or constitutional monarchy. I understand the former to mean that the whole legislative, judicial, and executive powers of the state are vested in the monarch, and there is no other independent and concurrent authority.[1] The latter means that besides the so-called monarch there are other political bodies which possess an independent and effective authority of their own, and share in the sovran power. These terms, absolute and constitutional mon-

[* The Creighton Lecture, University College, London, November 12, 1909, Cambridge University Press, 1910, 49 pp. The spelling of proper names will be found to differ in these essays, but in each case Bury's own forms have been retained.]

archy, are unsatisfactory, from a logical point of view. For they group together these two forms of government as subdivisions of the class monarchy, implying or suggesting that they have much more real affinity to one another than either has to other constitutions. This is evidently untrue: a constitutional monarchy is far more closely allied to a republic like France than to an absolute monarchy like Russia. The English constitution, for instance, in which legislation is effected by the consent of three independent organs, the Crown, the Lords, and the Commons, might be described more correctly as a triarchy than as a monarchy; and it seems to be unfortunate that monarchy should have come to be used, quite unnecessarily, as a synonym for kingship. "Limited monarchy", as Austin said long ago, "is not monarchy";[2] monarchy properly so called is, simply and solely, absolute monarchy. We have however an alternative term, "autocracy", which involves no ambiguities, and might, I venture to think, be advantageously adopted as the technical term for this form of government in constitutional discussions. And "autocracy" has a special advantage over "absolute monarchy". Autocracies are not all alike, in respect to the power actually exercised by the autocrat. Although not limited by any bodies possessing an independent authority, he may be limited effectually in other ways. Now we can properly speak of more or less limited autocracies, whereas it is an impropriety of language to speak of more or less absolute monarchies, as "absolute" admits of no degrees.

Originally, and during the first three centuries of its existence, the Roman Empire was theoretically a republic. The Senate co-existed with the Emperor, as a body invested with an authority independent of his; but the functions which it exercised by virtue of that authority were surrendered one by one; it became more and more dependent on him; and by the end of the third century the fiction of a second power in the state was dropped altogether, although the Senate was not abolished.[3] From that time forward, under the system established by Diocletian and Constantine, until the fall of the Empire in the fifteenth century, the government was simply and undisguisedly an autocracy.

Now one broad distinction between autocracies may be found in the mode of accession to the throne. The sovranty may be hereditary or it may be elective. If it is elective, the sovranty is derived from the electors who, when the throne is vacant, exercise an independent and sovran authority in electing a new monarch. If it is hereditary, if the right of the autocrat depends entirely and indefeasibly on his birth, then we may say that his sovranty is underived; the succession is automatic, and there is no moment at which any other person or persons than the monarch can perform an act of sovran authority such as is implied in the election of a sovran. This difference may involve, as we shall see, important consequences.

In the case of the Roman Empire, the Imperial dignity continued to be elective, as it had been from the beginning, and the method of election remained the same. When the throne was vacant a new Emperor was chosen by the Senate and the army. The initiative might be taken either by the Senate or by the army, and both methods were recognised as equally valid. It was of course only a portion of the army that actually chose an Emperor—for instance, if the choice were made in Constantinople, the guard regiments; but such a portion was regarded as for this purpose representing all the troops which were scattered over the Empire. The appointment did not take the formal shape of what we commonly understand by election. If the soldiers took the initiative, they simply proclaimed the man they wanted. If the choice was made by the Senate, the procedure might be more deliberate, but there seems to have been no formal casting of votes, and the essential act was the proclamation.[4] It sufficed that one of these bodies should proclaim an Emperor to establish his title to the sovranty; it only remained for the other body to concur; and the inauguration was formally completed when the people of Constantinople had also acclaimed him in the Hippodrome—a formality always observed and reminiscent of the fact that the inhabitants of the new capital of Constantine had succeeded to the position of the old *populus Romanus*.[5]

The part which the Senate played in the appointment of an Emperor, whether by choosing him or by ratifying the choice of the army, is constitutionally important. The Senate or *Synklêtos* of New Rome was a very different body from the old Senatus Romanus. It was a small council consisting of persons who belonged to it by virtue of administrative offices to which they were appointed by the Emperor. In fact, the old Senate had coalesced with the Consistorium or Imperial council, and in consequence the new Senate had a double aspect. So long as there was a reigning Emperor, it acted as consistorium or advisory council of the sovran, but when there was an interval between two reigns, it resumed the independent authority which had lain in abeyance and performed functions which it had inherited from the early Senate.

But it was not only when the throne was vacant that it could perform such functions. The right of election might be exercised by the Senate and the army at any time. It was a principle of state-law in the Early Empire that the people which made the Emperor could also unmake him, and this principle continued in force under the autocracy. There was no formal process of deposing a sovran, but the members of the community had the means of dethroning him, if his government failed to give satisfaction, by proclaiming a new Emperor; and if anyone so proclaimed obtained sufficient support from the army, Senate, and people, the old Emperor was compelled to vacate the throne, retiring into a monastery, losing his eyesight, or suffering death, according to the circumstances of the situation or the temper of his supplanter; while the new Emperor was regarded as the legitimate monarch from the day on which he was proclaimed; the proclamation was taken as the legal expression of the general will. If he had not a sufficient following to render the proclamation effective and was suppressed, he was treated as a rebel; but during the struggle and before the catastrophe, the fact that a portion of the army had proclaimed him gave him a presumptive constitutional status, which the event might either confirm or annul. The method of deposition was in fact revolution, and we are accustomed to regard revolution as something essentially unconstitutional, an appeal from law to force; but under the Imperial system, it was not unconstitutional; the government was, to use an expression of Mommsen, "an autocracy tempered by the legal right of revolution".

Thus the sovranty of the Roman autocrat was delegated to him by the community, as represented by the Senate, and the army, and, we may add, the people of Constantinople.[6] The symbol of the sovranty thus delegated was the diadem, which was definitely introduced by Constantine. The Emperor wore other insignia, such as the purple robe and the red boots, but the diadem was preeminently the symbol and expression of the autocracy. The dress only represented the Imperator or commander-in-chief of the army, and no formalities were connected with its assumption. It was otherwise with the crown, which in the Persian Kingdom, from which it was borrowed, was placed on the king's head by the High-priest of the Magian religion. In theory, the Imperial crown should be imposed by a representative of those who conferred the sovran authority which it symbolised. And in the fourth century we find the Prefect, Sallustius Secundus, crowning Valentinian I, in whose election he had taken the most prominent part. But the Emperors seem to have felt some hesitation in thus receiving the diadem from the hands of a subject; and the selection of one magnate for this high office of conferring the symbol of sovranty was likely to cause enmity and jealousy. Yet a formality was considered necessary. In the fifth century, the difficulty was overcome in a clever and tactful way. The duty of coronation was assigned to the Patriarch of Constantinople. In discharging this office, the Patriarch was not envied by the secular magnates because he could not be their rival, and his ecclesiastical position relieved the Emperor from all embarrassment in receiving the diadem from a subject. There is some evidence, though it is not above suspicion, that this plan was adopted at the coronation of Marcian in A.D. 450, but it seems certain that his successor Leo was crowned by the Patriarch in A.D. 457. Henceforward this was the regular practice. In the thirteenth century we find Theodore II postponing his coronation until the Patriarchal throne, which happened to be vacant, was filled. But although it was the regular and desirable form of coronation, it was never regarded as indispensable for the autocrat's legitimate inauguration. The last of the East Roman Emperors, Constantine Palaeologus, was not crowned by the Patriarch; he was crowned by a layman.[7] This fact that coronation by the Patriarch was not constitutionally necessary, though it was the usual custom, is significant.

For it shows that the Patriarch, in performing the ceremony, was not representing the Church. It is possible that the idea of committing the office to him was suggested by the Persian coronations which were performed by the High-priest, but the significance was not the same. The chief of the Magians acted as the representative of the Persian religion, the Patriarch acted as the representative of the State.[8] For if he had specially represented the Church, it is clear that his co-operation could never have been dispensed with. In other words, no new constitutional theory or constitutional requirement was introduced by the assignment of the privilege of crowning Emperors to the Patriarch. It did not mean that the consent of the Church was formally necessary to the inauguration of the sovran.

I will make this point still more evident presently in connection with another important feature of the constitution to which we now come. If you look down the roll of Emperors, you will find that only a minority of them were actually elected in the ways I have described. In most cases, when an Emperor died, the throne was not vacant, for generally he had a younger colleague, who had already been invested with the Imperial dignity, so that no new election was necessary. This practice[9] by which a reigning Emperor could appoint his successor modified the elective principle. The Emperor used to devolve the succession upon his son, if he had one; so that son constantly succeeded father, and the history of the Roman Empire is marked by a series of hereditary dynasties. The constitution thus combined the elective and the hereditary principles; a device was found for securing the advantages of hereditary succession, and obviating its disadvantages by preserving the principle of election. The chief advantage of hereditary monarchy is that it avoids the danger of domestic troubles and civil war which are likely to occur when the throne is elective and there are two rival candidates. Its chief disadvantage is that the supreme power in the State will inevitably devolve sometimes upon a weak and incapable ruler. The result of the mixture of the two principles, the dynastic and the elective, was that there were far fewer incapable sovrans than if the dynastic succession had been exclusively valid, and fewer struggles for power than if every change of ruler had meant an election. It would be interesting to trace, if we had the material, how the inhabitants of the Empire became more and more attached to the idea of legitimacy—the idea that the children of an Emperor had a constitutional right to the supreme power. We can see at least that this feeling grew very strong under the long rule of the Macedonian dynasty; it is illustrated by the political rôle which the Empress Zoe, an utterly incompetent and depraved old woman, was allowed to play because she was the daughter of Constantine VIII.* But the fact remained that although a father invariably raised his eldest son, and sometimes younger sons too, to the rank of Augustus, the son became Emperor by virtue of his father's will and not by virtue of his birth. The Emperor was not in any way bound to devolve the succession upon his son.[10] Now what I ask you to observe is that when a reigning sovran created a second Emperor, whether his son or anyone else, there was no election. The Senate, the army, and the people expressed their joy and satisfaction, in the ceremonies which attended the creation, but the creation was entirely the act of the Emperor. The constitutional significance is evident. The autocratic powers conferred upon an Emperor by his election included the right of devolving the Imperial dignity upon others. It was part

[* *v. infra* references *p.* 112 *note.*]

of his sovranty to be able to create a colleague who was potentially another sovran.

This difference between the appointment of an Emperor when the throne is vacant and the appointment of an Emperor as colleague when the throne is occupied is clearly and significantly expressed by the difference between the coronation acts in the two cases. In the former case the act is performed by a representative of the electors, almost always the Patriarch; in the latter case it is regularly performed by the reigning Emperor. It is he who, possessing the undivided sovranty, confers the Imperial dignity and therefore with his own hands delivers its symbol. Sometimes indeed he commits the office of coronation to the Patriarch, but the Patriarch is then acting simply as his delegate.[11] This difference is a confirmation of the view that the Patriarch, in discharging the duty of coronation, acts as a representative of the electors, and not of the Church. For if the coronation had been conceived as a religious act, it must have been performed in the same way, in all cases, by the chief minister of the Church.

But now you may ask, is the term autocracy or the term monarchy strictly applicable to the Empire? Monarchy and autocracy mean the sovran rule of one man alone, but, as we have just seen, the Emperor generally had a colleague. Both in the early and in the later Empire, there were constantly two Emperors, sometimes more. In the tenth century, for instance, in the reign of Romanus I, there were as many as five— each of them an Augustus, each a Basileus.[12] This practice is derived from the original collegial character of the proconsular Imperium and the tribunician power, on which Augustus based his authority. But, although the Roman Imperium or Basileia was collegial, the sovranty was not divided. When there were two

Emperors only one exercised the sovran power and governed the State; his colleague was subordinate, and simply enjoyed the dignity and the expectation of succession. Though his name appeared in legislative acts and his effigy on coins, and though he shared in all the Imperial honours, he was a sleeping partner. With one exception, which I will notice presently, the only cases of Imperial colleagues exercising concurrent sovranty were in the period from Diocletian to the death of Julius Nepos, when the Empire was territorially divided. Diocletian and Maximian, for instance; the sons of Constantine, Arcadius, and Honorius; were severally monarchs in their own dominions. But except in the case of territorial division, the supreme power was exercised by one man, and monarchy is therefore a right description of the constitution. In the reign of Constantine IV, the soldiers demanded that the Emperor should crown his two brothers. "We believe in the Trinity", they cried, "and we would have three Emperors". But this must not be interpreted as a demand that each member of the desired Imperial trinity should exercise sovran authority. Such a joint sovranty was never tried except in one case, and a clear distinction was drawn between the Basileus who governed and the Basileus who did not govern. The exceptional case was the peculiar one of two Empresses, who ruled conjointly for a short time in the eleventh century. I will mention this case again, in a few minutes, when I come to speak of the position of Empresses.

And here I must dwell for a moment on the name *Basileus* and another Greek name *Autokrator*, which were employed to designate the Emperor. In the early Empire, Basileus was used in the East and especially in Egypt, where Augustus was regarded as the successor of the Ptolemies, but it was not used officially by the Em-

perors; it was not the Greek for Imperator. The Greek
word adopted to translate Imperator was Autokrator,
and this is the term always used in Imperial Greek inscriptions. By the fourth century Basileus had come into
universal use in the Greek-speaking parts of the Empire;
it was the regular term used by Greek writers; but it was
not yet accepted as an official title. Nor was it adopted
officially till the seventh century in the reign of Heraclius. It has been pointed out by Bréhier[13] that the
earliest official act in which an Emperor entitles himself
Basileus is a law of Heraclius of the year 629. In the
earlier diplomas of his reign he uses the old traditional
form Autokrator. Bréhier, however, has failed to see the
reason of this change of style, but the significant date
A.D. 629 supplies the explanation. In that year Heraclius completed the conquest of Persia. Now, the
Persian king was the only foreign monarch to whom the
Roman Emperors conceded the title Basileus; except
the Abyssinian king, who hardly counted. So long as
there was a great independent Basileus outside the
Roman Empire, the Emperors refrained from adopting
a title which would be shared by another monarch. But
as soon as that monarch was reduced to the condition
of a dependent vassal and there was no longer a con-
currence, the Emperor signified the event by assuming
officially the title which had for several centuries been
applied to him unofficially. The Empire was extremely
conservative in forms and usages; changes were slow in
official documents, they were slower still in the coinage.
It is not till more than a century later that Basileus begins to be adopted by the mint. By this change Basileus
became the official equivalent of Imperator; it took the
place of Autokrator; and it was now possible for Autokrator to come into its own and express its full etymo-
logical significance. Thus we find a strongly marked

tendency in later times to apply the term specially to the Basileus who was the actual ruler. Though he and his colleague might be acclaimed jointly as Autokrators; yet Autokrator is distinctly used to express the plenitude of despotic power which was exercised by the senior Emperor alone.[14] Thus we may say that in early times Basileus was the pregnant title which expressed that full monarchical authority which the system of Augustus aimed at disguising, and Autokrator was simply the equivalent of the republican title Imperator; while in later times the rôles of the two titles were reversed, and Autokrator became the pregnant title, expressing the fulness of authority which the familiar Basileus no longer emphasised.

Before we leave this part of our subject, a word must be said about the rights of women to exercise autocracy. From the foundation of the Empire the title of Augusta had been conferred on the wives of Emperors, and we find in early times the mothers of minors, like Agrippina and Julia Domna, exercising political power. But this power was always exercised in the name of their sons. At the beginning of the fifth century the Augusta Pulcheria presides over the government which acted for her brother Theodosius II while he was a minor. On his death without children, it is recognised that although she cannot govern alone, she nevertheless has a right to have a voice in the election of a new Emperor, and the situation is met by her nominal marriage with Marcian. Similarly, forty years later, when Zeno dies without a son, his wife, the Augusta Ariadne, has, by general consent, the decisive voice in selecting her husband's successor; her choice falls on Anastasius, and he is elected. But it is not she who confers the Imperial authority on Anastasius, it is the Senate and army, who elect him, in accordance with her wishes. In the following century, the political importance of Empresses is augmented by the exceptional positions occupied by Theodora the consort of Justinian, and Sophia the consort of Justin II. But so far, although an Empress may act as regent for a minor,[15] may intervene in an Imperial election, may receive honours suggesting that she is her husband's colleague rather than consort, she never exercises independent sovran power, she is never, in the later sense of the word, an Autokrator. Passing on to the close of the eighth century, we come to the Empress Irene, the Athenian lady who is famous as the first restorer of Image-worship. When her husband died, her son Constantine was too young to rule, and she governed in the same way as Pulcheria had governed for Theodosius. When Constantine was old enough to govern himself, Irene was unwilling to retire into the background, and although the son succeeded in holding the power in his own hands for some years, the mother was continually intriguing against him. The struggle ended in her triumph. She caused her son to be blinded, and five years she reigned alone with full sovran powers as Autokrator. This was a considerable constitutional innovation, and the official style of her diplomas illustrates, in an interesting way, that it was felt as such. She was, of course, always spoken of as the Empress, but in her official acts she is styled not "Irene the Empress" but "Irene the Emperor" (*Basileus*).[16] It was felt that only an Emperor could legislate, and so the legal fiction of her masculinity was adopted.

It was said in Western Europe, for the purpose of justifying the Imperial claim of Charles the Great, that the sovranty of the Empire could not devolve on a woman, and that Irene's tenure of power was really an interregnum; but the Byzantines never admitted this constitutional doctrine. Nevertheless they had a strong objection to the *régime* of women, except in the capacity of regents, and the precedent established by Irene was repeated only in the case of Zoe and Theodora, the two nieces of Basil II. We find each of these ladies exercising the sovran authority alone for brief periods, and we also find them ruling together. This is the instance, which I mentioned already, of the experiment of government by two autocrats. Their joint rule might have been pro-tracted, if they had been in harmony, but Zoe was ex-tremely jealous of Theodora, and in order to oust her she took a husband, who immediately assumed the auto-cratic authority, and Zoe fell back into the subordinate position of a consort.*

We may now pass to the consideration of the nature and amplitude of the Imperial supremacy. The act of proclamation conferred his sovran powers upon the Emperor. In early days the Imperial powers were de-fined explicitly by a law, the *lex de imperio*. We have the text of the law which was passed for Vespasian. But the practice of passing it anew on the accession of a new Emperor was discontinued, and under the autocracy, when all the legislative, judicial and executive powers were vested in the autocrat, there was no reason to de-fine what those powers were. In the sixth century, how-ever, in the legislation of Justinian, it is recognised that by the *lex de imperio* the people transferred its sovranty to the Emperor. In the eighth century we may be pretty sure that no one from the Emperor downwards had ever heard of the *lex de imperio*.[17] But although there was no constitution of this kind defining or limiting the mon-arch's functions, I will proceed to show that his power, legally unlimited, was subject to limitations which must be described as constitutional.

[* *v.* for the joint rule *pp.* 168–75, and for Theodora's sole rule *pp.* 198–200.]

For his legislative and administrative acts, the monarch was responsible to none, except to Heaven; there was no organ in the state that had a right to control him; so that his government answers to our definition of autocracy. But when the monarch is appointed by any body or bodies in the state, the electors can impose conditions on him at the time of election, and thus there is the possibility of limiting his power. In other words, an elective autocracy, like the Roman Empire, is liable to the imposition of limitations. The case of the Emperor Anastasius I is in point. The Senate required from him an oath that he would administer the Empire conscientiously and not visit offences upon anyone with whom he had had a quarrel. This exhibits the principle, which was constantly and chiefly applied for the purpose of preventing a new Emperor from making ecclesiastical innovations.

It was a recognised condition of eligibility to the throne that the candidate should be a Christian, and an orthodox Christian. The latest pagan Emperor was Julian. After him it would have been virtually impossible for a pagan to rule at Constantinople. After the Council of Constantinople in A.D. 381, which crushed the Arian heresies, it would have been impossible for an Arian to wear the diadem. This was expressly recognised in the situation which ensued on the death of Theodosius II. The most prominent man at the moment was Aspar, but he was an Arian, and on that account alone his elevation was considered out of the question. Up to that period it may be said that such conditions of faith were political rather than constitutional; but when the coronation ceremony was attended with religious forms, we may say that Christianity was coming to be considered a constitutional condition of eligibility. By religious forms, I do not mean the part which the Patriarch played in the act of coronation, which, as we have seen,

had no ecclesiastical significance, but other parts of the
ceremony, such as prayers, which were introduced in
the fifth century. It was at the accession of Anastasius I
that a religious declaration was first required from an
Emperor. Anastasius was with good reason suspected of
heterodoxy; he was in fact a monophysite. He was not
asked to make any personal confession of faith, but at
the Patriarch's demand, he signed a written oath that
he would maintain the existing ecclesiastical settlement
unimpaired and introduce no novelty in the Church.
We are ignorant whether such a written declaration was
formally required at all subsequent elections; probably
not; but it was, we know, imposed in a number of cases
where there was reason to suspect a new Emperor of
heretical tendencies. Ultimately, we cannot say at what
time, this practice crystallised into the shape of a regular
coronation oath, in which the monarch confesses and
confirms the decrees of the Seven Ecumenical Councils
and of the local synods, and the privileges of the Church,
and vows to be a mild ruler and to abstain as far as
possible from punishments of death and mutilation.[18]

The fact that such capitulations could be and were
imposed at the time of election, even though the Emperor's obligation to submit to them was moral rather
than legal, means that the autocracy was subject to
limitations and was limited. But apart from such definite capitulations, the monarch's power was restricted
by unwritten principles of government which bound
him as much as the unwritten part of the English constitution binds our king and government. The autocrat
was the supreme legislator; personally he was above the
laws, *solutus legibus*;[19] there was no tribunal before which
he could be summoned; but he was bound by the
principles and the forms of the law which was the great
glory of Roman civilisation.[20] He could modify laws, he

could make new laws; but no Emperor ever questioned the obligation of conforming his acts to the law or presumed to assert that he could set it aside. Although theoretically above the law, he was at the same time bound by it, *alligatus legibus*, as Theodosius II expressly acknowledges.[21] Basil I, in a legal handbook, explicitly affirms the obligation of the Emperor to maintain not only the Scriptures and the canons of the Seven Councils, but also the Roman laws. And the laws embraced the institutions. Though changing circumstances led to adaptations and alterations, the Byzantine conservatism, which is almost proverbial and is often exaggerated, attests the strength of the unwritten limitations which always restrained the Imperial autocracy.

The Senate, too, though it had no share in the sovranty, might operate as a check on the sovran's actions. For there were various political matters which the Emperor was bound by custom to lay before it. We have not the material for enumerating what those matters were, but among the most important were questions of peace and war and the conclusion of treaties. The Senate would obediently concur in the views of a strong sovran, and probably its meetings were generally of a purely formal nature, but it is significant that in the case of a weak Emperor (Michael I) we find the Senate opposing the autocrat's wishes and the autocrat bowing to its opinion.[22]

It is implied in what I have said that the Church represented a limit on the Emperor's power. From the ninth century onward, the Decrees of the Seven Councils were an unalterable law which no Emperor could touch.[23] At the same time, the relation of the State to the Church, of which I must now speak, illustrates the amplitude of his power. The Byzantine Church is the most important example in history of a State-Church.

Its head was the Emperor. He was considered the delegate of God in a sphere which included the ecclesiastical as well as the secular order. The Patriarch of Constantinople was his minister of the department of religion, and though the usual forms of episcopal election were observed, was virtually appointed by him. It was the Emperor who convoked the Ecumenical Councils, and it was the Emperor who presided at them either in person or, if he did not care to suffer the boredom of theological debates, represented by some of his secular ministers.[24] Canonical decrees passed at Councils did not become obligatory till they were confirmed by the Emperor; and the Emperors issued edicts and laws relating to purely ecclesiastical affairs, quite independently of Councils. The Patriarch Menas asserted in the reign of Justinian that nothing should be done in the Church contrary to the Emperor's will, and Justinian, who was the incarnation of sacerdotal monarchy, was acclaimed as High-priest Basileus ($\dot{a}\rho\chi\iota\epsilon\rho\epsilon\dot{v}s$ $\beta a\sigma\iota\lambda\epsilon\dot{v}s$). It is true that the voices of prominent ecclesiastics were raised from time to time protesting that ecclesiastical matters lay outside the domain of secular authority and advocating the complete freedom of the Church. But this idea, of which Theodore of Studion was the latest champion, never gained ground; it was definitely defeated in the ninth century, and the Emperor continued to hold the position of a Christian caliph. Thus the theory of State and Church in the Eastern Empire is conspicuously contrasted with the theory which in Western Europe was realised under Innocent III. In both cases Church and State are indivisible, but in the West the Church is the State, whereas in the East it is a department which the Emperor directs. In the West we have a theocracy; the Church represented by the Pope claims to possess the supreme authority in temporal as well as spiritual affairs. In the East relations are reversed; instead of a theocracy, we have what has been called caesaropapism. A papalist writer, who endeavours to demonstrate the Pope's universal supremacy, remarks that in point of jurisdiction a layman might be Pope; all the powers and rights of a Pope, in spiritual as well as secular affairs, would be conferred upon him by election.[25] This hypothesis of Agostino Trionfo was realised in the Eastern Empire.

There were occasional struggles between the Emperor and the Patriarch, usually caused by an attempt on the Emperor's part to introduce, for political reasons, some new doctrine which the Patriarch considered inconsistent with the Decrees of the Councils or the Scriptures. In such cases the Patriarch was defending the constitution against innovation; he was not disputing the Emperor's position as head of the Church. And in such cases the usual result was that the Patriarch either yielded or was deposed, the Emperor had his way, and the orthodox doctrine was not reinstated until another Emperor reversed the acts of his predecessor. Some Patriarchs might suggest that the Emperor, not being an expert in theology, ought not to interfere in matters of doctrine; but the normal relations were generally accepted as fundamental and constitutional.

The Patriarch had indeed one weapon which he might use against his sovran—the weapon of excommunication. He might refuse, and direct his clergy to refuse, to communicate with the Emperor. It was a weapon to which recourse was seldom taken. Another means of exerting power which the Patriarch possessed was due to the part which he took in the coronation. He might make terms with the new Emperor before he crowned him. Thus the Patriarch Polyeuktos forced John Tzimiskes to consent to abrogate a law which required the Imperial approbation of candidates for ecclesiastical offices before they were elected.

The constitutional theory which I have delineated is implied in the actual usages from which I have drawn it; but it was never formulated. Constitutional questions did not arise, and no lawyer or historian expounded the basis or the limits of the sovran power. In fact, the constitution was not differentiated in men's consciousness from the whole body of laws and institutions. They did not analyse the assumptions implied in their practice, and the only idea they entertained, which can be described as a constitutional theory, does not agree, though it may be conciliated, with the theory that I have sketched. If you had asked a Byzantine Emperor what was the basis of his autocracy and by what right he exercised it, he would not have told you that it had been committed to him by the Senate, the army, or the people; he would have said that he derived his sovranty directly from God. I could produce a great deal of evidence to illustrate this view, but it will be enough to refer to the words of the Emperor Basil I in his Advice to his son Leo: "You received the Empire from God"; "You received the crown from God by my hand".[26] Such a doctrine of the monarch's divine right naturally tended to reflect a new significance on the part which the Patriarch played in the Emperor's inauguration. But it found an explicit symbolic expression in the new custom of unction, which perhaps was practised (though opinions differ on this point)[27] as early as the ninth century. In crowning, the Patriarch expressed the will of the State; in anointing, the will of the Deity. This theory, logically developed, implies the view which Dante expresses in his *De Monarchia*, that the Electors when they choose the Emperor are merely voicing the choice of the Deity. It was quite in accordance with the prevailing religious sentiments; it enhanced the Emperor's authority by representing that authority as a divine gift, and perhaps it sometimes enhanced his sense of responsibility. But although calculated to place the sovran above criticism, this theory of divine right did not affect the actual working of the constitutional tradition which determined the appointment of Emperors and the limitations of their power. Its chief interest lies in its relation to the political theories which were evolved in the Middle Ages in Western Europe. It has been observed by Mr Bryce,[28] as a striking contrast between the Eastern and Western Empires, that, while the West was fertile in conceptions and theories, displaying abundant wealth of creative imagination, in the East men did not trouble themselves to theorise about the Empire at all. The inspiration, in the West, came in the first place from the fact that the Holy Roman Empire was always an ideal, never fully realised, "a dream" (to use Mr Bryce's words), "half theology and half poetry". The Eastern Roman Empire, on the other hand, was always an actual fact, adequate to its own conception; there it was—there was no mistake about its being here and now; there was much in it to cause pride, there was nothing to stir imagination. In the second place, there was no need, in the Eastern Empire, to evolve theories, as nothing was in dispute. In the West a great constitutional question arose, of far-reaching practical importance, touching the relations of the two rival authorities, the Pope and the Emperor. It was to solve the political problem set by their rival pretensions that Dante wrote his *De Monarchia*, William of Ockham his *Dialogue*, Marsilius of Padua his *Defensor pacis*. In the East no such problem arose, inasmuch as the Emperor was recognised as the head of the Church, and there was therefore no stimulus to evolve political theories. Yet if a similar problem or need had arisen, I cannot help thinking that the medieval Greeks, though they were incapable of producing a Dante, would have proved themselves not less ingenious than Western thinkers in political speculation. But it is instructive to observe that the claim of the Eastern Emperor to derive his sovranty directly from God is the same theory of Divine Right which was asserted by the Western Imperialist writers. Dante affirmed this theory most forcibly; William of Ockham and Marsilius affirmed it too, but they tempered it by the view that the Empire was originally derived from the people, thus combining, as it were, the Divine pretensions of the later autocrats of Constantinople with the democratic origin of sovranty which is asserted in the lawbooks of Justinian.

I have endeavoured to show how the autocracy of the later Roman Empire was a limited autocracy. Every autocracy, every government, has of course natural limitations. The action of the monarch is limited by public opinion; there will always be some point beyond which he is afraid to venture in defying public opinion. It is also limited by the fact that he has to employ human instruments, and their personal views and qualities may modify or compromise or thwart the execution of his will. Further, if he rules over a highly organised society, he may be restrained from sweeping measures by the knowledge that such changes will involve other consequences which he does not desire.[29] These natural limitations affect all autocracies, all governments, in various modes and degrees. But apart from them, the Roman autocracy had definite restrictions which must be described as constitutional.[30] In what is miscalled a limited monarchy, the king may have legal rights which it would be unconstitutional to exercise. The action of the English crown, for instance, is restricted not merely by the statutory limits, such as are imposed on it by the Bill of Rights or the Act of Settlement, but by unwritten constitutional usage, which is obligatory. In the same way the action of the Roman autocrat was limited by a tradition and usage which were felt by him and by the community to be absolutely binding. The sanctions in the two cases are different. An English king is hindered from exceeding the constitutional bounds of his authority by the power which Parliament possesses of bringing the government to a standstill, as it can do by refusing to grant supplies or to pass the Mutiny Act. The more powerful Roman monarch was forced to conform to the institutions, customs, and traditions of his society by the more drastic sanction of deposition. The Russian autocrat, Peter the Great, abolished the Patriarchate of Moscow; it would have been an impossibility for the Roman Emperor to abolish the Patriarchate of Constantinople or to introduce any serious change in the organisation of the Church. The integrity of the Church was indeed secured against him not merely by this moral force, but by capitulations which, in consequence of the elective character of the monarchy, he could be obliged to swear to at his accession and which were finally embodied in a coronation oath. Here there was a religious sanction superadded.

The limitations tended to maintain the conservative character for which Byzantium is often reproached, and were in fact one of the results of that conservatism. They were efficacious, because the autocrat himself was usually imbued deeply with this conservative spirit, being a child of his age and civilisation; whilst the complex and elaborate machinery, furnishing the channels through which he had to act, was a powerful check on his freedom. It must, I think, be admitted that the autocracy of the Eastern Empire suited the given conditions, and probably worked better than any other system that could have been devised. The government was not arbitrary, and the evils from which the subjects of the Empire suffered were due (apart from the calamities of war) to economic ignorance and bad finance, such as prevailed everywhere alike in the ancient and the middle ages, and would have pressed as heavily under any other form of government. The freedom and absence of formality in the method of appointing the sovran made it possible to meet different situations in different ways; and if we examine the roll of Emperors from Constantine the Great in the fourth to Manuel Comnenus in the twelfth century, we must admit that the constitution secured, with a few dark but short intervals, a succession of able and hard-working rulers such as cannot, I think, be paralleled in the annals of any other state during so long a period.

NOTES

1 This differs somewhat from Sidgwick's definition, in *Development of European Polity*, p. 10: "What is meant by calling him [an Absolute Monarch] 'absolute' is that there is no established constitutional authority—no human authority that his subjects habitually obey as much as they obey him—which can legitimately resist him or call him to account".

2 *Lectures on Jurisprudence*, 1, 241 (ed. 1885).

3 The *Roman* Senate however seems to have retained some nominal sovranty; for under the *régime* of Theodoric it had the power, like the Emperor, *constituere leges* (a power which Theodoric did not possess). Cp. Cassiodorus, *Variae*, 6, 4, § 1, 2 (p. 177, ed. Mommsen).

4 This (ἀναγόρευσις) is the technical word applied to the whole procedure of inauguration.

5 In the early Empire, the Roman people took the initiative in proclaiming Pertinax; they forced the Praetorians to proclaim him; but undoubtedly it was the proclamation of the latter that conferred the Imperium. In the later Empire we find a section of the people of Constantinople taking the initiative in proclaiming the

nephews of Anastasius, on the occasion of the Nika revolt against Justinian.

6 Cp. for instance Leo Diaconus, II, 12, where Polyeuktos says that the sons of Romanus II were proclaimed Emperors "by us (the Senate) and the whole people".

7 Nicephorus Bryennius, who was proclaimed Emperor in the reign of Michael VII (11th cent.) and was suppressed, placed the diadem on his own head, Anna Comnena, *Alexiad*, 1, 4.

8 This is brought out by W. Sickel in his important article "Das byzantinische Krönungsrecht bis zum 10 Jahrhundert", in the *Byzantinische Zeitschrift*, VII, 511 *sqq.* (1898), to which I must acknowledge my obligations. For the details of the coronation ceremonies see F. E. Brightman's article in the *Journal of Theological Studies*, II, 359 *sqq.* (1901).

9 It was introduced by the Augustus in the form of the co-regency, for a full discussion of which see Mommsen, *Staatsrecht*, II, 1145 *sqq.* (ed. 3).

In the Hellenistic kingdoms (Macedonia, Syria, Egypt) there is material for instructive comparisons in regard to the combination of the elective and dynastic principles, and co-regencies.

10 This principle was asserted by Andronicus II who endeavoured to exclude his grandson (Andronicus III) from the throne. The civil wars which resulted represent, from the constitutional point of view, a struggle between this principle and the idea of legitimacy to which the Byzantines had become strongly attached.

11 The regular form of phrase is ἔστεψε διὰ τοῦ Πατριάρχου (cp. Theophanes, 417₂₅, 426₂₇, 480₁₁, 494₂₆). More explicitly Kedrenos, II, 296; Romanus I was crowned by the Patriarch ἐπιτροπῇ τοῦ βασιλέως Κωνσταντίνου (who was a minor). In the normal ceremony of crowning a colleague, described in Constantine Porph. *De Cer.* 1, 38, the Patriarch hands the crown to the Emperor, who places it on the new Emperor's head (p. 194).

12 The colleague is often designated as ὁ δεύτερος βασιλεύς, or as συμβασιλεύς (and we may suppose that the description of Otto II as *co-imperator* of his father was borrowed from this); if a child, he is distinguished as "the little Emperor" (ὁ μικρὸς βασιλεύς), and this, no doubt, explains why Theodosius II was ὁ μικρός. The description, applied to him when a minor, survived his boyhood, because it served to distinguish him from his grandfather and namesake, Theodosius the Great. In one case, we find the term *rex* strangely applied to a second Emperor. It occurs on a bronze coin of the year 866–7, in which Basil I was colleague of Michael III.

The obverse has *Mihael imperat(or)*, the reverse *Basilius rex* (Wroth, *Catalogue of the Imperial Byzantine Coins of the British Museum*, II, 432). I do not know how to explain this eccentricity which is contrary to all the principles of the Roman Imperium. The western title *Romanorum rex*, which in the eleventh century began to be assumed by Western Emperors before they were crowned at Rome and was afterwards appropriated to their successors, cannot be compared.

13 *Byzantinische Zeitschrift*, xv, 151 *sqq.* (1906).

14 It came into official use in the eleventh century, as a reinforcement of Basileus (β. καὶ αὐτ.), and in Latin diplomas we find it translated by *moderator*, Basileus by *Imperator*. A colleague could only use the title Autokrator by special permission of the senior Emperor (Codinus, *De Officiis*, c. 17, pp. 86, 87, ed. Bonn). But the distinction was drawn as early as the ninth century, for in Philotheos (A.D. 900), *Kletorologion* (*apud* Const. Porph. *De Cerimoniis*, p. 712), we find ὁ αὐτοκράτωρ βασιλεύς explicitly contrasted with ὁ δεύτερος βασιλεύς.

15 If an Emperor foresaw his approaching death and his colleague was a minor, he could make arrangements for the regency in his will. This was done, *e.g.* by Theophilus and by Alexander.

16 Zachariä von Lingenthal, *Jus Graeco-romanum*, III, 55 (Εἰρήνη πιστὸς βασιλεύς). The point is brought out in the *Chronicle* of Theophanes (p. 466, l. 25, ed. De Boor): Constantine VI causes the Armeniac soldiers to swear not to accept his mother Irene εἰς βασιλέα. The later force of the term αὐτοκράτωρ comes out in the same passage (l. 15).

17 In this connexion, however, may be noted the remarkable notion of establishing a democracy, attributed to the Emperor Stauracius (A.D. 811) by the contemporary chronicler Theophanes (ed. De Boor, p. 492). He was on his deathbed at the time and wished to be succeeded by his wife, the Athenian Theophano (a relative of Irene) as sovran Empress. He threatened democracy as an alternative. We should like to know what his idea of a democracy was.

18 Codinus, *De Officiis*, c. 17.

19 *Digest*, I, 3, 31; *Basilica*, II, 6, 1.

20 *Basilica*, II, 6, 9, καὶ κατὰ βασιλέως οἱ γενικοὶ κρατείτωσαν νόμοι καὶ πᾶσα παράνομος ἐκβαλλέσθω ἀντιγραφή. The meaning of *lex generalis* (briefly, an edict promulgated as applicable to the whole Empire) is explained *ib.* 8, which is based on *Cod. Just.* I, 14, 3. The Emperor could not enact a special constitution—applicable to a section, district, or town—which was contrary to the provisions of a *lex generalis*.

21 *Cod. Just.* i, 14, 4, digna vox maiestate regnantis legibus alligatum se principem profiteri: adeo de auctoritate iuris nostra pendet auctoritas.

22 The functions of the Senate seem to have closely resembled those of the Synedrion in the Hellenistic kingdoms. Compare the account of a meeting of the Synedrion of Antiochus in Polybius, v, 41–42. It may be noticed that during the minority after the death of Romanus II, it is the Senate that appoints Nicephorus II to the supreme command of the Asiatic troops (Leo Diaconus, ii, 12). The importance of the Senate is illustrated by the political measure of Constantine X who "democratised" it: see Psellos, *Historia*, p. 238 (ed. Sathas, 1899); C. Neumann, *Die Weltstellung des byzantinischen Reiches vor den Kreuzzügen*, p. 79.

23 This principle had been already laid down by Justinian in regard to the first four Councils, the decrees of which he places on the same level as Holy Scripture: *Nov.* 151, a′, ed. Zachariä, ii, p. 267.

24 The best general account of the relation of State and Church in Byzantium will be found in the late Professor Gelzer's article in the *Historische Zeitschrift*, N.F. vol. L, 193 *sqq.* (1901). At the Seventh Ecumenical Council (A.D. 787) the presidency was committed to the Patriarch Tarasios, evidently because he had been a layman and minister, not (like most of his predecessors) a monk.

25 Augustinus Triumphus, *Summa de potestate Ecclesiastica*, i, 1, p. 2, ed. 1584 (Rome): si quis eligatur in Papam nullum ordinem habens, erit verus Papa et habebit omnem potestatem iurisdictionis in spiritualibus et temporalibus et tamen nullam habebit potestatem ordinis.

26 *Paraenesis ad Leonem*, in Migne, *P. G.* cvii, pp. xxv, xxxii.

27 See Photius, in Migne, *P. G.* cii, 765 and 573. Cp. Sickel, *op. cit.* 547–8, and on the other hand Brightman, *op. cit.* 383–5.

28 *The Holy Roman Empire* (last ed. 1904), 343 *sqq.*

29 This is noted by Sidgwick, *Development of European Polity*, p. 10.

30 For an analysis of the conception of *unconstitutional* as distinguished from *illegal* see Austin, *Jurisprudence*, i, 265 *sqq.* (ed. 1885).

9. ROMAN EMPERORS FROM BASIL II TO ISAAC KOMNÊNOS*

PART I

The eleventh century is the turning point in the Middle Ages; in it new currents are beginning to flow and old currents are beginning to ebb. It was in the eleventh century that Normans founded their kingdom in southern Europe and conquered England; it was in the eleventh century that Gregory VII introduced a new spirit into western Christendom; it was in the eleventh century that the crusade movement began. The mere mention of the Crusades, Gregory VII, and the Normans sufficiently indicates the new currents that flowed in western Europe. A change was taking place at the same time in the Eastern Roman Empire, a change which implied and led to its decline; and if we do not misunderstand the system of medieval Europe, unduly isolating the Byzantine world from the occidental kingdoms as if they did not act and react upon one another, we must assume that the new tide in the West was causally, or rather reciprocally—for reciprocity is generally the right category in history—connected with the ebb in the East. The most obvious indication of this connection is the commercial change which resulted in the transference of trade from the Greeks, who had hitherto almost monopolised it, to the rising republics of Italy. The chief external event in the Eastern Empire was the succession of the house of Komnênos to the house of Basil the Macedonian, whose descendants had worn the purple for two centuries. This change of

[* I.e. A.D. 976–1057. Reprinted from *English Historical Review*, vol. IV, part I, pp. 41–64, part II, pp. 251–85 (1889).]

dynasty meant the triumph and preponderance of the wealthy aristocratic families of Asia Minor; it was the outward sign of a great inward change which had been taking place since the reign of Basil II. The final separation of the Greek and Latin churches occurred at this period (1054); but as they were really alienated long before, this is an event of only second-rate importance. Of much more interest are the projects of the patriarch Kêrularios to make the Church independent of the State, in fact to do what Hildebrand did in the West. Another movement of the time which deserves attention is the revival of literature under the auspices of Michael Psellos, who reclaimed Greek prose from the barbarism into which it was falling.

There is a plentiful lack of contemporary authority for the last years of the Macedonian dynasty. For a few events at the beginning of the reign of Basil II (976–1025) we have a page or two of a contemporary author, Leo Diakonos; but for the rest of his long reign and for that of his brother Constantine VIII we have only the later chronographers, Kedrênos and Zônaras. For the following Emperors, until the accession of Isaac Komnênos, Finlay's only Greek sources were Kedrênos and Zônaras, for we need hardly take into account such writers as Glykas or Manassês. But since Finlay wrote his history the labours of M. Constantine Sathas have rendered a new source accessible, the contemporary history of Michael Psellos.[1] This history was so diligently utilised by Zônaras that the original does not supply us with any new facts of great importance; but nevertheless it is invaluable, as we learn a large number of inter-

[1] *Bibliotheca Græca Medii Ævi*; vol. IV, *Pselli Historia Byzantina et alia opuscula* (1874). The opuscula are three Ἐπιτάφιοι λόγοι, on Michael Kêrularios, Constantine Leichudês, and Joannes Xiphilinos, three personages of whom we shall have more to say. Vol. V of this series contains other "words" of Psellos, including a large collection of letters.

esting details, not to mention that the work of a contemporary has always a flavour which no compilation can have. There may be sufficient foundation for the paradoxical statement of M. Amédée Thierry that details are the soul of history, to warrant us in collecting and recording the new points which may be gleaned from Psellos. Accordingly, as the subject has not been worked up, I propose to give a sketch of Byzantine history from Basil II to the deposition of Michael VI, confining myself almost entirely to what Psellos has recorded, and consequently omitting altogether some important wars of which Finlay, reproducing Kedrênos and Zônaras, has given so full an account, that a repetition here seems unnecessary. It will be advisable at the outset to say something more of Psellos and the nature of his history, and also to notice briefly our other authorities.

1. *Sources.* The history of Psellos is a Ἑκατονταετηρίς; it embraces a period of one hundred years, beginning with the accession of Basil II (976) and ending with the accession of Nikêphoros Botaneiatês (1077). For the first three reigns (of Basil, Constantine, and Rômanos) it is a short and meagre record of things which he had not witnessed, though he had doubtless heard many facts on first-hand authority, but with the accession of Michael IV in 1034 it becomes more complete and detailed, and at the same time assumes the value of contemporary history. In order to understand and appreciate its value we must give a short outline of the author's career.[1]

He was born in 1018, and thus at the accession of

---

[1] M. Sathas has prefaced his edition with a full biographical account of Psellos. His original name was Constantine; he was renamed Michael when he took the monastic vows. How little is generally known of Psellos and his works is apparent in the short notice in the *Encyclopædia Britannica.*

Michael the Paphlagonian was sixteen years old. He had seen the Emperor Rômanos in a public procession not long before his death. Thus for the reign of Rômanos he may be considered a contemporary writer in the same sense that Cicero's authority might be called contemporary for the history of Livius Drusus. His father's fathers had been consuls and patricians; his mother was of good family and herself a clever woman who used to assist her son, when a boy, in preparing his lessons. He studied rhetoric and philosophy, giving the preference to the latter, and in his studies "chummed" with an older friend, Joannês Xiphilinos, whom he assisted in philosophy and in return received help in jurisprudence. Under Michael IV he was appointed judge at Philadelphia, and in the short reign of Michael V held the post of under-secretary (ὑπογραμματεύς), through the influence probably of his friend Constantine Leichudês, whom that Emperor appointed chief minister. Leichudês did not fall with his master; Constantine IX retained his services, and Psellos won the marked affection of that impressionable sovran and became his trusted confidant, holding the post of secretary. Constantine was induced to refound, in a sort of manner, the university of Constantinople, and Psellos filled the chair of philosophy. Towards the end of this reign Leichudês was deposed, and Psellos, fearing, as he tells us, the weathercock nature of his master, determined to embrace the spiritual life and retired to a monastery, in spite of the Emperor's expressed wishes. Theodôra recalled him to court after Constantine's death, and he took part in the administration of Michael VI. He was one of the embassy sent by that monarch with proposals to Isaac Komnênos, under whose sovranty he succeeded Leichudês as Prime Minister. We need not touch on his political conduct in the following reigns, his education of Michael VII, and his relations to Rômanos Diogenês, as this paper will not go further than the accession of Isaac.

From this brief sketch we may see that the memoirs of Psellos as a distinguished contemporary who was initiated in the arcana (ἀπόρρητα) of political events are of the highest value. Through his artificial, often irritatingly artificial, rhetorical style,[1] his descriptions of the Emperors and Empresses whom he knew give an impression of reality and life. He presents us with pictures of men and women of the time more vivid than we could ever get from writers like Zônaras. He had seen Rômanos like a living corpse, when a boy of sixteen; he had seen George Maniakês, standing ten feet high, and looked up at him as at a pillar or a mountain; he had stood by the side of Constantine Monomachos when he witnessed the seafight with the Russians; he had stood by his side when an arrow narrowly missed him during the siege of Tornikios; he knew by personal experience that the queen Sklêraina was an excellent listener; he was an intimate friend of the first minister Leichudês and the great patriarch Michael Kêrularios; he was first minister himself.

In the rather pretentious preface to his chronography Joannês Skylitzês, whom George Kedrênos copies, enumerates some of his predecessors in the field of history. He remarks of Psellos and others that they do not give accurate details, but "merely record a list of the Emperors, stating who succeeded whom, and nothing more".[2] In regard to Psellos this criticism is in one way

---

[1] As examples I may quote ὡς εὐθὺς τὸ κράτος διαδεξόμενον τοῦ κρατοῦντος τῷ κρατήσαντι πάθει καταναλωθέντος, where κρατήσαντι is chosen as a verbal antithesis to κράτος ἀκρατοῦντος (p. 61). Again (p. 131), ὁ βασιλεὺς Βασίλειος ἐν τοῖς βασιλείοις ἀπεθησαύρισε.

[2] καὶ ἄλλοι ἐπεχείρησαν οἷον ὁ Σικελιώτης καὶ ὁ ὑπέρτιμος Ψελλὸς καὶ ἕτεροι σὺν τούτοις· ἀλλὰ τῆς ἀκριβείας ἀποπεπτώκασιν ἀπαρίθμησιν μόνην

entirely false; in another way it expresses in exaggerated terms a certain truth. The events which Psellos does describe he describes in far more elaborate detail than Kedrênos himself, who gives us the dry bones; in this respect the criticism is false. But, on the other hand, many events of importance are not even mentioned by Psellos, as he tells us plainly himself; and so far the criticism has an element of truth. Skylitzês prides himself on giving us all, even the smallest, bones; Psellos gives us a selection of bones and flesh together. Psellos is quite aware of this, as we may see from a passage in which he states the scope and nature of his history. He does not attempt to describe, he says, all events in order and each in detail from its beginning to its conclusion, nor to enumerate every military engagement however trifling, and the other things which *accurate* historians describe.[1] He aims at a succinct relation, not at an ambitious history; and he therefore omits many things worthy of record, and, instead of dividing his history chronologically, simply dictates the most critical events and what most impressed itself on his recollection. "I do not note in detail every event, for it is my design to follow a middle course between the ancient historians of old Rome on the one hand, and our modern chronographers on the other, avoiding the roundabout flow of the former and not imitating the bald conciseness of the latter, so that my narration may neither weary the reader nor omit capital events".

ποιησάμενοι τῶν βασιλέων καὶ διδάξαντες τίς μετὰ τίνα γέγονεν ἐγκρατὴς καὶ πλέον οὐδέν (ed. Bonn, p. 2). The word ἀκρίβεια means accurate fulness of detail, not accuracy in our sense of trustworthiness. Both Skylitzês and Psellos might be called fond of detail, for "detail" is ambiguous. The remark already quoted from Thierry, *Les détails sont l'âme de l'histoire*, refers to details in the sense in which we should use the word of Psellos.

[1] See his history, pp. 135, 136. τοῖς ἀκριβέσι τῶν συγγραφέων would include Skylitzês.

Thus Psellos' intention was to compose readable memoirs in contrast to the prevailing style of Byzantine history, which he considered dry and wearisome. By his neglect of chronology he completely breaks through the stereotyped method. There was consequently a sort of opposition between Psellos and contemporary historians like Joannês Skylitzês, who held fast by the old method; there were, in fact, two historical schools—one instituted by Psellos, whose influence on historiography in method as well as in style was permanent, inasmuch as the best historians of the following centuries adopted a midway method.

While he often omits important facts, such as the Patzinak war in the reign of Constantine IX, he devotes pages to minor details of court life which he had personally observed, and he deems it necessary to apologise for such digressions.[1] He says he will not describe the grief exhibited by Constantine when his queen Sklêraina died, for such a description would be a descent to triviality (σμικρολογεῖσθαι καὶ οἶον λεπτολογεῖν). "But if I myself am sometimes guilty of that against which I warn writers of history to guard, it is no wonder, for the notion of history is not so absolutely bounded, so shaved off on every side, as not to leave some loopholes and passages for egress; but if anything take advantage of a loophole, the historian must quickly recall the waif, and must arrange his matter so as to bear on the general theme, considering all else as merely secondary".

His general view of history is, that it is directed by providence.[2] "I am wont to refer to the *pronoia* of the Deity the arrangement of the larger events of history, indeed to attach to his prevision all events that do not arise from the perversion of our human nature". Thus,

[1] P. 134. [2] P. 64.

as an orthodox member of the church, he believed in a combination of design and freewill.

Michael Attaleiatês was a younger contemporary of Psellos.[1] He dedicates his history to the Emperor Nikêphoros Botaneiatês, the predecessor of the great Alexios, and beginning with Michael IV gives a short eclectic sketch of the years 1034–1057, somewhat similar in compass, though different in style, to the sketch given by Psellos of the reigns of Basil, Constantine VIII, and Rômanos. His history becomes more complete with the revolt of Komnênos as that of Psellos with the accession of Michael IV. Although slight, the preliminary sketch is valuable, for Attaleiatês was a man superior in judgment and insight to the average Byzantine chronographer, and we shall have occasion to refer to it. He tells us in his introductory remarks that though he was distracted with official business which occupied him every hour of the day, it seemed good to him to undertake yet an additional labour and "digest a few things in a short and simple style—as is meet for historians, if the subject be not agonistic and therefore demanding an artificial method, but historical and superior to irrelevant prolixity—not concerning what I received from others by hearsay, but concerning what I myself witnessed and beheld, in order that things worthy of narrative may not be overwhelmed in the profundities of oblivion by the lapse of time". It seems to me evident that this pointed remark in regard to style is intended as a criticism on Psellos, whose florid and elaborate style Attaleiatês thought unsuitable for history, and himself followed the unadorned baldness of the older chronographers.

[1] Besides his history, published in the Bonn series of *Scriptores Byzantini*, there is also extant his διάταξις, or will, containing regulations for a charitable institution (πτωχοτροφεῖον) which he founded; it has been published in the first volume of Sathas' *Bibliotheca Græca Medii Ævi*.

Finlay did not know the history of Attaleiatês—there is not a single reference to it in his *History of Greece*; and it seems to have also escaped the notice of his learned editor.[1]

Joannês Skylitzês, also known as Thrakêsios,[2] was a contemporary of Attaleiatês and Psellos, and wrote a history of the Eastern Roman Empire from 811 to 1081. He held the offices of kuropalatês, drungarios of the guards, and protovestiarios, but we do not hear that he had any political influence. His history was plagiarised in a wholesale manner by George Kedrênos, who probably lived at the close of the century and wrote a universal history from the foundation of the world to the accession of Isaac Komnênos. The latter part of Skylitzês' history (1057–1081) is printed at the end of the Bonn edition of Kedrênos. A Latin translation of the whole work of Skylitzês, by J. B. Gabius, was published at Venice in 1570. Between Skylitzês and Attaleiatês there are very close resemblances, and I agree with Hertzberg that Skylitzês followed Attaleiatês. His criticism on Psellos was mentioned above.

Joannês Zônaras lived in the first half of the twelfth century, and probably finished his *Epitome of Histories* before 1150. He is so much superior in calibre to writers like Theophanês and Kedrênos that Hertzberg ranked him not among chronographers but among historians. From this judgment, however, Hirsch dissents.[3] Zônaras

---

[1] Mr Tozer mentions in his valuable notes almost every source of which Finlay was not aware. Besides Attaleiatês, I have noticed the omission of Kritobulos, the historian of the Ottoman conquest of Constantinople, who imitates Thukydidês. Whereas the other Greek historians, Phrantzês, Dukas, and Chalkokondylês, are patriots, Kritobulos is unique as writing in the Turkish interest; his hero is Mohammed.

[2] Called Thrakêsios by Kedrênos (I, 5) and Zônaras (IV, 196). He was probably a native of the Thrakêsian theme.

[3] F. Hirsch, *Byzantinische Studien*, p. 391: *Zonaras bemüht sich allerdings, wie wir gesehen, an einigen Stellen, verschiedenartige Berichte zu verarbeiten, aber*

complains at the beginning of his work of lack of books, and L. Dindorf, who examined carefully the sources of the earlier part of the work, concluded that his library was really very scanty. Whatever materials he lacked, he did not lack the history of Joannês Skylitzês, which he quotes, nor that of Psellos, which he also refers to and has utilised very largely, reproducing it even verbally, and constantly adopting from it expressions with a difference. It will not be amiss to give one or two examples, as Zônaras, whose judiciousness was recognised by Gibbon, deserves attention, and the sources of the later portion of his history have not been adequately investigated.

Psellos.

P. 36: ἐλπίσας τε ἀπὸ τῆς περὶ τὸν δημόσιον ἐπιμελείας τὰ ἀπολωλότα αὐτῷ ἐν ἴσῳ ἀνακτήσασθαι μέτρῳ πράκτωρ μᾶλλον ἢ βασιλεὺς ἐγεγόνει ...τοὺς παῖδας λογιστεύων πικρῶς.

P. 12: ἐντεῦθεν ἕτερος ἀνθ’ ἑτέρου ὁ βασιλεὺς γίνεται...ὕποπτος οὖν εἰς πάντας ὦπτο καὶ σοβαρὸς τὴν ὀφρὺν τάς τε φρένας ὑποκαθήμενος καὶ τοῖς ἁμαρτάνουσι δύσοργος καὶ βαρύμηνις.

Zônaras.[1]

P. 131: ἵνα γὰρ τῶν ἀπολωλότων ἰσοστάσια κτήσηται πράκτωρ ἀντὶ κρατοῦντος ἐγένετο καὶ πικρὸς λογιστής.

P. 115: ὁ δὲ ἀλλοιότερος ἦν ἢ τὸ πρότερον· σοβαρός τε γὰρ ἐγεγόνει καὶ τὸ ἦθος ὑποκαθήμενος καὶ πάντας ὑπώπτευε καὶ τὴν ὀργὴν ἐτύγχανεν ἀπαραίτητος.

er verfährt dabei doch mit wenig Kritik. Hirsch gives a very good account of Skylitzês. For the ninth and for the first half of the tenth century Hirsch's book is invaluable.

[1] The pages of Zônaras referred to are those of the 4th vol. of L. Dindorf's ed. (1871).

P. 14: ἀθυμίας τε ἐνε-
πίμπλατο … νέφους τὴν
κεφαλὴν πληρωθεὶς … τὰ
μέλη παραλυθεὶς καὶ
νεκρὸς ἔμψυχος γεγονὼς
μετὰ βραχὺ καὶ αὐτὴν ἀπέρ-
ρηξε τὴν ψυχήν.

P. 115: ὅθεν ἐκεῖνος διὰ
ταῦτα νέφει περισχεθεὶς
ἀθυμίας παρεῖτο τὰ μέλη
καὶ ἔμπνους ὦπτο νεκρὸς
καὶ βραχύ τι διαλιπὼν
οἰκτρῶς τὸν βίον ἐξέλιπεν.

The later chroniclers, Glykas, Ephraem, Joel, and Constantine Manassês,[1] have no independent value. Events in "Italia"—by which Byzantine writers meant Calabria and Longibardia—and their Latin historians do not concern us here; but the chronicler, Lupus Protospata, it may be mentioned, is occasionally useful in supplying us with a date, and for the separation of the Greek and Latin churches, of which the Greek historians are silent, there is an important though short chapter in Leo of Ostia, the historian of Monte Casino.

2. *Basil II and Constantine VIII.** It is usual to say that Basil succeeded John Tzimiskês, and was succeeded by his brother Constantine. But, strictly speaking, Basil and Constantine were joint Emperors, although practically Basil was sole sovran, as his brother was a man of pleasure who, preferring horse-racing to State business, and a lady's chamber to the council-room, took no part in the administration. On their accession (976) Basil was twenty years old and Constantine seventeen, and it struck Psellos as a very remarkable and praiseworthy act of the latter to resign to his abler brother all claim to a share in the imperial power.

Basil was like Henry V of England. Wild and addicted to pleasure before and for some years after his accession, he suddenly exhibited a complete change of character,

---

[1] Manassês writes occasionally a good "political" verse.
[* John Tzimiskês, A.D. 969, Dec. 25, Basil II, A.D. 976, Jan. 10–1025, Dec. Constantine VIII (IX), A.D. 976, Jan. 10–1028, Nov.]

and proved an energetic and brilliant monarch. Psellos was acquainted with men who had seen him. "Most of our contemporaries", he says, "who saw the Emperor Basil regarded him as a tart man, abrupt and rough in character, prone to anger and obstinate, abstemious in his mode of life, and abhorring all delicate living. But, as I heard from historians of his time, he was not such at first, but having been dissolute and luxurious in his youth, he changed and became serious, for circumstances acted on his nature like an astringent; the loose strings were stretched and the gaps closed in. At first he was wont to indulge openly in wild revels, he used to engage in amours, he loved conviviality; but after the two revolts of Sklêros and the revolt of Phôkas and other insurrections, he left the shores of luxury with full sail, and devoted himself to the serious things of life".

The first overt act which manifested the inward change in Basil's character was the deposition and banishment of the eunuch Basileios, who was chamberlain and "President of the Senate", a title which had been instituted for him by Nikêphoros Phôkas. Basileios was a half-brother of the Emperor, who, feeling himself incompetent and disinclined through youth and inexperience to undertake the administration, abandoned the reins entirely to his namesake, who was personally very much attached to him. The stature, form, and bearing of the eunuch were imperial, and as John Tzimiskês had vested the civil government altogether in his hands, he was experienced in political affairs. Basil gave him "voice and hand" over all, military as well as civil, affairs; and thus the chamberlain was like an athlete performing while the Emperor stood by as a spectator, not intending, however, to place a crown on his head, but in order to learn a lesson, and at some future time perform in like manner himself. The act by which he loosed the leading-strings and ceased to play a secondary part in the Empire took place, according to Psellos, soon after the suppression of the rebellion of Bardas Phôkas in 989. If this be correct, the power of Basileios had lasted for thirteen years. But Kedrênos (Skylitzês), the "accurate" historian, places his fall some years sooner—namely, after the subjugation of the first rising of Bardas Sklêros. Finlay, accepting the statement of Kedrênos, assigns the change in Basil's policy as the cause of the discontent and revolt of Phôkas. Psellos assigns no reason for it except that as the relation of the Emperor Nikêphoros he felt he had a claim to the throne, and he states clearly that the fall of the eunuch was subsequent to the revolt of Phôkas. Having narrated that pretender's strange death and how his head was brought to Basil, he writes, "From this time forward the Emperor becomes a different person . . . he became suspicious, haughty, reserved, and wrathful. Nor did he wish any longer to leave the administration to his chamberlain, but was ungracious to him", etc.[1] By the use of the pluperfect tense[2] Zônaras avoids committing himself to either opinion. He places his description of the change in Basil and the fall of the eunuch after the revolt of Phôkas, following herein the order of Psellos; but by his mode of expression, "he *had become* haughty", etc., he leaves it undetermined at what time the change took place.

Whatever the date may have been, Basil did not concern himself to smooth the way for the removal of his minister from office. He managed the matter with brutal simplicity, causing him to embark in a ship which carried him to exile. He then proceeded to examine all the acts of his ministry, and undid those which seemed aimed at personal display or private patronage, pro-

[1] P. 12.   [2] ἐγεγόνει, p. 115.

fessing ignorance of them. He even dismantled the splendid monastery which the president, who was immensely wealthy, had built; and so, as he said, turned the refectory into a reflectory, because the monks would be obliged henceforward to reflect seriously how to obtain the necessaries of life.[1] Basileios was utterly overwhelmed with grief at this unkind treatment, and with disappointment at having to say a long farewell to all his greatness. His noble form became a living corpse, a literal monument of the sudden change of fortune, and he soon died. At the same time Basil began to apprehend the difficulties that attend on an Emperor's office, and the seriousness of his position so impressed him that he became quite ascetic, abstaining from all good cheer, wearing no ornaments on his person, not even a chain on his neck, nor a diadem on his head, nor a chlamys bordered with purple; superfluous rings he put away from him, and eschewed many colours in his clothes. He was completely preoccupied with the problem how to make all the acts of his rule concur "to produce an imperial harmony".[2]

The second revolt of Sklêros followed hard upon the death of Phôkas, his old rival. In regard to this revolt Psellos states a fact which Skylitzês[3] seems not to have known or not to have believed, and Zônaras does not record. From their narratives we should conclude that the hostility of Sklêros was only momentary, and that

---

[1] P. 13: οὐκ ἀνῄει ἄχρις οὗ φροντιστήριον, ἰδεῖν χαριεντισάμενος εἰπεῖν, τὸ μοναστήριον δέδρακε, διὰ φροντίδος τιθεμένων τῶν ἐν αὐτῷ, ὅπως ἂν ἑαυτοῖς τὰ ἀναγκαῖα πορίσαιντο.

[2] ὅπως ἂν τὰ τῆς ἀρχῆς εἰς ἁρμονίαν βασιλικὴν συμβιβάσειε.

[3] Kedrênos, II, p. 446: ἄρτι δὲ τοῦ Φωκᾶ ἀποθανόντος κατὰ τὸν Ἀπρίλλιον μῆνα τῆς δευτέρας ἰνδικτιῶνος τοῦ ͵ϚΥϠϚ΄ ἔτους καὶ τῆς κατ᾽ αὐτὸν ἀποστασίας διαλυθείσης ἀδείας λαβόμενος ὁ Σκληρὸς πάλιν ἀνελάμβανεν ἑαυτὸν καὶ τὴν προτέραν ἐσωμάσκει ἀποστασίαν. ὅπερ πυθόμενος ὁ βασιλεὺς γράμμασι παρῄνει, κ.τ.λ. . . . τούτοις δὲ τοῖς γράμμασι μαλαχθεὶς . . . κατατίθεται τὰ ὅπλα.

his reconciliation with Basil took place almost immediately, certainly before the end of the year 989. But Psellos tells us that his rebellion, which began in the summer of that year, lasted many years longer. He did not venture on an engagement with the imperial troops, but strengthened and increased his army and cut off the traffic and means of communication with the capital, and intercepted supplies. His army was devoted to him —won by his kindness and good fellowship; he used to call each soldier by his name, eat at the same table with his men, and share the same wine-bowl. But he felt age with stealing steps creeping over his frame, and at the last listened to an embassy of Basil, who seems to have been at the end of his wit to disembarrass himself of the opposition of the able general.

Now the manner in which Psellos states the duration of the hostility of Sklêros is peculiar.[1]* "This tyranny which began in summer did not cease in the autumn, nor was it circumscribed even by the limit of a year, but for many years the mischief surged". It is, I think, a legitimate conjecture that the negative clauses refer to, and are intended to refute, a prevailing view, which was shared by Skylitzês, and which Psellos considered an historical error. If this be so, the opposition between the historical schools was not confined to style and method.

Zônaras took from Psellos his account of the meeting between Basil and Sklêros, but he omitted what is perhaps the most interesting point about it—the advice which the aged, now blind, commander gave to the young Emperor, who asked him as a general for his opinion as to the best policy for maintaining absolute power and avoiding rebellions. The advice which he

---

[1] *History*, p. 15...ἀλλ' ἐπὶ πολλοῖς ἔτεσι τουτὶ διεκυμαίνετο κακόν.
[* v. note 58, p. 216, vol. v, Bury's *Gibbon*, 1898 ed.]

gave, says Psellos, was not strategic, but unprincipled ($\pi\alpha\nu o\hat{\nu}\rho\gamma o\varsigma$)—as we should say, Machiavellian. It was to do away with too exalted offices, to allow no military officer to be too rich, to wear them out with unjust exactions, so that their private affairs may claim all their attention, not to introduce a wife into the palace, to be to none easy to deal with, and to be chary of imparting to others his secret resolves.

This advice of a man who knew the condition of the Roman Empire well indicates clearly the danger which was threatening the Macedonian dynasty, and, staved off for a time by Basil's personal vigour, finally over-threw it—the power of the wealthy Asiatic aristocrats, who by their wealth could convert the imperial regiments which they commanded into private armies of their own.

Basil's subsequent policy was conceived fully in the spirit of his old opponent's advice. The law of *allêlengyon*, by which the rich taxpayers of a district were bound to make up the deficiencies of the poorer, is an instance of the "unjust exactions". The loyalty of terror, and not the loyalty of goodwill, was what he wished to secure. He managed the whole administration himself, and as he grew older experience made him quite independent of the wisdom of councillors. As Psellos expresses his policy of imperial absolutism, he steered the State not according to enacted laws, but according to the un-written laws of his own well-constituted nature; and in this spirit he paid no attention to educated men, but utterly looked down on them. This was a feature of Basil's reign; culture was not patronised, but dis-couraged and scorned by the Emperor.[1] Nevertheless we

---

[1] This feature should doubtless be connected with the policy of de-pressing the nobility and higher classes who represented the culture of the Empire. The education of Basil's nieces Zôê and Theodôra was com-

are told that there was a large number of philosophers and rhetoricians in those days. On which fact, which strikes him as curious, Psellos makes the comment that to these men culture was an end in itself, not a mere means to favour or money, "whereas now money is the end".

Psellos does not enter on the subject of Basil's campaigns, but he has some interesting remarks on his military system. One of his peculiarities was to pay no attention to the traditional habit of limiting the season of campaigns. It was usual to set forth in the middle of spring and retire before the extreme heat began. Basil, with "adamantine" indifference, despised heat and defied cold when he had an object in view, and like other great generals made season wait on occasion. His great principle in tactics was to preserve the ranks unbroken; he considered that this was the one secret which would save the Greek phalanxes from rout, and he was punctilious in punishing that too eager bravery which led a man to step out before his fellows or leave his column. When soldiers on one occasion openly grumbled at his mode of battle, he calmly replied with a smile, "There is no other means by which we can cease waging war".

His personal appearance is minutely described by Psellos. His stature was rather under-sized, but not disproportionate; on horseback he looked incomparable, like the statue of a master sculptor, presenting inflexibly the same pose both uphill and downhill. His face was an exact circle; his forehead neither retreated nor protruded. His eyes were bright and flashing, and the brow, avoiding the extremes of a feminine straight line and the grim aspect lent by an overhanging shape, expressed his

pletely neglected. His secretaries were obscure men of little training, but he wrote his despatches in so simple and unvarnished a style that no great ability was required (p. 19).

innate pride. He wore a thick beard and whiskers which he was fond of twirling, particularly when he was angry or perplexed in thought; he had also the habit of sticking out his elbow and resting his fingers on his hips. He spoke in short abrupt sentences, more like a peasant than a gentleman, and when he indulged in laughter his whole frame assisted in the operation.

3. *Constantine VIII.** On Basil's death in 1025 his brother and sleeping colleague, if we may use the expression, at the advanced age of seventy became ruler of the Empire. His chief achievement was to spend the immense treasures which Basil had accumulated, and which were so large that he had to build subterranean treasure vaults. The money in the treasury amounted to 200,000 lb. of gold.[1] The arrears of two years' taxes were due when Basil died; these he rigorously collected. He was now an old voluptuary, utterly unfit to conduct the government, in which he had never taken any interest. He cared only for horse-racing, hunting, and dice-playing, or for tasting luxurious dishes. He had always been weak-minded, and his originally firm physique was so worn with age and indulgence and gout that, instead of meeting in the field the barbarians who were threatening the Empire, he preferred to buy them off. It was his custom to forestall conspiracies by depriving of sight those whom he suspected, and he inflicted the same penalty on any one who actually conspired. That the notion of justice was alien to him is further shown by his habit of overwhelming persons in his immediate environment with a bounty which he did not extend further. He was too capricious and flighty

[* Constantine VIII (IX), A.D. 976, Jan. 10–1028, Nov.]

[1] If Zônaras means *pounds* by the pedantic word *talents*, the sum exceeds nine million pounds sterling. (Finlay, II, p. 387.) I am afraid that Psellos (whom Finlay elsewhere calls a pedant) is originally responsible for the affected word *talents*.

to cherish resentment like Basil, and he often repented of his own severity.

Although his education was only superficial, he had a mother-wit and a remarkable fluency of speech—in this, too, contrasting with his brother—so that when he dictated business letters or despatches the fastest writer could not keep up with him.

It was Basil's custom to transact all business as far as possible himself. Constantine, on the other hand, transacted no business himself, except occasionally the dictation of letters. He entrusted the administration to six eunuchs of his household.[1]

His wife Helena, the daughter of Alypios, a man of distinction, bore him three daughters, of whom their childless uncle Basil had been extremely fond. The eldest, Eudokia, was unlike her family in being of equable and soft disposition; she was permitted at her own request to retire into a monastery. The other two, Zôê and Theodôra, who were of a prouder and more domineering temper, were destined to play a prominent part during the following years. When his death was approaching, the Emperor chose Rômanos Argyropôlos to be his successor as the husband of his second and fairest daughter Zôê, then forty-eight years old. The fact that he was already married was no impediment; his wife cut off her hair and sought the retreat of a convent.

Zônaras states that Constantine had originally destined Theodôra to be the wife of Rômanos, but that she refused.[2] Psellos makes a contrary statement—namely, that before the selection of Rômanos the Emperor's choice fell on his second daughter. Moreover, he omits to mention a circumstance recorded by Zô-

---

[1] Their names are recorded by Kedrênos.
[2] Vol. IV, p. 128: ἡ γὰρ τρίτη διὰ τὸ τὴν ἐκείνου εὐνέτειραν ἄκουσαν διαζυγῆναι αὐτοῦ παραιτήσασθαι τὴν μετ᾽ αὐτοῦ συμβίωσιν λέγεται.

naras and Kedrênos, that the first intention was to name Constantine Dalassênos as his successor.

4. *Rômanos III.** We are informed by Psellos that from the accession of Rômanos his narrative will become fuller; "for the Emperor Basil died when I was an infant, and Constantine when I was just beginning my lessons; I was never in their presence, nor did I ever hear them speaking, and I know not whether I saw either of them, as I was too young to remember. But Rômanos I saw and on one occasion met him. Thus my account of Basil and Constantine is derived from others, whereas I can describe Rômanos from personal knowledge".

Rômanos was well born and well educated, but Psellos expresses contempt for the amount and quality of his learning. "He thought that he knew far more than he did". He was ambitious to rival Marcus Antoninus and pose as a philosopher on the throne. It became the fashion to talk metaphysics at court, but it was mere pretence and show, due to no real concern for truth; and the learned of that time, says Psellos, had not reached further than the portals of Aristotle and only knew by rote a few catchwords of Platonism, never really penetrating into the secrets of metaphysics.

Another mania of Rômanos was warfare, of which he knew absolutely nothing. When he did not talk of the insoluble problems of parthenogenesis, his conversation was of greaves and corslets. He had high-flying schemes of subjugating all the eastern and all the western nations; he burned to rival the exploits of Alexander, Hadrian, or Trajan. His expedition against the Saracens in 1030 ended in a complete fiasco. Contrary to the advice of his officers he had rejected the proposals of the Caliph for peace, as he could not bring himself to give up the delightful prospect of cutting trenches, diverting the

[* Rômanos III, Argyros, A.D. 1028, Nov. 12–1034, Ap.]

courses of rivers, laying ambushes, and performing the military operations described in ancient history. The great Basil made war in order to be at peace; Rômanos made war for its own sake. Psellos says that he began the war without a pretext, but we read in Kedrênos that Spondylês, governor of Antioch, had suffered a serious defeat in the last month of 1029, which endangered the safety of Syria, so that Psellos is probably exaggerating for the sake of effect the sexagenarian Emperor's childish fancy to do what he read of.

Thus Rômanos "raught at mountains with out-stretched arms, yet parted but the shadow with his hand". He had ascended the throne with high fan-tastical hopes of a brilliant and long reign, and perhaps the foundation of a new dynasty, and he held court with more splendour and practised a more profuse liberality than most sovrans. He had inaugurated his reign with popular measures, abolishing, for example, the *allêlengyon*. But the discomfiture at Azaz acted like cold water, and moreover placed his finances in a very unsatisfactory condition. Consequently, when he re-turned to Constantinople after his unlucky experiences, his domestic policy changed. He abandoned the idea of being a second Trajan or Hadrian, and set before himself the far more practical ideal of a Byzantine financier—"a less strange life". For his subjects this meant that he became a tyrant instead of a liberal if fantastic sovran. His object was to recruit the treasury for the money he had staked for the glory he had not won. He waked from their slumbers old and forgotten claims, dormant since the proverbial archonship of Eukleidês, and visited with bitter visitation the monetary deficiencies of the fathers upon the children. In these matters he did not sit as an impartial judge, but acted as an advocate of the exchequer.

The use to which he put the results of his financial abilities was such that not even the court, much less the mass of his subjects, derived any benefit from all the money that streamed into the treasury. For Rômanos had yet another mania. He desired not only to rival Basil I or Constantine the Great as the founder of a new dynasty, to imitate Alexander or Trajan as a general, to rank with Aurelius as a crowned philosopher; he wished also to emulate Solomon and Justinian as a builder. Justinian had built the immortal church of the Divine Wisdom; Rômanos determined to build a church to the mother of God on a grand scale. "A whole mountain was excavated" to supply the stones, and the art of excavation was reckoned a branch of philosophy; the workmen engaged in the edifice were ranked with the assistants of Pheidias and Polygnôtos. The work continued interminably, for the original design was not followed out, but modified and enlarged as it progressed. The sources of gold were being exhausted, and yet the church was not approaching completion.

Rômanos looked on this as a work of piety and undertook it professedly from pious motives, but Psellos says of course that they were only sham. It is interesting to read the philosopher's comments on the propriety of spending money on costly buildings for divine service. "It is good", he says, "to love the comeliness of the house of the Lord, as the psalmist says, and the habitation of his glory, and often to prefer throwing away money on it to winning happiness from other things. This is good, and who will gainsay those who are consumed with zeal for the Lord? But the principle holds good only when there is nothing to interfere with this pious end—when it does not involve injustice and harm to the public weal. Care that there should be nothing indecent in the Lord's house does not imply that even walls, encircling pillars, and swinging drapery, or expensive sacrifices are necessary to serve God, the true requisite being a mind encircled with godliness, a soul hued with the intellectual purple, even actions, and the fair affection of heart which really consists in an unaffected manner. The Emperor understood syllogisms, and the puzzles of Sorites and Nobody, but he had no practical philosophy". He was not content with building the church; he added to it a monastery which he supplied with the greatest luxury.

While the Emperor's thoughts were occupied with building, intrigues were carried on at court of which he seems to have been intentionally ignorant. The Empress Zôê had cause for dissatisfaction and very good reason for laying plans for future contingencies. At the time of his accession, although he himself was sixty-five and Zôê almost fifty years old, Rômanos had cherished the hopes of founding a dynasty. But when charms and aphrodisiacs proved unavailing, and he found that there was no prospect of issue, he began to show a neglect to his wife, which she felt derogatory to her royal birth, and lived apart from her, an arrangement which, being a delicate liver, she could not endure. Moreover, as she had no child and as the Emperor's sister Pulcheria had great influence with her brother, and was not well disposed to herself, the prospect of what might happen on his death seemed precarious, and the state of his health indicated that he could not live long.

The most trusted counsellor of the Emperor was a eunuch named Joannês, a very clever man of low origin who held the post of *orphanotrophos*, or head of an institution for the support of orphans. We shall have occasion to learn more about his personal qualities when we come to the history of the next reign. He and Zôê were on very bad terms, and perhaps we may suppose that he

influenced the Emperor in his behaviour towards her.
But he had a very handsome brother named Michael,
a youth of regular features, with bright eyes and a fair
pink and white complexion. One day when the Emperor and Empress were sitting together, Joannês by
imperial direction introduced his brother for inspection.
The Emperor having addressed a few questions to him
dismissed him, bidding him remain in attendance within
the palace, but the Empress saw and loved. For a long
time she kept her feelings a secret, but, unable longer
to endure the pangs, she changed her behaviour to
Joannês and became quite amicable, courting opportunities of conversation with him; and casually introducing the topic of his brother she desired him to
convey to Michael a permission to enter her presence
whenever he wished. Joannês, at first unsuspicious, soon
ascertained the state of Zôê's affections, which were
manifested clearly in her next interview with Michael.
Grasping the situation and seeing the prospect of unlimited power by the devolution of the sovranty on his
brother, he prepared Michael for the part he was to play.

The intrigue soon became an open scandal. Zôê, in
the extravagance of her passionate admiration, used to
array her lover in cloth of gold and rings; she was seen
to place him on the throne with a sceptre and a crown.
Pulcheria and her adherents indignantly informed the
Emperor of what he could not, except intentionally,
have avoided seeing. He felt no *tremor cordis* at Zôê's
virginalling on Michael's palm. He merely for form's
sake summoned the young man and questioned him on
the matter, and when he denied the allegations on oath,
professed to consider the informants calumniators and
the alleged adulterer a most loyal servant. One point
in Michael's favour was his liability to epileptic fits,
which might be thought to unfit him for offices of gal-

lantry; and it might be supposed that this circumstance really disarmed the suspicions of Rômanos. But Psellos learned from a well-informed person who moved in the court at that time, and was acquainted intimately with the course of the love-drama of the Empress and Michael, that Rômanos was perfectly aware that Zôê was madly in love with Michael, but was quite indifferent and determined to overlook it. And we can well understand that on the head of Rômanos, old and worn with disease, and devoid of affection for Zôê, the horns sat lightly. His sister Pulcheria, who led the party which disapproved of the intrigue, died soon afterwards, and then Joannês and Michael had a free field.

Psellos gives a description of the wasting disease which consumed the frame of Rômanos. He had himself seen him in a procession looking like a corpse; his hair had fallen off, and he used to stop and draw breath every few steps. It was generally believed that his death, which took place in a bath, was accelerated by poison administered by Zôê (1034).

The officials of the palace, both those attached to the Basilian family, and also the adherents of the late Emperor, advised Zôê to wait, nor in such weighty matters take a too hasty step. But her mind was quite made up, inasmuch as her affections were engaged, and she was incited to speedy action by Joannês. Michael the Paphlagonian was placed on the throne the same evening, and all the residents in the palace paid him the usual homage. Two commands were sent to the prefect of the city, that he should come early on the morrow with the members of the Senate to recognise the new Emperor, and that he should make arrangements for the obsequies of the deceased. The ceremony of homage consisted in the senators advancing one by one into the presence of the King and Queen, seated on thrones, and laying their heads on the ground before each; they then kissed the right hand of the Emperor, but not that of the Empress.

Psellos was in Constantinople at this time, a lad yet unbearded, and witnessed the funeral of Rômanos. The corpse, which was not, as with us, covered in a coffin, but carried in an open bier, was so changed that it was unrecognisable. The face was swollen, and the colour was not that of a dead body, but resembled persons who have been injured by drugs. Whether Rômanos was really poisoned was a question on which contemporaries could only entertain suspicions, but their suspicions seem to have been very strong.

5. *Michael IV.** Even from Zônaras it might be seen that Michael IV was by no means a bad Emperor. The energetic part he took in the Bulgarian expedition just before his death was really heroic, if heroism means the surrender of personal interests and endurance of pain for impersonal ends. But in Psellos we can see his judgment and ability far more clearly than in Zônaras, who gives us an abridgment of Psellos. He tells us plainly that he is combating against a prevailing opinion, detrimental to Michael; he has in fact made himself Michael's apologist. We may assume with tolerable certainty that he owed some of his information to Constantine Leichudês, who became a member of the Senate at this time, and through whose influence probably Psellos himself became judge at Philadelphia. "I am well aware", he says, "that many chroniclers in treating of his life will give an account diverging from ours; for the suspicion of the reverse of what was really the case was more prevalent in his times. But I, having partly had to do myself with the actual affairs, and having partly learned the secrets of state from persons who were

[* Michael IV, the Paphlagonian, A.D. 1034, April 11–1041, Dec.]

in close attendance on him, am a competent judge of the matter, except my eyes and ears be impugned".

As a contemporary, Psellos is the best authority we have, and his whole account of the reign of Michael IV gives us the impression of an impartiality which unfortunately we cannot always give him credit for. But his favourable representation of the Emperor's character is confirmed by the shortly expressed judgment of Michael Attaleiatês—"he left behind him many tokens of virtue".[1] "If we leave out of sight", says Psellos, "his conduct before his accession, he will rank among the few elect monarchs".

Michael is an instance of a man who suddenly became mature. For a short time at the beginning of his reign, he made the palace a sort of playground, gratifying the whims of the Empress and careless of everything serious, just like a boy. But he suddenly became conscious of the magnitude of supreme power and the responsibilities devolving on a true king, and, immediately rising to the situation, he put away childish things and proved that his nature was not superficial. It struck Psellos as notably admirable that he made no sudden change in the administration, but graduated all his alterations. He introduced no novelty in the ordinary practices, annulled no law, made no change in the Senate. To personal friends to whom he had pledged himself before his accession he kept his word, but did not immediately place them in high posts; he gave them subordinate positions as a preliminary training for advancement. His unwearying solicitude both provided that the provincial cities were well governed, and secured the Empire against invasion.[2]

[1] *History*, p. 10: πολλὰ τῆς ἀρετῆς καταλιπὼν εἰκονίσματα. Skylitzês' judgment is also favourable (Kedrênos, ii, p. 534).
[2] παντοδαπὸς ἦν περὶ τὴν τῆς ἀρχῆς πρόνοιαν, οὐ μόνον τὰς ἐντὸς τῶν ἡμετέρων ὁρίων πόλεις εὐνομουμένας ποιῶν ἀλλὰ καὶ τοῖς πέριξ ἔθνεσι

He bestowed particular diligence on the efficiency and improvement of the army, "the sinews of Rômaioi". The administration of the finances he left entirely to his brother Joannês, who was experienced in that department.

Like Rômanos, his predecessor, Michael was very religious, but he was not like him a *dilettante*: he was really in earnest. He was not only a constant church-goer, but he cultivated the society of theosophists, whom Psellos calls philosophers and distinguishes from the metaphysicians, such as Rômanos used to patronise; they were the philosophers who despise the world, and live with beings that are above the world. Michael sent out to the highroads and hedges, searched high and low throughout the whole Empire to find such men, and when they arrived in his palace showed them the most extravagant veneration, rubbing their dirty feet with his own hands, and kissing them. He even went so far as to wrap secretly his imperial person in their rags. He used to set them on a couch, and lie at their feet on a stool. Those who had bodily sores or infirmities, and had thereby become disgusting to their fellowmen, were the objects of his special devotion; he used to wash them like a servant, and actually place his face on their sores.

Psellos speaks in tones of praise of this extravagant method of realising a spiritual life, which seems to us a sort of monomania. But Michael was really sincere, and we must remember that he had no "Hellenic culture" to preserve him from these aberrations of a self-annihilating gymnosophic asceticism, which seems so ludicrous in a sovran. He was not only ascetic himself, he also encouraged asceticism in others, and he laid out large sums in endowing monasteries for both male and

τὰς ἐφ᾽ ἡμᾶς ἀναστέλλων ἐφόδους τοῦτο μὲν πρεσβείαις τοῦτο δὲ δώροις τοῦτο δὲ μαχίμων ἐπετείοις ἀποστολαῖς. (*Hist.* p. 58.)

female recluses. He built a new hall at Constantinople, called the Ptôchotropheion, a sort of refectory for poor religious people. His zeal for saving lost souls extended itself to unfortunate females, of whom there was a very large number in the capital. As "such persons are apt to be deaf to salutary advice", he did not think it judicious to reclaim them by moral lectures, nor did he think of using violence. He built a very large and fine reformatory or penitentiary in the city, and then proclaimed to all women who made a trade of their persons, that if any of them wished to live in plenty, she had only to repair to this refuge and take the monastic habit. A large swarm of the "ladies of the roof"[1] presented themselves, and were enrolled as recruits in the army of God. What the social effects of this step were, if "a large swarm" is to be taken literally, we can only conjecture from the well-known measure which was tried at Venice. Such an effect, however, could only have been momentary; for as Michael's object was not directly to repress prostitution, but to save lost souls, and as he passed no repressive measure, the curtailed supply would, in a very short time, again equal the demand.

Persons ill disposed to the Emperor put a malicious construction on his religious practices, asserting that before he ascended the throne he had had communication with evil spirits with which he had made a compact to deny God, and so lose his soul on condition of obtaining the Empire. This is an interesting instance of the medieval superstition of compacts with the devil.

It was Michael's close connection with his family that prevented his good qualities from being appreciated; his affectionate brothers proved his greatest misfortune,

---

[1] καὶ πολὺς ἐντεῦθεν ἑσμὸς τῶν ἐπὶ τοῦ τέγους ἐκεῖθεν συνέρρευσεν (p. 67). Five hundred years before Theodôra and Justinian had made efforts to reclaim prostitutes.

their vulgar grasping natures tarnishing the lustre of his. They were a sort of nemesis which attended his elevation. The eldest and chief of them, who possessed most political talent, was Joannês the orphanotrophos, of whom I must now give a more detailed account. Psellos, when old enough to be a capable observer, had seen him and heard him speaking, and been in his company while he was transacting business; and he had observed his character carefully. He sums up his good and bad qualities in a businesslike manner which reminds us of Ammianus Marcellinus. He was keen and ready of wit, as could be seen by the flash of his eye; in the transaction of business he was most diligent and hardworking, and very experienced; his keenness was manifested particularly in public finances. He did no evil to any one, but put on a sour face in order to frighten people, and often deterred men from bad actions by his threatening looks. Hence he was really a tower of defence for the Emperor, for night and day his thoughts were busy with the interests of the State, though this did not prevent him from attending banquets and public festivals. Nothing that went on escaped his many-eyed vigilance, which was so great that he used often in the dead hours of the night to walk through the whole city—"like lightning", says Psellos—easily escaping observation himself, for having been originally a monk he continued to wear a monastic dress. His excellent information on all that went on exercised a wholesome terror, which prevented gatherings and meetings that might look like illegal conspiracies.

Such were his laudable qualities, over against which Psellos places his profound dissimulation. He always adapted his words and looks to his company, and he had the habit of gazing at a person steadily when he was at some distance, and on his approach behaving as if he had not been aware of his presence before. If any one made a new suggestion which seemed likely to prove advantageous, he would pretend that he had himself decided on the course proposed long since, and rebuked the suggestor for his tardiness, who passed out crestfallen, while Joannês put the suggestion in practice and was under no obligation to its real author. He was ambitious to behave with princely grandeur and dignity, but the inner man continually exposed itself; he was not to the manner born. He used occasionally to indulge in potations, and it was then especially that his vulgarity came out in indecent behaviour. Yet even on such occasions he did not forget the absorbing cares of power. Psellos often met him at banquets, and wondered how a man unable to refrain from intoxication and laughter could draw the car of government. But when he was drunk he measured the behaviour of each of his fellows, and called them to account afterwards for what they said or did, so that men were more afraid of him drunk than sober. He was a strange compound, this man, dressed in his monastic gown. To the decency which such a dress might seem to demand he did not dream of paying any regard, though, in deference to some new imperial law which concerned the monastic orders, he might occasionally pretend some outward conformity. For dissolute livers he entertained a contempt, but to gentlemen of liberal culture and refined habits he felt a repugnance and tried to diminish their influence.

The shiftiness which he displayed towards the world in general was, in relation to his brothers, replaced by an unvarying affection. The other brothers are represented to have been a worthless lot. If Joannês was far inferior in virtue to Michael, he was far superior to the other three, Nikêtas, Constantine, and Geôrgios. They utilised their kinship to the Emperor as a cover for deeds of injustice of which Joannês did not approve; while Joannês was so fond of his brothers that he took care that the Emperor should not hear of them, and if anything did come to his ears used his influence to protect them from the imperial anger. Nikêtas was made duke (δούξ) of Antioch, where he signalised himself by an act of perfidy. The citizens, who before his arrival had wreaked summary vengeance on a tax collector who had behaved indecently towards them, shut the gates in fear lest Nikêtas should punish them. He bound himself by oaths to grant a plenary pardon, but when he was admitted put a great number to death and sent many of the chief men to the capital.[1] Some time after this Nikêtas died, and his brother Constantine, a eunuch like Joannês, succeeded him as duke of Antioch, and in that office relieved Edessa from a Saracen siege. He was soon raised to the rank of domestikos, or commander of the eastern armies. Geôrgios, of whom we hear least, was made protovestiarios; he too was probably a eunuch. The whole family was very unpopular:

> And what is Edward but a ruthless sea?
> What Clarence but a quicksand of deceit?
> And Richard but a ragged fatal rock?

And the Emperor Michael was involved in the unpopularity of the family with which he was identified.

Joannês was a man of boundless activity and resources. His object was to secure the succession for his own family—to found a Paphlagonian dynasty; and as Michael's health was very bad it was imperative to take precautions in good time. A scheme of personal ambition which he attempted to execute failed. This was his own

---

[1] Zônaras, IV, 138. The citizens of Antioch were suspected of a degree of goodwill towards Constantine Dalassênos which was inconsistent with their loyalty to the throne. Dalassênos was considered a dangerous person, and kept in strict confinement.

election to the patriarchal chair, which involved the deposition of the then patriarch Alexios, to compass which Joannês formed a cabal of clerical dignitaries who conspired to unseat Alexios on the ground that he had not been canonically elected. Alexios was equal to the occasion, and pointed out that if his election had not been canonical, the invalidity of all the appointments he had made during his tenure of office would follow of logical necessity. This manifesto caused the majority of the clergy to take the part of Alexios, and the scheme of Joannês fell through. If he had been successful—if Alexios had been a weaker man or had happened to die in the reign of Michael IV—Joannês would have been in so secure and influential a position that he might have saved his family dynasty from the catastrophe in which the conduct of Michael Kalaphatês involved it. Alexios was probably never well disposed to the Paphlagonian family, but he was a firm adherent of the Basilian house.

The epileptic fits to which the Emperor was subject became so constant that he was obliged to lead a life of great seclusion, and when his imperial duties made it necessary to hold an audience, purple curtains and curtain-pullers were so placed that if the least sign indicated that the disease was about to seize him his agony could in a moment be concealed from view, as it were in a separate room. And when he rode abroad he was accompanied by a guard which used to form a circle round him, so that if he were overtaken by a fit he should not be a public spectacle. In the intervals between the fits he was always actively engaged. But Joannês perceived that the sands of his life were running quickly down, and he framed a plan for securing the succession to his family, which consisted in the timely elevation of a nephew to the rank of Cæsar, and the adoption of him by the Empress Zôê as her son.

Besides his four brothers Joannês had a sister named Maria, who was the wife of a ship-tarrer (caulker) named Stephanos. The brother-in-law had taken his share in the successes of the family, and had been appointed to succeed George Maniakês in Sicily, where, as might be expected, he conducted affairs with such gross incompetency and corruption that the rich island was lost to the Saracens, with the exception of Messênê, which was preserved by the bravery of its commandant Kekaumenos Katakolôn. Psellos saw Stephanos after he had been transformed in the game of fortune from a pitch-smearer of ships to a military commander, and was highly amused with the figure he cut. He looked out of place on his steed, and his dress looked out of place on him; he was like a pygmy trying to act Hêraklês, but unable to manage the lionskin and wield a club bigger than himself. This man and Maria had a son named Michael, who was surnamed Kalaphatês after his father's profession. He had not been forgotten in the family preferments, and had been appointed captain of the bodyguard. On him the choice of Joannês fell to succeed his brother, for he seems to have been the nearest relative eligible,[1] and he decided to have him proclaimed Cæsar. It required some adroitness to suggest this to the Emperor and obtain his consent, as it is a matter of difficulty even for brothers to introduce to monarchs the subject of their own mortality.

Psellos professes to give a full account of the conversation which passed between Joannês and Michael. That some such conversation did take place we have no reason to doubt, though of course the actual words put into their mouths by Psellos are as fictitious as the dialogue of the Athenians and Mêlians in Thukydidês. It has a considerable value, however, as a dialogue

---

[1] Nikêtas was dead; Constantine and Geôrgios were eunuchs.

imagined as probable by a contemporary, and in this aspect claims our attention. Joannês begins by reminding the Emperor of his own unwavering loyalty and brotherly attachment. When the Emperor demands the aim of this prelude, he goes on to say: "Do not imagine that the ears of the majority of your subjects have not heard and their eyes seen that you suffer both from a secret and from an undisguised disease. That you are really in no danger on this account I know full well, but yet the tongues of men refrain not from discussing the possibility of your death; and this leads me to fear that, having got into their heads the idea that you are about to die immediately, they may combine against you and elect a new Emperor and place him in the palace. For myself and our family I feel less concern, but I am alarmed in your behalf lest such a good and excellent monarch should pay for want of prudence. He will escape the danger but not the reproach of not foreseeing the future". This punctiliously deferential speech is interesting as showing the tone in which Joannês would have spoken to his brother. He then proposed his plan, and Michael consented. As a greater security it was arranged that Zôê, who as an heiress of the old Basilian dynasty was very popular, should adopt him as her son. A public festival was proclaimed and the ceremony was performed.

Michael never loved Zôê, who was past fifty when their *liaison* began. For a time he acted the lover, but the part soon became tedious, and he not only grew cold, but, feeling suspicious that she might treat him as she is supposed to have treated Rômanos, he kept her in strict confinement in the women's apartments, cut down her income, and prevented access to her except by the special permission of a guard whom he appointed to superintend her. Zôê behaved under this treatment

with the greatest self-control and patience, never even
bestowing on her appointed keeper a hard word or look.
The brothers did not trust this meek behaviour, which
they viewed as consummate acting; they looked on Zôê
as a caged lioness, and the meeker she seemed the greater
precautions they took. The Emperor soon gave up
living with her altogether. He suffered from dropsy, and
was indisposed for conjugal life; and this indisposition
was confirmed by the admonitions of his spiritual
advisers.

The Bulgarian war which immediately preceded and
hastened Michael's death—the rising of the false Doli-
anos, the double desertion of the genuine Alusianos, and
the heroism of the Emperor—has been related fully by
Zônaras, closely following Psellos, and by Finlay. We
need not repeat it here. The Emperor after his ex-
hausting labours returned in triumph, but nigh unto
death, for which he prepared by assuming the monastic
order. The ceremony was performed in the church of
the Anargyroi which he had built himself, and when it
was concluded the ex-Emperor was cheerful "like a
man light and fleet for a journey", but his household
and brothers, especially Joannês, were plunged in de-
spondency. When the Empress heard the news, she immediately proceeded on foot to the monastery, but
Michael refused to see her. Shortly afterwards the time
for a hymnal service arrived, and Michael arose from
his couch to attend it, but found that his imperial shoes
had not been changed nor monastic foot-gear provided.
He was obliged to totter barefoot to the chapel, and
when he returned to repose he died. He was a man who,
under more favourable circumstances, might have been
an efficient ruler and have won the praise of historians;
but he was sorely let and hindered, on the one hand by
his ill health, and on the other hand by his kinsfolk.

PART II

6. *Michael V.** The irony of history forcibly impressed itself on the philosopher Psellos as manifested in the elevation of Michael V. Joannês the orphanotrophos had secured this elevation with the express purpose of preserving his own power and the position of his family; and destiny or providence made use of the same means for the ruin of Joannês himself and his family's utter catastrophe. *L'homme propose.*

Michael V is represented by historians to have been a man of no principle and no conscience. He is said to have been skilled in dissembling, hiding the fire of hatred under the ashes of goodwill—*cineri doloso*;—he is said to have been ungrateful to his benefactors. When he was made Cæsar—an honour perhaps which he had not dreamed of—he sketched out in his imagination (we are informed by Psellos) plans of action to be followed when his uncle Michael died. His chief feeling was detestation of his own family, and he determined to get rid of his relations, especially Joannês, by death or banishment—to stamp out his whole stock.

> And till I root out their accursed line
> And leave not one alive, I live in hell.

The more virulent his feelings, the more friendly to all did he appear in the meantime, but the quicksightedness of Joannês was not deceived by the dissimulation of his most unnatural nephew, whose real sentiments he suspected. But he decided to take no step at once. Michael on his part became aware of Joannês' suspicions, and the dissembling friendliness deceived neither. Michael IV did not like his nephew; he showed him no

[* The second article began here. Michael V, Kalaphatês, A.D. 1041, Dec. 14–1042, Ap.]

consideration nor honour, except in the mere formal ceremonies in which he assisted as Cæsar, and kept him in a sort of banishment outside the city, not permitting him to appear in court, except in obedience to a command. But his uncle Constantine, who was jealous of the influence of Joannês, saw that it might be a profitable game to ingratiate himself with the apparent heir, and accordingly flattered him and lent him money.

On Michael's abdication of the throne, the family clique took their measures cautiously; and caution was necessary, as the city was excited and ready for a tumult. Psellos was a witness of the circumstances. They took no step without the countenance of the Empress, so that the elevation of Michael Kalaphatês should appear altogether due to her, and the adopted son made the most lavish protestations and took the most solemn oaths that she should be sole sovran and that he would merely act as a sort of hired minister to put her wishes into execution. Zôê was won, and, her attitude repressing the threatening populace, the new Emperor was consecrated and crowned. For the first day he was on his good behaviour towards both the Empress and his uncle Joannês, calling her, with emphatic repetition, "Empress", deferring to the opinion of "my lady", addressing Joannês as "my lord" and placing him next himself at table. All except Joannês were taken in by this conduct and thought him a most deserving and judicious young man. "His uncle", they said, "made a good choice".

This respectful deference was very soon dropped, and his uncle Constantine, who had been immediately created a *nobelissimos*, encouraged him to exhibit the coldness he felt towards Joannês. The latter did not say much, but concocted a plan, which came under the notice of Psellos but was not generally known, to replace the Emperor by one of his cousins, a certain Constantine. In order to provide against miscarriage he actually induced the Emperor, in a moment when he was indisposed to transact business, to sign a paper in which there was a clause that if any of his cousins were to attempt usurpation the matter should pass unpunished. But the plan came to nothing.

The smouldering envy between uncle and nephew soon burst into flame, the occasion being a difference of opinion between them, of which Constantine the nobelissimos availed himself to heap abuse and reproaches on Joannês for arrogance and disloyalty. Joannês immediately withdrew from the city accompanied by a personal retinue, expecting that his nephew would repent and beseech him with importunity to return, and a large number of senators, not from love but from the same expectation, withdrew with him. Michael did not in the least regret his uncle's departure, but he was alarmed at the secession of the members of the *synkletôs*, and therefore wrote a letter to Joannês, in which he reproached him for his conduct and summoned him to a private interview in the palace. Joannês went, expecting reconciliatory overtures, but found that the Emperor had not kept his appointment, being absent at a horse-race. Considering this a sign that the breach was final, he left the city. Soon afterwards the Emperor sent a vessel to his place of retreat, with a mandate to present himself at the palace, which he obeyed. As the vessel was about to enter the great harbour, Michael, who was watching its approach from the palace windows, gave a preconcerted signal to the captain not to moor but to turn the vessel back. Then a second vessel came up which carried the orphanotrophos to a distant place of banishment.

In one point at least, Joannês and his nephew were of

diametrically opposite disposition. The uncle was remarkable for his unswerving attachment to his kindred; the nephew abhorred his relations with the most consistent detestation, making an exception in favour of Constantine. "The names of kinship, the common bond of kindred blood, appeared to him mere childishness, and it would have been nothing to him if one wave had engulfed all his relations". When he had disposed of Joannês he proceeded to gratify these disagreeable sentiments by emasculating most of the members of his family, many of whom were respectable men with wives and children.

This policy of exterminating his own family seems so obviously self-destructive for an Emperor in the precarious position of an upstart, that one might almost conclude that the young man must have been mad. Nobody had any reason to object to the banishment of the unpopular orphanotrophos, whose Argus-like supervision, oppressive taxation, and restless ambition had not conduced to making many friends. Once he was gone, the temerity of Michael hurried on the catastrophe; for "beggars mounted run their horse to death". His policy was to depress and show disfavour to the officials and persons of rank, removing or limiting their powers and privileges; and on the other hand to concede privileges to the populace and humour it, so as to rest his tenure of the throne on the many and not on the few. Tradesmen and retail dealers who profited by his *ad captandum* measures showed their goodwill by strewing silken carpets in the streets when he rode abroad; and this deluded him into the idea that he might with impunity try to set aside the old Basilian dynasty, by hanging on to which he had himself obtained power. This misconception of the popular mind led to his fall.

He had got rid of one political power which he disliked, his uncle. There was another political power which he disliked more, but whose position was more dangerous to assault. This was the Empress Zôê, on whom, as he found out too late, his position really depended. After the first days of his reign, during which he had lavished marks of deference towards her, he had "elbowed her aside" and kept her in confinement, withholding her income and not even permitting her to be attended by her own servants. But this was only preparatory. He hated her so much, we are told, that he was ready to bite his tongue out for having ever called her mistress. He determined to banish her, "that the beast might have the palace to house in all to himself".[1] He accused her of practising poisoning—it is said, with the most absurd details—and condemned her to exile. She was conveyed with only one maid to Prince's Island,[2]—the island where another Empress, Irene the Athenian, had been kept in confinement before she was removed to Lesbos. One of the persons who escorted her related to Psellos that, as the ship was starting, the Empress, looking up at the palace, apostrophised it with a rather theatrical lament. The Emperor ordered that her hair should be cut off, and thus she was sacrificed, "I know not if to the Lord", says Psellos, "but at least to the passion of the Emperor".

The next step was to give official publicity to this act. He first announced it to the Senate, and the Senate

[1] Psellos, *History*, p. 86: ἵν' ἔχοι μόνος ὁ θὴρ ἐν τοῖς βασιλείοις αὐλίζεσθαι. He consulted the astrologers as to his project; they forbade it; he laughed at them (*ib.* 87–88).

[2] Attaleiatês, p. 13: νῆσος δὲ αὕτη τῆς βασιλευούσης οὐ πόρρω is rendered in the Latin translation which accompanies the text in the Bonn edition by *insula hæc reginæ non longe abest*. Did the translator understand τῆς βασιλευούσης or not? If he did, he has not succeeded in expressing the meaning. In a passage in Kedrênos relating to the Chrysargyron tax which Anastasios abolished, I noticed that the word οὖρον was rendered *mulus* by the Bonn translator!

approved of the measure. He then caused a manifesto to be read aloud in the forum of Constantine in order to justify himself to the people.[1]

The great explosion that followed this ill-advised act of Michael made a deep impression on eye-witnesses. Psellos introduces his account of it with a solemn preparation as for a great scene in history—too great for human powers to narrate. He speaks of it in language that we might expect to be used about such an event as the French Revolution.[2]

The Emperor was congratulating himself on the success of his cherished scheme while the storm was gathering in the city. The usual routine of business and pleasure had been interrupted; all ages, sexes, and classes formed small groups and muttered their dissatisfaction. There was a threatening gloom over the whole city—grief at the Queen's misfortune and wrath with the audacity of the despot. On the second day the mutterings became distinct, and the half-formed wish to avenge the banished Empress assumed a definite shape. Officials of rank and public men joined with the populace, the classes with the masses, in the excitement; all were ready to lay down their lives for Zôê, and the Emperor's foreign guard could not allay the tumult. The women behaved like Mænads. Psellos says that he saw women, who had never been outside the female apartments in their lives before, coming forth in public, shouting and beating their breasts. The rioting inhabitants armed themselves with any implement they could lay hands on—axes, clubs, bows, or stones.

[1] This is recorded by Attaleiatês, p. 14: the Emperor in order to calm the anger of the Byzantines, when his act became known, ἔγγραφόν τι ποιεῖται τούτοις κατὰ τὸν ἐπισημότερον τόπον τοῦ φόρου ἐπαναγνωσθησόμενον, in which manifesto he threw all the blame on Zôê. The bill was called a πιττάκιον.

[2] P. 90: τὸ μέγα ἐκεῖνο καὶ δημοσιώτατον ἀπετελέσθη μυστήριον.

At this time Psellos was in the Emperor's ante-chamber. He was an under-secretary, and happened to be dictating some State document when the sound as of horses tramping struck his ears, and anon came a messenger with the news that the whole people had unanimously risen against the Emperor. To most persons in the palace it seemed incredible, but Psellos had observed the prognostics in the city, and understood that the spark had burst into a flame which it would require many rivers to quench. He immediately got to horse and rode to see the tumult himself, which he describes rhetorically. It is easy to read between the lines here that the philosopher had quite made up his mind beforehand to desert the Emperor, for whom he has no good word.

The mob first attacked the houses of all the relations of the Emperor, among them the house of Constantine the nobelissimos. The eunuch armed his household and at their head made a desperate rush through the crowds, and traversing the streets like fire reached the palace. There he found the Emperor sitting in dismay, utterly at a loss what to do, unable even to rely on his foreign guards, some of whom had deserted. He received his uncle with kisses of joy, and they decided to bring back Zôê from the adjacent island, to which she had been banished. Zôê sympathised, whether really or feignedly, with Michael's misfortune, and readily consented to show herself to the people. She appeared in purple robes on a balcony overlooking the hippodrome, but the device had not the desired effect; the mob was not imposed upon.

The life of Theodôra, Zôê's younger sister,[1] had been

---

[1] In the reign of Rômanos she had been compelled through Zôê's enmity to retire to a convent. From Kedrênos, II, 537, we learn that she lived at Petrion.

so recluse that Michael V was hardly even aware of her existence. A happy thought struck some of the leaders of the insurrection—to lead her forth from her retirement at Petrion and proclaim her Empress. This idea was carried out in a surprisingly orderly manner. One of her father's servants—a foreigner, *but* noble in form and spirit, according to Psellos—was appointed their guide, and they marched in regular order to her dwelling. At first the surprised princess, inured to her mode of life and perhaps afraid, would not listen to their proposals, and shut herself up in the sanctuary; they were obliged to force her by threats with drawn daggers. She was dragged from the altar, arrayed in royal attire, and borne on horseback to the church of St Sophia, where high and low acknowledged her as Empress. The participation of the patriarch Alexios in this movement is mentioned by Attaleiatês, not by Psellos.

The Emperor gave up all for lost, and exchanging his robes for the garb of a suppliant went by ship with his uncle to the famous monastery of Studiòn,[1] which presently became the place of a strange scene. When his flight became known, general exultation, displayed in songs and dances, prevailed, but also the desire of revenge.

Psellos rode with a friend, a captain of the guard, to the church at Studion, whither the greater part of the mob was thronging. There he saw the fugitive Emperor clinging to the altar and his uncle standing on the right side of it, both so disfigured and changed that Psellos could not feel any vestige of anger against them, but was so overwhelmed and aghast at the violent change that he could not refrain from weeping. The multitude, however, was not of as soft stuff as the philosopher; they stood around like wild beasts, eager to devour their prey.

[1] Situated in the south-west corner of Constantinople.

Psellos was standing hard by the altar, and the two hunted fugitives were quick enough to notice that he was affected, and catching at the chance they came to him for help. He "gently rebuked" Constantine for his evil counsels, and asked the Emperor what ill he had suffered at the hands of his mother Zôê. The nobelissimos denied any participation in the Emperor's acts, and remarked that if his advice had been followed his own kindred would not have been reduced to their present state. The Emperor could make no excuse.

In the afternoon a messenger, accompanied by a number of civil and military officials, arrived with orders from Theodôra to remove the fugitives elsewhere. But they were so much frightened by the threatening countenances of the crowd that they refused to leave the altar, and it was necessary to drag them from it. They were carried in mulecarts to a place called the Sigma, where their eyes were put out. The operation is described in Psellos: in undergoing it the Emperor behaved as a coward, his uncle with more fortitude. This punishment of the Emperor seemed a political necessity, as it was feared that Zôê, whose dislike of her sister was one of her strongest feelings, might restore the deposed monarch.

Michael V is generally looked upon as a sort of moral abortion, a monster without a virtue. Psellos and Zônaras, following Psellos, represent him as such, and in the preceding pages I have kept closely to Psellos' account.

But if we look merely at his actions and leave for a moment out of consideration a particular historian's view of his character—remembering that that historian was probably biassed, as he was an actor on the opposite side—we cannot pass a judgment of pure unmodified damnation. The two acts to which most prominence is given are the banishment of Joannês and the banishment of Zôê. The former of these seems to have been foolish for Michael's own interest, but can have been by no means unpopular, as Joannês was hated. During the long supremacy which he had enjoyed in the reign of Michael IV he had probably become overbearing and dictatorial, and may have made himself very offensive to the new Emperor if the latter had independent ideas and wished to act on them. The banishment of Zôê shows that Michael had not appreciated the conservative feeling which prevailed in the Empire, and attached itself to the Basilian dynasty as a sort of central rallying-point. In itself the exile of Zôê was hardly more or less flagitious than that of Joannês. She was probably a troublesome and meddlesome old woman, and of course we need not believe all that Psellos tells us of the deep-seated detestation, without any apparent ground, that Michael felt towards her.

Some other acts, reversing acts of the previous reign, deserve commendation. He delivered the able general George Maniakês from the confinement in which he had been placed by Michael IV, and made him magister and catapan of "Italy". He also released Constantine Dalassênos, who had been persecuted by Joannês. He made Psellos' own friend Constantine Leichudês, who afterwards won high repute as an able and upright statesman, his chief minister.[1]

Psellos is not by any means above the suspicion of partiality; his account of the reign of his pupil and pet Michael Parapinakês is a sufficient proof of this. In the present case it was not his interest to say a word for

---

[1] We learn this fact from Psellos' funeral oration on Leichudês, p. 398: εἶτα δὴ ὁ μετ' ἐκεῖνον ἄρξας, εἰ καὶ μὴ ἐγνώκει τὴν ἐπιστήμην τοῦ κράτους, ἀλλ' οὖν ἄρτι τοῦ ὀχήματος ἐπιβάς, καὶ δεδιὼς ὅπερ ἐπεπόνθει, πρὸς οὐδένα τῶν πάντων ἢ πρὸς τὸν ἄνδρα τοῦτον ἀπέβλεψεν· οὐκ ἔφθασε δὲ τοῦτον ἀναβιβάσας ἐπὶ τὸ ὄχημα, κ.τ.λ.

Michael V, as afterwards it was not his interest to speak good words of Rômanos Diogenês. He joined the general insurrection, as probably Leichudês also did, and he was a strong partisan of the next Emperor, Monomachos, whose power was founded on the ruins of Kalaphatês.

These considerations may lead us to conclude that Michael V, after all, was not so very diabolical; that the chief diabolical quality he possessed was perhaps that of not being so black as he was painted. But this view becomes stronger and less negative when we compare a neglected passage in the history of Michael Attaleiatês.[1] There we read that before his elevation this Emperor's views on politics were blamed and blameworthy, but that after his succession he was very highly praised for his honourable behaviour to the Senate and to his other subjects, in which respect he surpassed previous monarchs, conferring honours and dignities on many; moreover for his concern for the maintenance of order and his zeal for justice. This passage is sufficient to make us pause before accepting an extreme view unfavourable to Michael.[2]

It seems to me that Michael V conceived the bold idea of making a new start in the direction of reform, but

---

[1] ἦν δ' ἀνὴρ ἐπὶ μὲν τῆς προτέρας διαγωγῆς κακιζόμενος καὶ τοῖς ἐπαινετῶς πολιτευομένοις μὴ συναπτόμενος, ἐπὶ δὲ τῆς βασιλικῆς ἀναβάσεως καὶ λίαν ἐγκωμιαζόμενός τε καὶ σεμνυνόμενος οἷα φιλοτίμως ἄρτι πρῶτον ὑπὲρ τοὺς πρὸ αὐτοῦ βεβασιλευκότας τῇ συγκλήτῳ καὶ τοῖς ἄλλοις προσφερόμενος ὑπηκόοις καὶ τιμαῖς περιβλέπτοις καὶ ἀξιώμασι πλείστους ὅσους καταγεραίρων καὶ τὴν εὐνομίαν εἴπερ τις ἄλλος σπουδάζων ἀνεγερθῆναι καὶ τῶν ἀδικουμένων ἐκδικητὴς ἀναφαινόμενος ἀπαραίτητος καὶ δικαιοσύνην τῶν ἄλλων ἁπάντων ὑπεραίρων καὶ προτιμώμενος.— Hist. p. 17.

[2] Le Beau's words may be taken as typical of the general feeling of historians about this Emperor: *Plus indigne de régner par la bassesse de son cœur que par celle de sa naissance, il était fourbe, injuste, ingrate, ne reconnaissant ni les droits de la parenté ni ceux de l'amitié ... etc.* (XIV, 308, ed. Saint-Martin).

that the conservative elements—the *inertia*—were too strong for him. It had not escaped his observation that his predecessor was weighed down and impeded by his relations; and he consequently concluded that one condition of success was to make a clean clearance of his kinsmen. Joannês would never have fallen in with his new plans, but Constantine, who was merely a time-server, humoured him. The banishment of Zôê was also necessary to his designs, for she was a remnant of the old order of things.

The irrelevant consideration that his conduct to Zôê was ungrateful, combined with his unkind treatment of his relations, has obscured the attitude and the aims of Michael V, and perverted the judgment of historians in his regard. We have no reason to blame his political tendencies; it is his blunder in banishing the Empress that condemns him.

7. *Zôê and Theodôra.** The women's apartments in the palace were now changed into a council-chamber. There was some difficulty at first in the joint rule of two old sisters, between whom suspicion and dislike had prevailed for many years. Zôê was the eldest, but it was the proclamation of Theodôra that had overthrown Kalaphatês. The difficulty was solved by unexpected graciousness on Zôê's part; and Theodôra, in accordance with her retiring disposition, yielded precedence to her sister. State business was transacted and audiences were held just as usual, and the general loyalty was more pronounced than towards an Emperor.[1] Those who had

[* A.D. 1042, Ap.–June.]
[1] τό τε πολιτικὸν πλῆθος καὶ τὸ στρατιωτικὸν συμφωνοῦντας ὑπὸ δεσπότισι (Psellos, *Hist.* p. 104); cf. Zônaras, p. 155. Psellos adds an expression of wonder that no family seemed so favoured of Heaven as the Basilian, "though the root was fixed and planted not lawfully, but by bloodshed and slaughter"; the members of the family were all incomparable in both beauty and size.

held office under Kalaphatês were not disgraced nor deposed.

Zôê was quick in apprehension, but not fluent of speech; Theodôra, on the other hand, fluent and less swift-witted. Theodôra was fond of hoarding, Zôê extravagant in her liberality.

But the reign of the two women could not last, for the administration was neglected or mismanaged and the expenditure ruinous. Neither of them understood anything of finances or political affairs; they mixed up the trivialities of a lady's bower with the imperial business. The court was kept up with a degree of extravagant splendour and display that drained the treasury. The palace was full of flatterers, and Zôê spent the military funds in profusion to these nimble caperers.

This waste and height of brilliance were the beginnings, says Psellos, of the subsequent descent—the condition of state bankruptcy which ensued. A strong man's hand at the helm was imperatively required. Zôê's jealousy of her sister induced her to satisfy this requirement and choose a third husband. She fixed first on Constantine Dalassênos, a nobleman who had suffered from the ascendency of the Paphlagonian family, to which his birth, his position, and his high spirit had made him an object of alarm.[1] In the reign of Michael IV he had been confined in the island of Platy; Michael V released him, but made him become a monk. Zôê summoned him to the palace on some pretext, but his independent manner and his uncompromising spirit disappointed the Empress, who was used to smooth words, and she rejected him. Her choice then fell on a man, distinguished for beauty and sensual attractions, though not for rank or position,[2] Constantine Arto-

---

[1] Constantine VIII (IX) had thought of choosing him as his successor.

[2] οἶον πρὸς ἔρωτας ἐφελκύσασθαι καὶ μὴ μαχλοσύνῃ προσκειμένην ψυχήν (Zônaras, p. 155). This is not taken from Psellos, who merely says,

klinas, who had been a secretary of Rômanos III, and was then suspected of carrying on an intrigue with Zôê. The disposition of Rômanos was not jealous, but Michael IV found a pretext for removing him from Constantinople. It was fated, however, that Zôê should be obliged to make yet a third choice, for death suddenly carried off Artoklinas. This accident blew good to another Constantine, who had been banished by Michael IV to Mitylênê, Constantine Monomachos. Zôê recalled him from exile, married him, and raised him to the throne. The Monomachoi[1] were an old family, and Constantine had made a brilliant second marriage, which had joined him in affinity with the Emperor Rômanos. Pulcheria, the sister of Rômanos, was the wife of Basil Sklêros; Constantine married their only daughter. But this alliance did not procure him any appointment. His father Theodosios had conspired against Basil, and a cloud of suspicion continued to rest over the son.

8. *Constantine IX.** From Rômanos III to Michael VI the Basilian dynasty continued; for of the five Emperors three were husbands of Zôê, one was her adopted son, and one was the nominee of Theodôra. Thus the acci-

---

τὸ δὲ εἶδος ἀξιωματικὸς καὶ λαμπρός. Nor does Psellos mention the suspicion recorded by Zônaras that his death was caused by poison administered by his wife.

[1] ῥίζης ἀρχαίας τῶν Μονομάχων (Psellos, *Hist.* p. 110). In the *Epitaphios* on Leichudês, Psellos speaks of Constantine thus: ὁ καὶ τὴν κλῆσιν ὁμώνυμος τῷ τὴν οὐρανόπολιν ταύτην οἰκίσαντι καὶ τὴν προσηγορίαν φερώνυμος, μόνος τοῦ κράτους προκινδυνεύσας καὶ ὑπὲρ πάντας ἀξιόμαχος γεγονὼς καὶ ὑπὲρ τῆς κοινῆς τοῦ γένους μονομαχήσας εὐκλείας, κἀντεῦθεν τὴν ἐπωνυμίαν ὥσπερ ἀριστεῖον ἀνειληφώς (p. 398). Here of course there is only a play on the name Μονομάχος, which was a family name, not an ἐπωνυμία. One of the characteristics of Psellos' style is a love of speaking of people without mentioning their names, as though the names were something trivial, and it were more dignified to indicate by a periphrasis or indirection.

[* Constantine IX (X), Monomachos, A.D. 1042, June 11–1054, Nov.]

dent of the long lives of these women lends a sort of
continuity to the history between Constantine VIII and
Isaac Komnênos. But in the first part of this period the
actual government of the Empire passed into the hands
of a Paphlagonian family, and the attitude of Constantine IX was opposition to this administration,[1] an
opposition which one of themselves, Michael V, had
already initiated. This contrast is indicated by his choice
of ministers. His first chief counsellor was Michael
Kêrularios,[2] who had been concerned in a revolt against
Michael IV, and when after a short time he became
patriarch, he was replaced by Leichudês, who had held
the same position under Michael V. Thus his ministers
were trained and learned men. One of the most important events of his reign was the revival of letters,
which had been on the wane since Constantine VII;
influenced by Leichudês and the polymath Psellos,
Monomachos patronised learning, in which respect he
was the forerunner of the Komnênoi.

Psellos gives us a long account of this reign, which he
compares to an ocean; for he had lived through so many
very short reigns that the supremacy of Monomachos,
which lasted thirteen years, seemed quite long. In de-
scribing the chief men and women at his court we may
begin with the Emperor himself.

Love of pleasure and fickleness of disposition were the
chief characteristics of Constantine; he was a thoroughly
frivolous man. In a long banishment he had suffered
many hardships, and when he ascended the throne his
idea was to recompense himself for past pains by the
greatest possible measure of enjoyment. He looked on

---

[1] The eyes of Joannês, the orphanotrophos, were put out in 1043,
May 2.

[2] Psellos: ἐγκωμιαστικὸς εἰς τὸν μακαριώτατον πατριάρχην κῦρ Μιχαὴλ
τὸν Κηρουλλάριον (p. 324).

the palace as a haven of rest which he had reached having endured the stress of the waves; and all he cared for was good cheer and the presence of smiling faces. He had no conception, says Psellos, that the function of a king is the performance of services beneficial to the *subjects* and demanding a mind constantly awake and alive. Consistently with this view he left the entire public administration to others, devoting very little time himself to business, and gave himself up to the life hedonistic; and as Zôê's inclinations were similar she was very well content. "He that must steer at the head of an Empire ought to be the mirror of the times for wisdom and for policy". Constantine did not even try to be wise or politic; his utter indifference reacted ruinously on the State, though his ministers seem to have been "indifferent honest".

He had a vulgar love of buffoonery and a childish love of triviality; any one who could make him laugh pre-possessed him and was sure of promotion. Here we touch on a bad feature of his reign. There were fixed and definite conditions, and grades of promotion to rank; Constantine declined to be restricted by them and lavished titles and posts on the favourites of an hour. He filled the Senate with persons who had no right to be there. The consequence was that these honours became valueless, as they meant nothing. This profusion of titles was at least cheap, but unfortunately he was equally generous and unjust in spending the public money, following the example set by Zôê and Theodôra in their short reign before his accession. The State was really sound, says Psellos, before his accession; but his un-principled principles as to the lack-duty privileges of the Emperor affected it with many germs of disease.

Nevertheless he had some good qualities; he was sharp-witted and very good-natured. Psellos, who endeavours to treat him impartially and does not scruple to censure severely many of his acts and points out his defects, had a high opinion of his personal character, and comparing him with Alexander, "the two Cæsars", and other great men of ancient ages, says that while inferior to these in bravery he excelled them in other good qualities. Whenever he passed a sentence of imprisonment or banishment, he felt a pang of remorse for his severity; and he was so afraid of his own clemency that he used to bind himself secretly by oath not to commute the sentence he had passed. He was beneficent and compassionate in cases that came under his immediate notice. For example, it happened that a rich man had been accused and found guilty of peculating money from certain military funds. The fine which was adjudged was larger than all he was worth, and he had the prospect of not only present penury but a debt which would be transmitted to his children. The claimant of the fine being the public exchequer, it was impracticable to supplicate an inexorable thing. The man gained an audience of the Emperor, at which Psellos was present as secretary; and professed his readiness to pay everything he possessed, if only the surplus should not be handed down as an inherited obligation to his children. He began to strip off his clothes in token that he would surrender everything. The Emperor was moved to tears, and ended by paying the whole debt for him.

We may be sure that Constantine was not really badly intentioned. It was his fortune and not his fault that it was an impossibility for him to be serious. He was a bad Emperor, but a sufficiently amiable man. We can understand the leniency of an historian towards him, and are not surprised at the favourable judgment of Attaleiatês, who says that he was a good Emperor till the end of his reign, when in a most unexpected manner he began a system of exactions.[1] "He was generous in giving, and knew how to confer benefits in imperial style", solicitous for military successes, but addicted to luxury and lechery. The commendatory clause about his generosity reminds us of a remark of Psellos, that the unwise profusion which he himself censures will furnish to other historians a theme for praise. Attaleiatês goes on to mention his love of amusement and buffoonery, and notes especially that he provided an elephant and a camelopard, of which animals he gives long descriptions, for the delectation of the Byzantine populace. He gratified his love of magnificence and followed the fashion of preceding monarchs by building a monastery and church, dedicated to St George, with charming meadows attached to it. He also erected a hospital.

The Emperor and the Empress Zôê, who was now too old to be jealous, continued very good friends till her death in 1050. Theodôra fell back into her old secluded life, and her chief worldly pleasure consisted in hoarding money. Neither she nor Zôê cared for parks or gardens, or houses fitted with splendour and refinement. Zôê's taste was quite peculiar: she had a passion for perfumery. If you had entered her sleeping apartment, you might have thought you were in the workshop of a city mechanic. You would first be conscious of a very strong heat, which in winter might not be unwelcome, but in summer would drive the visitor away. The heat proceeded from an immense fire in the chamber, where you would have seen several maidservants engaged in the processes of brewing and mixing unguents and perfumes; one perhaps measuring the requisite quantities of the ingredients, another blending them, another boiling or

[1] *Hist.* p. 47: ἀνὴρ πολιτικὸς (which we may in the case of Constantine interpret by the negative of its antithesis, "not military") καὶ γένους ἐπισήμου γενόμενος δωρηματικός τε καὶ βασιλικῶς εὐεργετεῖν ἐπιστά-μενος, κ.τ.λ. On his accession Constantine ἡγάθυνε τὸ ὑπήκοον (p. 18).

distilling them, and Zôê herself, impervious to the heat
at midsummer, directing or assisting them. One who
desired to win her favour had only to send her a rare
spice or a precious perfume. She used her compounds
for the purposes of divine worship, for she was very
religious.

As the Empress was thus wholly devoted to the odours
of sanctity, the Emperor was sufficiently free to prosecute his amours. He had been married twice, and when
his second wife, who belonged to the family of the Sklêroi,
died, he fell in love with her niece Sklêraina, but did not
marry her from religious scruples, which however did
not hinder him from becoming Zôê's husband. Sklêraina was his faithful companion during his exile, and
in the day of his prosperity he did not forget her. As
Psellos says, reminding us of a certain remark of Théo-
phile Gautier, when he looked upon Zôê with the eyes
of sense he saw Sklêraina with the eyes of the spirit, and
when he held the Empress in his arms, his beloved was
in the bosom of his soul. His first step was to recall
Sklêraina to the capital, to which he obtained his wife's
consent. He kept her at first in a private residence, and
set building operations afoot in order to have an excuse
for visiting her, without exciting suspicion, several times
a month,[1] and he used to entertain his attendants there
with such sumptuous repasts that it was their interest to
smooth the way for these secret trysts. He used to lavish

[1] Psellos, *History*, p. 127: ἵνα δὲ πρόφασις εἴη τῷ βασιλεῖ ἐκεῖσε φοιτᾶν
οἶκον ἑαυτοῦ πεποίηται τὴν σκηνὴν καὶ ἵνα δὴ μεγαλοπρεπὴς γένηται καὶ
πρὸς βασιλικὴν ὑποδοχὴν ἐπιτήδειος θεμελίους τε ἔξωθεν μείζονας
καταβάλλεται, κ.τ.λ....Προσεποιεῖτο γοῦν ἑκάστοτε ὅ,τι δήποτε τῶν
οἰκονομουμένων καὶ τοῦ μηνὸς πολλάκις ἀπῄει, πρόφασιν μὲν ὀψόμενός
τι τῶν γιγνομένων, κ.τ.λ. Zônaras (IV, p. 178) says that the Emperor
began the building of the monastery of Mangana for the same reason,
λέγεται δὲ τῆς οἰκοδομῆς ἄρξασθαι διὰ τὴν ἐρωμένην αὐτῷ, τὴν Σκλήραιναν
λέγω, ἵν᾽ ἐκείνη προσφοιτᾷ συνεχῶς, ἐν τῷ οἴκῳ τοῦ Κυνηγίου ἐχούσῃ
τότε δὴ τὴν κατοίκησιν. Thus the house of Kynêgios was the σκηνή.

the imperial treasures on his mistress, and as an example of his gifts Psellos mentions that, having found one day in the palace a bronze casket with carved work, he filled it with money and sent it to Sklêraina. But he soon became bolder, and finally introduced her to the palace, where Zôê treated her amicably and conferred on her the title of Sebastê. A contract of friendship between the mistress and wife was drawn up in a written form, and the blushing Senate, which was summoned to give its countenance to this measure of amity, praised the document as if it had fallen from heaven. On that day the two ladies sat together in the Emperor's company, and Zôê did not betray the least chagrin, whether her feelings were really indifferent or her long experience of Emperors and court life made her deem dissimulation advisable. But when the newcomer was once installed Zôê never visited her husband until she had assured herself that he was alone.

Sklêraina was not remarkable for beauty, but was sufficiently goodlooking to give no opening for malicious remarks. Her sympathetic disposition and graceful manners won the heart of Psellos; and the stylist goes so far as to say that her "speech was like nothing else, refined and flower-like, with a quite sophistic excellence in the rhythms; a sweet style ran along her tongue spontaneously, and when she described aught, indescribable charms hovered around". She was a very good listener, and was fond of Greek mythology, on which she used often to question Psellos. We can picture to ourselves the young philosopher of twenty-five entertaining the imperial lady with fluent accounts of old Greek stories, full of plays upon words, and not unseasoned with adroit compliments and elegant adulation.

He tells an anecdote that Zôê attended by her court, her sister Theodôra and the Sebastê, who had not been seen in public with the imperial sisters before, went in procession to a spectacle; and a bystander expert in flattery cried aloud οὐ νέμεσις, without finishing the quotation.[1] Sklêraina said nothing at the time, but afterwards received an explanation of the words, and rewarded the man who had pronounced them most richly. She conciliated the goodwill of Zôê and Theodôra by making them presents suitable to their whims—coins to Theodôra, to Zôê Indian perfumes and scented woods, very small-sized olives and very white laurel-berries. With the expenses of the three ladies the treasures which Basil accumulated "with toil and the sweat of his brow" were gaily and quickly spent on amusements. Psellos does not mention the tumult which Kedrênos alleges to have taken place in September 1044, owing to a general feeling of indignation against the influence of the mistress who seemed to be ousting the wife and sister-in-law. The multitude cried, "We will not have Sklêraina to reign over us, nor on her account shall our purple-born mothers (μάμαι) Zôê and Theodôra die". Zôê herself quieted this disturbance. Not long after, its cause was carried off prematurely by asthma, and the Emperor was inconsolable. Psellos declines to describe his puerile grief.

One of the personages at the Byzantine court in this reign was Boilas, a man who had a defect in his utterance and behaved as a sort of court jester. It was his defective speech and odd pronunciation that gained him the favour of Constantine, who delighted in nothing more than in personal oddity and silly conversation. He soon became so fond of this man—"this hypocrite", as

---

[1] See Homer, *Il.* III, 156—

οὐ νέμεσις Τρῶας καὶ ἐϋκνήμιδας Ἀχαιοὺς
τοιῇδ' ἀμφὶ γυναικὶ πολὺν χρόνον ἄλγεα πάσχειν.

Homer was perhaps as familiar in educated Byzantine society as Shakespeare is in England nowadays.

Psellos calls him, for his real character was knavery—
that he could do nothing without him. He loaded him
with the highest titles and granted free access to himself
at all times, free use of all the private entrances and
rooms of the palace. Boilas had all the privileges of an
Emperor's fool. He managed even to gain access to the
women's apartments. He boldly asserted with oaths
that both Zôê and Theodôra had brought forth children,
and gave a detailed account of Theodôra's confinement,
repeating even the very words she uttered. These au-
dacious inventions made him so formidable that the
Empresses opened all the secret doors to him, and he
received innumerable gifts.[1]

"But he was not content with this good fortune", says
Zônaras; "he also coveted the Empire". Zônaras does
not tell us what put this idea into his head, but we learn
the reason from Psellos. After the death of Sklêraina the
Emperor loved a young Alan princess, whom he kept
as his concubine, and after the death of Zôê conferred
on her the title of Sebastê.[2] Boilas became enamoured

---

[1] Attaleiatês (p. 18) states that on the accession of Constantine IX [X]
Theodôra retired to her old solitary life. This seems to imply that she
left the palace, which is in accordance with the fact that before Constantine's death she was conveyed to the palace by ship (Kedrênos, II,
610). Moreover, when Sklêraina was installed in the palace, it is mentioned that she and Zôê resided on either side of the Emperor's apartments, μέσον δὲ σκηνοῦντος τοῦ βασιλέως ἑκατέρωθεν ᾤκουν παραλλὰξ
ἡ βασιλὶς καὶ ἡ Σεβαστή (Zônaras, p. 160); the residence of Theodôra is
not mentioned. Nevertheless the incident recorded above about Boilas
(see Psellos, Hist. pp. 172–3) implies that Theodôra resided in the palace,
and when we compare the passage of Psellos from which the statement
of Zônaras seems to be taken, we are led to the conclusion that Zônaras
mistranslated it. Διανειμάμενοι δὲ τὰς οἰκήσεις ὁ μὲν βασιλεὺς τὸ μέσον
ἔλαχε τῶν τριῶν αἱ δὲ πέριξ ἐσκήνουν τὸ δὲ ἄδυτον εἶχεν ἡ Σεβαστή.
Zônaras took τῶν τριῶν as meaning Constantine, Zôê, and Sklêraina;
whereas it really means Zôê, Theodôra, and Sklêraina, and αἱ δὲ refers
to Zôê and Theodôra. τὸ ἄδυτον means the innermost apartments, they
would correspond to the altar, πέριξ to the two aisles, τὸ μέσον to the
nave of a church.

[2] He did not marry her because he had been already married three
times, and from a feeling of respect for Theodôra.

of her, and, not being able to succeed in his suit while Constantine was alive, conceived the notion of slaying him and ascending the throne. The design seemed to present no difficulty, as the Emperor had complete confidence in him and was accustomed to sleep unguarded. But it was betrayed within less than an hour before its intended execution. One of the persons whom Boilas had taken into his counsels suddenly entered the Emperor's chamber out of breath, and, having told him that his dear friend Boilas was about to assassinate him, fled to the chapel altar and confessed the whole conspiracy. Constantine could hardly believe that it was a fact, and was half glad at escaping the danger, half angry at the chance of losing his indispensable favourite. When the conspirator was brought to trial in fetters, he could not bear the sight and cried, "Undo the fetters, for my heart is softened with pity for him". He then tried to put his defence into his mouth, and at last Boilas approached him, and, kissing his hands and placing his head on his knees, said all he wanted was to sit on the throne with a diadem of pearls. The Emperor leaped with joy, but his sister Euprepia and the Empress Theodôra were so vexed at his folly that for mere shame he sent the delinquent for a few days in mock banishment to an island hard by the capital. The attachment of Boilas to the Alan princess was not however extinguished, and the Emperor himself one day in the company of Psellos observed him making erotic signs to her, but looked on the matter as a joke.

Constantine Leichudês was invested with the administration of the Empire in 1043 when Kêrularios became patriarch. Leichudês was an able and cultured man who had made a study of rhetoric and had dipped deeper into the secrets of law than most of the Byzantine statesmen of the time, having sat at the feet of Joannês

Xiphilinos. He was an intimate friend of Psellos, who probably owed his advancement to him and honoured him with a panegyrical oration after his death. From it we learn that he was born at Constantinople of good family, and was very precocious as a boy. He carried the rhetorical powers with which he was naturally gifted to great perfection; and he made his rhetorical and legal studies react upon each other—a point on which Psellos strongly insists.[1] We must not, of course, give too much weight to the glowing terms of eulogy in which his friend, the philosopher, speaks of his administration. He says that when Leichudês came to the helm he showed himself at once fully equal to the very varied duties that demanded his attention, and displayed the most astonishing versatility;[2] he had the useful power of being all things to all men. Skylitzês also bears witness to the high reputation he bore as a minister;[3] but his capacity is best attested by the fact that he held the same office under Isaac Komnênos and was elected patriarch after the fall of Kêrularios. In everything, we are told by Psellos, he aimed at symmetry; his dress was neither very plain nor very rich, his table neither poorly furnished nor luxurious, his step measured, his speech at once dignified and fluent. In State documents his

[1] For his law studies see *Epitaphios*, p. 395; cf. *History*, p. 188. "He was a canon of orthography (correct writing), a manual of rhetoric, a chalk-line of legislation".

[2] *Epitaphios*, p. 401: οὗτός τε γὰρ πρὸς τοὺς διαφόρους τὰς γνώμας διάφορος ἦν.

[3] Skylitzês (Kedrenos, vol. II, Bonn ed.), p. 644, recording his election to the patriarchate, speaks of him as ἀνὴρ μέγιστον διαλάμψας τοῖς βασιλικοῖς καὶ πολιτικοῖς πράγμασιν ἀπό τε τοῦ Μονομάχου καὶ μέχρι τοῦ τηνικάδε καιροῦ καὶ μέγα κλέος ἐπὶ τῷ μεσασμῷ τῆς τῶν ὅλων διοικήσεως ἀνενεγκάμενος καὶ τῆς τῶν Μαγγάνων προνοίας καὶ τῶν δικαιωμάτων φύλαξ παρὰ τοῦ εἰρημένου βασιλέως καταλειφθείς. The expression by which the chief minister was denoted was ὁ παραδυναστεύων τῷ βασιλεῖ, but in the time of Constantine IX the phrase ὁ μεσάζων came into use; hence τῷ μεσασμῷ in this passage.

style was simple, pure, and ordinary; but he could write good "Attic".

It was probably by his suggestion that Constantine changed the constitution of the Senate and made the qualification merit instead of birth. He made an important reform in the administration of justice, by which the judges in the various themes were to commit their sentences to writing and deposit them in public registers. And there is no doubt that his influence contributed largely to the revival of the study of philosophy, rhetoric, and law, under the able guidance of Constantine, Psellos, and Joannês Xiphilinos.

The university of Constantinople which had been founded by Theodosios II lived for only three centuries. The study of letters declined in the seventh century, and the Emperor who founded the great dynasty of the iconoclasts, Leo III, abolished the university because the professors refused to support his religious doctrines. In the ninth century Theophilos licensed Leo, the famous scholar of his day, to give public lectures; and Constantine VII, himself a prolific author, encouraged the writing or compiling of books on an extensive scale. But there was no organised system of teaching in the Empire, no recognised body of men to whose judgments questions of learning might be deferred. Constantine IX had the honour of being the second founder of the university, though on a far more modest scale than the scheme of Theodosios. Two chairs were instituted, one for law and one for philosophy. The site of this new academy was a church of St Peter.

Psellos, who was the prime instigator of this revival of letters, gives an account of his first interview with Constantine, which is amusing from its naive self-conceit. He was well known at court, having been under-secretary in the preceding reign, and had a high repute for his learning and fluent speech. "My tongue", he writes, "has a certain flowery grace even in simple utterances, and without any intention or preparation certain natural qualities of sweetness distil from it"; he knew this from the manifest effect he produced on interlocutors. When he appeared before the Emperor, he informed him of his family, and of the nature and scope of his studies; and the impressionable monarch was so enthusiastic at the philosopher's speech and manner that he hung upon his lips and wellnigh kissed him.

Psellos was appointed to the chair of philosophy, and his friend Joannês Xiphilinos to the chair of law. Xiphilinos was a native of Trapezûs who came to study at Constantinople. These two students, with their friends Leichudês and Joannês Mauropûs,[1] formed a sort of new literary movement in Byzantium. In particular Psellos revived Platonism, which he valued above the ecclesiastical Aristotelianism in vogue, and he introduced a new atticising style, which was followed by Anna Komnênê, Zônaras, Nikêtas, etc. A tendency to purism—exclusion of colloquial and Latin words—may be traced even at the end of the tenth century in Leo Diakonos, who, in this respect, shows a particularity which is quite foreign to Constantine Porphyrogennêtos, Theophanês, or John Malalas. But Leo was not a stylist like Psellos; we may consider him the model of Attaleiatês and Skylitzês. These writers do not scruple to introduce a foreign or vulgar word when their meaning requires it—for example, $\tau\zeta o\nu\kappa\alpha\nu\iota\sigma\tau\acute{\eta}\rho\iota o\nu$ or $\dot{\epsilon}\xi\kappa o\acute{\nu}\beta\iota\tau\alpha$, words which Psellos would avoid, or, if he strained a point and admitted them, would apologise for. For the *Hellênismos* on which the Princess Anna prided her-

---

[1] This scholar was a relation of Leichudês. He was afterwards appointed archbishop of Euchaitoi. Letters of Psellos to him are extant, and he speaks of him and Xiphilinos as "the two Johns", $\tau\grave{\omega}$ Ἰωάννη.

self she was altogether indebted to the movement initiated by Psellos, and but for his influence in the revival of
Platonic studies she could never have boasted that she
had studied Plato's dialogues.[1] To this resurrection of
the "divine" philosopher in the eleventh century is
perhaps ultimately traceable also the Platonism of
Gemistos Plêthôn, who wrote in the fifteenth century.
We must note that Psellos considered the study of Greek
philosophy necessary to the thorough comprehension of
Christianity.[2]

Joannês Xiphilinos was appointed custodian of the
laws, *nomophylax*, as well as professor of law. He was a
man renowned for piety as well as for learning, and bore
a high reputation. Modern writers on the *Jus Græco-
romanum* have not been aware of his identity, knowing
him only as he is cited in scholia on the Basilika by the
name Joannês Nomophylax, and only conjecturing his
date to be the middle of the eleventh century from the
fact that in one scholion his opinion is opposed to that
of Garidas, who was a distinguished lawyer of that age.[3]

---

[1] τὸ ἑλληνίζειν ἐς ἄκρον ἐσπουδακυῖα καὶ ῥητορικῆς οὐκ ἀμελετήτως
ἔχουσα καὶ τὰς Ἀριστοτελικὰς τέχνας εὖ ἀναλεξαμένη καὶ τοὺς Πλάτωνος
διαλόγους (Anna, Bonn ed. 1, 4). Compare an article by Mr Freeman on
"Some Points in the later History of the Greek Language", in which the
"Renaissance", as he calls it, is duly insisted on. "Go on to Leo the
deacon, still more go on to Anna Komnênê and Nikêtas.... We are
landed in a *Renaissance*" (*Journal for Hellenic Studies*, III, 377). Psellos
intervenes between Leo and Anna, and explains the "still more".

[2] In an exhortation to his pupils (*Opuscula*, ed. Boissonade, pp. 151–3,
quoted by Sathas, preface to vol. IV, p. li) he says: By studying Greek
metaphysics, "ye will be drawing fresh water from salt water like
mariners. For what do they? When in mid ocean they find themselves
unprovided with fresh water, they hang sponges over the sea, and com-
pressing the collected vapour into water have a perfectly sweet draught.
So ye likewise, if ye suspend your souls above the brine of Hellênic doctrines and convert the heavy and terrestrial sound which is wafted up
from them into a light and treble note, will perhaps hear the sweet melody
of the highest string".

[3] Attaleiatês, *Hist.* p. 21: ἐκαίνισε δὲ (Constantine IX) καὶ δέκρετον
δικῶν ἰδιωτικῶν ἐπὶ τῶν κρίσεων καλέσας τὸν τούτου προέχοντα—that

No one thought of identifying the scholiast on the Basilika with that Joannês Xiphilinos of whom Attaleiatês and Skylitzês give short notices.[1] This identification is demonstrated by the writings of Psellos.[2]

When Monomachos came to the throne, he sent a manifesto throughout the provinces to declare his accession and to promise to his subjects freedom of speech, the abolition of all abuses, and abundance of all blessings.[3] This was in fact a notification that his policy would be quite the reverse of that of the Paphlagonians. And until the last years of his reign he seems to have realised these promises, or allowed Leichudês to realise them, as far as the wars in which he was involved permitted him. But towards the end of his reign he became dissatisfied with the administration of his chancellor, because (says Psellos) he envied his power and felt uneasy under his restraint. It seemed as if Leichudês were the Emperor and Constantine the minister. But the true reason for this dissatisfaction was, we can have no doubt, that the Emperor wanted more money than Leichudês could provide, and Leichudês was not prepared to be

is Xiphilinos. Garidas flourished in the reign of Constantine Dûkas, and was the author of διαίρεσις περὶ φόνων (a tract which he dedicated to that Emperor) and a βιβλίον περὶ ἀγωγῶν. See Heimbach's notice of him in *Griechisch-römisches Recht*.

[1] Attaleiatês, p. 92: ἦν γὰρ τῆς συνόδου προεξάρχων καὶ τὴν πατριαρχίαν κοσμῶν Ἰωάννης ὁ ἐπικεκλημένος Ξιφιλῖνος ἐκ Τραπεζοῦντος μὲν ὡρμημένος ἀνὴρ δὲ σοφὸς καὶ παιδεύσεως εἰς ἄκρον ἐληλακὼς κἀν τοῖς πολιτικοῖς περίβλεπτος γεγονὼς καὶ ἀρετῆς εὐφρόνως ἐπιμελούμενος ὥστε τοῖς βασιλείοις ἔτι ἐμφιλοχωρῶν καὶ πρῶτα φέρων παρὰ τῷ βασιλεῖ τὴν μοναχικὴν πολιτείαν ἐν ἀκμῇ τῆς εὐημερίας καὶ τῆς ἡλικίας ἀσπάσασθαι καὶ τὸν ἀναχωρητικὸν βίον περὶ τὸ Ὀλύμπιον ὄρος ἑλόμενος χρόνον ἐπὶ συχνὸν ἦν διαλάμπων ἐπ᾽ ἀρετῇ καὶ φόβῳ θεοῦ. The corresponding passage in Skylitzês (p. 658) reproduces this, with some omissions, almost verbally.

[2] See especially his *Epitaphios* on Xiphilinos.

[3] Kedrênos, p. 542: παντὸς μὲν ἀγαθοῦ βλύσιν καὶ παρρησίαν πάσης δὲ κακίας ἀποτομήν. In the same place his promotions in the Senate and his largesses to the people are mentioned.

unscrupulous. Kedrênos refers this want of money to the expenses incurred in building the monastery of Mangana.[1] Psellos perceived a change in the sentiments of Monomachos towards Leichudês and told the matter to his friend, but he refused to make any alteration in his attitude. The Emperor deposed him—not suddenly, but gradually—and with this act we must connect the "great and unexpected change" for the worse which took place in the administration. "He attached himself to clever tax-collecting officers whom official language names *sekretikoi* [thus Attaleiatês apologises for using a non-Hellenic word]; with them he invented unforeseen fines and arrears, and, as it were, extracted the marrow of those who had any degree of wealth".[2] The prisons were filled with the bankrupt and ruined. Special dissatisfaction was given by seizing property destined for churches and supplies intended for monasteries. In another way too he injured the Empire. He disbanded the Iberian army in order that the treasury might receive in money the equivalent of the supplies which those provinces furnished in kind to the army. The chief of these unscrupulous financiers was a eunuch, the logothete Joannês.[3] He was a man of so little education that he could not speak or write grammatically correct Greek; his birth was base, and he was unfit for the higher branches of the administration; in fact, he was quite the reverse of Leichudês whom he succeeded. The new order of things was so oppressive that Constantine's death (January 1055) was universally felt to be a relief.

[1] Kedrênos, p. 602, where his new ministers are called δημοσίους... φροντιστὰς ἀσεβεῖς καὶ ἀλάστορας.

[2] Attaleiatês, p. 50: ἐκμυελίζων is the strong word used of this bleeding. The disbanding of the army of Iberia is recorded by Kedrênos.

[3] Our knowledge of Joannês is due to Zônaras (IV, 180), who says that he was the reverse in every respect of Leichudês. For some time before the deposition of the latter the two men were drawing the Emperor in different ways.

Yet before his end he seems to have repented his dismissal of Leichudês.[1]

The changes that had come over the spirit of the Emperor, who in small matters had always a character for instability and want of seriousness, produced a general feeling of uncertainty and want of confidence, which was shared by Psellos and his friends. He and Xiphilinos had always felt a leaning towards the spiritual life, and they considered that the time had come to take the step. So they took an oath together, which Xiphilinos at least kept with an equal mind until he was elected patriarch, to spend the rest of their lives in the seclusion of a monastery. They alleged bodily illnesses in order to obtain the Emperor's permission to retire; but with Psellos, "with whose tongue he was dreadfully in love", he was unwilling to part.[2] He first wrote most touching letters to him, which Psellos preserved, and when writing his history some years later was unable to read without weeping. When entreaties were of no avail, he used threats. But Psellos took the step of cutting his hair, and then Constantine, resigning himself gracefully, wrote an epistle of congratulation that he had chosen the better life and preferred the monk's gown to the soft raiment of a palace.

With Psellos and Xiphilinos vanished also the more refined tastes which their presence induced the Em-

---

[1] Skylitzês, p. 644: καὶ τῶν δικαιωμάτων φύλαξ παρὰ τοῦ εἰρημένου βασιλέως καταλειφθείς. For the deposition of Leichudês, cf. Psellos, *Epitaphios* on L., p. 405: καί γε θαυμάζων ἐπὶ πᾶσι τὸν αὐτοκράτορα ἐν τοῦτο ἐπαινεῖν οὐκ ἔχω ὅτι ὃν ἐπὶ πολλοῖς δοκιμάσας ἠκρίβωσε τοῦτον ὡς ἄρτι διαγινώσκων κατῃτιάσατο μεθιστᾷ τῆς ἀρχῆς οὐ τεταγὼς ἀπὸ βηλοῦ θεσπεσίοιο, τοῦτο δὴ τοῦ ἔπους· ᾐδεῖτο γὰρ τὴν τοῦ ἀνδρὸς ἀρετὴν καὶ ἀχθόμενος τούτῳ οὐδέ που παρακρημνίσας, ἀλλὰ βραχύ τι τοῦ ὀχήματος παρωσάμενος, ἵν' αἰδέσιμος αὐτῷ καὶ ἡ μετάστασις γένοιτο.

[2] Psellos used to serve up his philosophy in a light and superficial dress to suit the light and superficial mind of the Emperor. When he was tired of philosophy, he used to treat him to rhetoric (*Hist.* p. 196).

peror to cultivate. On their retirement he had recourse to amusements of the senses,[1] of which Psellos gives one instance. He caused a large basin to be dug in the middle of a park and to be filled with water up to the brim, so that it was on a level with the surrounding land. The Emperor used to lie in wait in order to observe and laugh at the mishaps of unwary persons who, advancing to pluck fruit from the trees with which the park was stocked, would sometimes walk into the water. He afterwards made a summer-house in this park close to the pond, in which he used constantly to bathe; and, perhaps from remaining in the water too long, he got an attack of pleurisy which brought on his death.

The military history of Constantine's reign has been given in full detail by Kedrênos. The chief events were the revolt of Maniakês, the Russian war, the Servian war, the Patzinak invasions, the Saracen war and loss of Armenia, the revolt of Tornikios, the invasions of the Seljuk Turks. Only three of these are described by Psellos—the revolts of Maniakês and Tornikios and the Russian war. Of the well-known circumstances of the life of George Maniakês we learn nothing new, but receive a vivid impression of his personal appearance. Psellos had seen and admired him standing nearly ten feet high, like a mountain or a pillar.[2] The expression of his countenance was not delicate nor pleasing, but like a volcano; his voice was as the voice of thunder, his hands were stalwart to shake walls to pieces or crush bronze gates between them, his gait was as a lion's, and his shadowy eyebrows gave him a grim look. In personal

---

[1] ἐπὶ τὰς ἐν αἰσθήσει πάλιν κατέφυγε χάριτας (p. 198).
[2] Cf. Constantine Manassês, l. 6284:

ἀνὴρ γιγαντοπάλαμος ὀξύχειρ ἀνδροφόντης
θρασύσπλαγχνος εὐκάρδιος πνέων ὀργῆς ἐκθύμου.

The chosen men who fought with him in the battle of Ostrovos were also γιγαντόσωμοι.

might and bravery he must have been equal to the bravest and mightiest western knight; and he was a worthy fellow of the adventurous Norseman Harald Haardrada, with whom he sailed in the Ægean and fought in Sicily, and, if we may believe the saga, sometimes quarrelled.[1] It was in the reign of Rômanos in Syria that Maniakês first gained reputation as a warrior and a general. At the beginning of the reign of Michael IV he was despatched to Sicily against the Saracens, and the castle of Maniakês still exists at Syracuse to attest his successes. On an absurd accusation of conspiracy he was recalled to Constantinople and imprisoned (1040), but was released by Michael V. Sicily had in the meantime been lost, but he was appointed commander in Calabria and Longibardia, and there he won a battle near Monopoli which was as fruitless in its results as the great victory of Remata had been in Sicily. A private wrong determined him to return to the East, and his conduct was interpreted as treasonable. Psellos blames Constantine for his want of tact in dealing with Maniakês. At the beginning he should have loaded him with honours, and at least subsequently, when he heard rumours that he intended to revolt, he should have feigned ignorance. Moreover, he sent the most unfit messengers—the men who were most likely to provoke the general. Maniakês was killed by a stray arrow in the battle near Ostrovos; otherwise he might have anticipated Isaac Komnênos.

Psellos was an eye-witness of the naval engagements

[1] The sources for the career of Harald Haardrada in southern Europe are: (1) Annalista Saxo (Pertz, VI, 695); (2) Adam of Bremen (Pertz, VII, 339, 31, and 341, 24); (3) Theodosius Monachus, *De regibus veteribus Norvagicis* (*Script. Rer. Dan.* V, 333, cap. 25); (4) the Saga of Harald in the Heimskringla of Snorro, for which see *Script. Hist. Island.* VI, 125, or Laing's translation of the Heimskringla; (5) the runic inscriptions on the lions formerly in the Peiræus, now in the arsenal of Venice, interpreted by Rafn.

with the Russians, which took place in the Bosphorus within sight of the palace in the summer of 1043. A tumult between some Greeks and the Russian traders resident in Constantinople, in which one distinguished Russian was killed, furnished the pretext of the expedition. This fact we learn from Zônaras, but it is completely ignored by Psellos, who informs us that this expedition had been designed and delayed for many years. Basil Bulgaroktonos had completely cowed the Russians, but after the death of his brother Constantine they began to revive their hostile projects. The reign of Rômanos, however, seemed to them too brilliant, and they were themselves too ill prepared to venture; but when Michael IV, a nobody, came to the throne, they decided to hesitate no longer. But before their preparations were completed Michael died, and in a few months afterwards Constantine IX became Emperor.[1] Though they had no reason for making war on him, they determined to do so, lest their preparations should go for nothing. It seems to me that the silence of Psellos as to the ostensible pretext of the war is not only intentional, but pointed; that he not only disregarded it as a mere pretext which had nothing to do with the real cause, but ignored it in pointed opposition to a contemporary historian who laid undue weight on it. During the engagements Psellos was standing beside the Emperor, and he gives a clear account of what happened, which Zônaras follows.

The revolt of Leon Tornikios took place several years later (1047). He was a sort of second cousin of the Emperor on the mother's side, and resided in Adrianople. He was very intimate with Euprepia, the Emperor's rich sister, who was a woman with a mind of her own,

---

[1] These observations are unsatisfactory, in that Psellos does not explain why the preparations of the Russians occupied so long a time.

on whom her brother consequently looked with suspicion and treated with caution as a strong-minded person cleverer than himself. She seldom visited him, and when she did so spoke out her sentiments with sisterly frankness.[1] The Emperor suspected her intimacy with Tornikios, and gave him an appointment in Iberia. His enemies accused him in his absence of treasonable intention, but it was not till Euprepia defended him (this point is omitted by Zônaras) that Constantine sent persons to cause him to become a monk. When he returned in monastic guise to the capital, the Emperor jeered at him, but Euprepia opened her house to him. The dissatisfied Macedonian faction, "men most ready to devise anything wild and most energetic in executing it", most punctilious in concealing and faithful in keeping their secret compacts, fixed on Leo as the most suitable leader, and conveyed him secretly to their headquarters, Adrianopolis, which Psellos is not guilty, like Zônaras, of calling Orestias.

The first important step was to win the troops stationed in the western provinces to their side, and in this they soon succeeded. The Emperor was not popular with the army, and Zônaras describes their desertion to the usurper as entirely due to this. Nevertheless it does not appear that they were quite so ready to take his part, for according to Psellos the leaders of the revolt were obliged to resort to a ruse in order to gain the support of the military captains. They sent round a number of agents to the different regiments with the news that the

---

[1] Psellos, *Hist.* p. 149: [τὴν δ' ἑτέραν] οὔτε τι λαμπρὸν ἐξ ἀρχῆς κομῶσαν καὶ εἰς περιφάνειαν τύχης ἐληλυθυῖαν, φρονήματός τε πλήρη τυγχάνουσαν καὶ γυναικῶν ἁπασῶν ὧν ἐγὼ τεθέαμαι σταθηροτάτην τε οὖσαν καὶ δυσπαράγωγον, κ.τ.λ. Zônaras, IV, 163: γυνὴ γενναία τε καὶ σταθηροτάτη τὸ φρόνημα καὶ εἰς τύχης ἐλάσασα περιφάνειαν καὶ εἰς πλούτου δαψίλειαν—which shows that the text of Psellos as it stands can hardly be correct. Something more than τὴν δ' ἑτέραν must have fallen out before οὔτε. The name of Constantine's other sister was Helena.

Emperor was dead, and that Theodôra had selected the Macedonian Leo Tornikios, in consideration of his good family, his mental ability, and energetic disposition, as the new Emperor. He adds that in addition to the effect of this artifice hatred of the sovran was operative. When the preparations were complete, they advanced to the siege of the capital.

One of the first measures of Constantine when he heard of the revolt was to banish his sister Euprepia. As the troops of the East could not arrive for several days, and all the forces he could muster did not fully amount to 1000, it was out of the question for him to take the field; his only chance was to defend Constantinople until succour arrived. He was very unwell at the time, suffering from gout and a severe attack of diarrhœa; and a rumour spread in the city that he was dead. The citizens collected to consider the advisability of joining the usurper, and the Emperor, ill though he was, had to dispel the false rumour by appearance in public. In the meantime Leo was acting as if he were already monarch; for as he had no money the only way in which he could reward or secure partisans was to remit taxes, distribute titles, and appoint ministers. One quality in his favour was his military experience; men wished to see a soldier on the throne who could in person defend the Empire against Turks or Patzinaks, like Basil or John Tzimiskês; for the only thing military about Monomachos was his name.

The army encamped round the whole city, and the first assault took place in the early morning. Both the Emperor and the tyrant were conspicuous, the latter riding on a white horse, the former sitting on a balcony that overlooked the field of action. Among the spectators of the teichomachy and the attendants of the Emperor was Psellos.

The siege lasted for three days, which Zônaras, though he follows Psellos, has not carefully distinguished and in some respects has confounded.[1] On the first morning the chief hostilities consisted of the buffooneries of the Macedonians, who danced and acted in a manner insulting to the Emperor. Constantine himself had a narrow escape; an arrow aimed at him passed very close and grazed the side of a court minion who was standing by. This incident forced the Emperor and his company, including Psellos, to retire. In the afternoon the forces of the besieged were increased by some civilians who volunteered and a few soldiers who were extracted from the prisons. The night was spent in digging a trench round the city, and the next morning the besiegers found a larger force drawn up in front of the gates than they had seen the day before. At first they were afraid that the army from the East had arrived; but soon, perceiving that it consisted of a town mob, they leaped over the narrow and shallow trench with loud cries and put the tumultuary band to flight. If this assault had been followed up, a change in the sovranty might have taken place on that day, but Leo restrained the pursuit, hoping perhaps to enter the city as an Emperor invited by citizens, not as a victorious general taking possession of a vanquished town. The policy of Leo throughout was to conciliate the inhabitants of the capital, and Constantine said he was more afraid of these kindly words than of anything else. On the third day a stone was thrown at the usurper, and though it missed him forced him and his party to flee. This created a panic and saved Constantine. The besiegers remained a few days inactive before the walls, and then, abandoning the siege, retired to Arkadiopolis. In the meantime the eastern troops arrived, and Tornikios was deserted

---

[1] He has thrown the first and second days into one.

by his followers. His eyes were put out, and the same punishment befell Joannês Vatatzês, a man celebrated for his strength and bravery, who was a sworn comrade of Tornikios and generously refused to desert him in his extremity.

Joannês, the eunuch, and others induced Constantine shortly before his death to select Nikêphoros Prôteuôn as his successor. But the design was frustrated by the promptness of Theodôra, who immediately appeared in the palace and was recognised as Empress.

9. *Theodôra.** It was expected that Theodôra would choose a partner to share the duties and prerogatives of imperial power, and there were some complaints uttered when it was found out that she had no such intention. Nevertheless her rule seems to have been popular and to have called forth no disloyalty, though some grumbled —for example, the patriarch Kêrularios[1]—that the government of a woman exercised an effeminate influence on the Empire. Yet Psellos says that she showed no weakness, on the contrary a degree of decision which might almost seem hardness.

Her chief minister was Leo Strabospondylês, and Attaleiatês speaks in most favourable terms of his administration.[2] He was a man of sense and experience, and most careful to maintain the law. Even Psellos, who speaks unfavourably of him, admits that he possessed ability and does not impugn his honesty. But he

---

[* Theodôra, A.D. 1054, Nov.–1056, Aug.]

[1] Psellos, *Hist.* p. 207.

[2] P. 52: εἶτ᾽ ἀνενεγκοῦσα τῶν ἐλλογίμων ἀνδρί τινι ἱερωμένῳ τε (he was synkellos of the patriarch) καὶ συνέσεως γέμοντι καὶ πολυπειρίας οὐκ ἀποδέοντι (Λέων προσηγορία τῷ ἀνδρὶ) τὴν διοίκησιν τῶν πραγμάτων ἐπέτρεψεν. ἐπιεικῶς οὖν οὗτος ἐν ἅπασιν ἐνεργῶν καὶ κατὰ λόγον τοῖς παρεμπίπτουσι χρώμενος καὶ τὸν νόμον ποιούμενος βούλημα πᾶσαν εὐταξίαν καὶ εὐνομίαν πεποίηκε πολιτεύεσθαι. He refers the state of domestic peace (ἀστασίαστον) in Theodôra's reign to the fact that God was pleased with this ἀγαθοεργία.

had not, or did not choose to practise, the conciliatory manners of a courtier and the smooth arts of a diplomatist; he was not endowed with readiness and fluency of speech; he used to sit in silence and look at the ceiling, and was so careless or awkward in expressing himself that he often conveyed to his hearers exactly the opposite of what he intended. This want of a statesmanlike exterior—of political *éthos*, as Psellos says—created an unfavourable opinion; and his roughness made him unpopular. Yet he was free from all taint of bribery or avarice, and gave generous and magnificent entertainments.

The significance of the position of Leo in the reigns of Theodôra and Michael VI we can determine from two facts. He had been the minister of Michael IV,[1] and he was passed over by Constantine IX,[2] whose policy had been guided by opposition to the Paphlagonians. He seems to have been a rival of Constantine Leichudês, and the two men are contrasted by Psellos. I think I shall not be mistaken in conjecturing that Michael V, among his many reactionary acts, deposed Leo from office and appointed Leichudês in his place. Hence the administrations of Theodôra and Michael VI bear the character of a reaction against that of Constantine IX, just as that of Constantine was a reaction against the government of Michael IV, and as that of Isaac Komnênos was a reaction against the Macedonian Basilians.

Before her death[3] Theodôra placed the diadem on the head of a man already stricken in years, Michael VI,

---

[1] Zônaras, IV, 181: τὸ πάλαι τῷ βασιλεῖ Μιχαὴλ ὑπηρετήσαντι.

[2] Psellos, *Hist.* p. 206: ὁ γὰρ τὴν τῶν ὅλων πεπιστευμένος διοίκησιν …ἐπειδὴ μὴ τῶν πρωτείων ἠξίωτο παρ᾽ ἐκείνου (Constantine) μηδὲ παρὰ τῇ ἐκείνου εἱστήκει πλευρῷ, ὅπερ δὴ αὐτῷ ἔθος ἐν τοῖς προτοῦ βασιλεύειν ἐγίγνετο καὶ ζῶντι ἐμέμφετο καὶ ἀπεληλυθότι τῆς ἀτιμίας ἐμνησικάκησεν. These words express clearly enough Leo's position.

[3] August 30, 1056 (not 1057, as stated in Finlay's *Hist. of Greece*, II, 449).

whom Leo and his party selected as a man likely to be manageable and weak.

10. *Michael VI.** The position of the new Emperor rested on his nomination by Theodôra and on the support of a strong political party, headed by Leo the synkellos. By generosity and promotions he exerted himself to please the members of the Senate and the various civil functionaries; he also cultivated popularity with the people.[1]

But he was too old and too inexperienced to understand the political situation and the dangers which at that very moment were lurking around his throne; and so at the very outset he committed a radical mistake which produced the immediate operation of the very elements by which those dangers were threatened. While he showed marked kindness to the Senate and the people he pointedly and designedly ignored the army.

Now the army had been long discontented.[2] The soldiers were tired of Emperors ignorant of warfare, who devoted themselves to civil affairs and took little personal interest in the army, and the commanders felt keenly that their position was a very secondary one in the Empire; for the succession depended on the ministers, not on the generals.

And now that the Basilian line was extinct—connection with which had been a palladium for the preceding monarchs—it behoved the new sovran to deal most warily and delicately with the military power.

[* Michael VI, Stratiotikos, A.D. 1056, Aug. 22/30–1057, Aug.]

[1] Compare Psellos, *Hist.* p. 209 (Zônaras, IV, 182). He promotes too rapidly: οὐ γὰρ τῷ προσεχεῖ ἕκαστον συνίστα βαθμῷ, ἀλλὰ καὶ πρὸς τὸν ἐφεξῆς καὶ τὸν ἐπέκεινα ἀνεβίβαζεν.

[2] Psellos, *Hist.* p. 212: ἐβούλοντο μὲν καὶ πρότερον τὸ στρατιωτικὸν ξύμπαν τὸ κράτος Ῥωμαίων ὑποποιήσασθαι καὶ ὑπήκοοι γενέσθαι στρατηγῷ αὐτοκράτορι καὶ τὴν πολιτικὴν καταλῦσαι τῆς βασιλείας διαδοχήν.

But Michael was too old and stupid to see this.[1] He had the idea—a false generalisation derived from the reigns of his immediate predecessors—that his supremacy rested altogether on the civil power, and that the army, like a subordinate servant, was a *quantité négligeable*. He combined all the stubborn conservative tendencies of an old man with that love of making reforms in trivial matters which is perhaps also a characteristic of the old.[2]

He especially offended Katakalôn Kekaumenos, Duke of Antioch, whom he deprived of that post in favour of his own nephew Michael. Katakalôn and Isaac Komnênos, with a number of other distinguished officers, presented themselves before the Emperor to remonstrate with him on his injustice and imprudence; but he would not listen to them, and overwhelmed Katakalôn with reproaches. Psellos, who had been recalled to court by Theodôra, and was sometimes consulted by her and Michael, was present at this scene.

The insulted generals made another attempt to influence Michael through the medium of his counsellor Leo; but Leo did not attempt to mollify them and only exasperated them more. It is not necessary to suppose that they had any share in instigating the unsuccessful and unimportant insurrection of Theodosios Monomachos, which took place at about this time.[3]

---

[1] Manassês describes Michael as ἄνδρα τινὰ μακρόβιον πέμπελον τρομαλέον (l. 6331), and speaks of the military commanders as

καταφρονοῦντες Μιχαὴλ ἄντικρυς ὡς ἀνίκμου
κράμβης ἀφύλλου γηραιᾶς ἤδη διερρευκυίας.

See Kedrênos, II, p. 614. For example, he wished to enact that the heads of the citizens should no longer be covered δι' ἀγραμμάτων ὡς νῦν ἀλλὰ διὰ μεγαλογράμμων ὀθονίων ἐκ βυσσοῦ πορφυρᾶς ἐξυφασμένων.

[3] Zônaras, IV, 184. The Byzantine populace jeered at the feeble attempt of Monomachos in words that, if the text of Zônaras is correct,

They determined to overthrow Michael, and unanimously selected Isaac as his successor. Having made this arrangement, they withdrew from Constantinople to their estates in Asia Minor to mature their plans and collect their forces. Isaac took his measures with the utmost caution, and perfect order prevailed in his camp. Money was absolutely necessary for his success, and he raised it by regular and accurately defined impositions, and by intercepting all the wealth that happened to be on its way to the capital. Along with the rich and influential noblemen Katakalôn and Rômanos Sklêros, Isaac hoped to have the aid of Nikêphoros Bryennios, the commander of the Macedonian regiments and governor of Kappadokia, who had been also offended by the Emperor. But in the Anatolic theme, where he took up his quarters, he quarrelled with Opsaras, who was loyal to Michael, and his eyes were put out.[1] The rebels took up their quarters at Nikaia.

But in Constantinople itself there was not an undivided adherence to the Emperor. There was a large party which wished to dethrone him, and which was, we need not hesitate to assume, in direct communication with the leaders of the insurrection. What lent this party special weight was that the patriarch Kêrularios was hostile to the government and the Emperor; and Kêrularios, of whom I shall have more to say, was a man of unusual energy and importance. One can hardly avoid conjecturing that he and Isaac had arranged the whole matter between them before the latter left the capital.

are appropriately feeble: ὁ δημώδης ὄχλος ἐπεγγελῶντες ῥήματά τινα συνθέντες ἐπῇδον αὐτῷ· τὰ δ᾽ ἦσαν,

ὁ μωρὸς ὁ Μονομάχος, εἴ τι ἐφρόνει, ἐποίησε.

Let us hope that the words had at least the form of a "political" verse, and ran, by a slight transposition,

ὁ Μονομάχος, ὁ μωρός, ἐποίησ᾽ εἴ τι 'φρόνει.

[1] See Zônaras, IV, 185.

In this position of affairs Michael VI took counsel with men who had played a prominent part in the days of Monomachos, but whom he had hitherto gladly dispensed with.[1] In particular he asked the advice of Psellos. Psellos suggested three things: first, that he should become reconciled with the patriarch, as he might be able to give most powerful assistance to the usurper;[2] secondly, that he should send a conciliatory embassy to Isaac; thirdly, that he should collect all the military forces available (the western troops, some eastern troops that had been left in the capital, the foreign guards), obtain succour from neighbouring States, and appoint a competent general.

The first part of this advice was not followed, and the second part was set aside until the third had been tried. Michael appointed Theodôros, a eunuch of the Empress Theodôra,[3] and Aaron, a relative of the wife of Isaac Komnênos, to the command of his troops, and they encamped over against Nikaia. But neither soldiers nor commanders were loyal. "The commander of the forces", says Psellos—"his name I need not mention—was a waverer, or rather, as I fancy, a partisan".[4] Further on he tells us that the president Theodôros had a secret understanding with Komnênos. Hence we may conclude that the unnamed commander was

---

[1] Psellos, *Hist.* p. 214: ἄλλους τε πλείστους μετακαλεῖται τῶν γενναίων μὲν τὰς γνώμας τηνικαῦτα δὲ κατολιγωρηθέντων· καὶ δῆτα κἀμὲ εἰσποιεῖται καὶ ὅτι μὴ ἔχοι πάλαι ἐγκόλπιον ὡς ἄτοπόν τι πεποιηκὼς σχηματίζεται.

[2] *Ibid.*: ἐπεὶ γὰρ ἐγνώκειν ὅτι ἐκ διαφόρου γνώμης τῷ μεγάλῳ ἀντικαθεστήκοι ἀρχιερεῖ καὶ δυσόργως εἶχεν ἐκεῖνος αὐτῷ γνώμην αὐτῷ πρώτην ταύτην εἰσήνεγκα πᾶσαν αὐτῷ διαφορὰν διαλύσασθαι...ἐν τοῖς τοιούτοις μάλιστα δυναμένῳ καιροῖς καὶ συνεπιθησομένῳ τοῖς τυραννεύσασιν εἰ μὴ προλάβοι τοῦτον εἰς ἀκριβεστάτην οἰκείωσιν. It is quite possible that Psellos knew of the intentions of Kêrularios.

[3] Theodôra had created him *proedros*, and afterwards commander of the eastern army (Psellos, p. 216).

[4] ἀμφιρρεπὴς ἦν ὡς δ' ἐγῷμαι μονομερής.

Aaron. The result was that the Emperor's army was defeated.

After some days Michael resolved to send an embassy to Komnênos. He engaged on this commission three men of moderation and distinction, who were not identified with his own policy, and who would carry weight with the revolutionists. He first called Michael Psellos, on whose persuasive fluency he doubtless relied as a valuable auxiliary, and asked him to undertake the negotiation. Psellos says he was unwilling and yielded only to entreaties, making the condition that he might select a colleague. He chose Leo Alôpos, a distinguished member of the Senate,[1] and they chose a third, Constantine Leichudês. They helped the Emperor to compose a letter, of which the purport was to offer the rank of Cæsar to Komnênos.

The envoys sent a notice beforehand to Komnênos of their approach, and obtained a sworn promise of their personal safety in his camp. They were received with great cordiality and rejoicings; and in an interview with Isaac on the evening of their arrival nothing passed between them but commonplace civilities.[2]

The next morning Isaac, surrounded with imperial pomp, gave them a public audience. The doors of his tent were suddenly thrown open that the splendour might all at once burst on the amazed multitude, with whose cheers and shouts the ears of Psellos and his companions were dinned. When the noise ceased they saw Isaac in sumptuous raiment, sitting on a raised gilt throne, resting his feet on a footstool. His fixed eyes testified to the preoccupation of his mind, and his face

---

[1] κἀγὼ αἱροῦμαι τὸν κάλλιστόν τε καὶ συνετώτατον καὶ ὃν μάλιστα ᾔδειν τὴν σὺν ἐμοὶ θαρρήσοντα ἔξοδον. We learn his name from Zônaras.

[2] μηδέ τι πλέον παρ' ἡμῶν μαθεῖν ἠβουλήθη ἢ ὅσον τὰ περὶ τὴν πορείαν καὶ εἰ εὐκυμάντῳ τῷ πλῷ ἐχρησάμεθα.

bore marks of the recent conflict. The historian describes in full the successive circles of guards or attendants which stood around the throne, among whom the most striking were the foreign mercenaries, "the Italians and Tauroskythians". The ambassadors, at the sovran's sign, approached near the throne, and after an interchange of civilities a gentleman-in-waiting called upon them officially to state their commission. Psellos was put forward as spokesman, and he gives an elaborate account of his diplomatic speech. He began with an encomium on the rank of Cæsar and the dignities attached to it, and amid interruptions from the audience went on to speak of the adoption of the Cæsar by the Emperor. He finished with an appeal to Isaac to desist from his usurpation.

The speech was received with unfavourable clamours, which Komnênos was obliged to quiet by assuring the soldiers that the eloquence had produced no effect on him. He then dismissed the assembly and gave the envoys a private audience, at which he informed them that for the present he would be quite satisfied with the rank of Cæsar on condition that the Emperor named no other successor before his death, and deprived none of his companions of honours he had bestowed on them; he also required a certain measure of power, so far as to have the bestowal of some subordinate civil and military appointments. He also asked them to obtain the removal of the minister "of short stature", who was hostile to him and unpopular—Leo Strabospondylês we may presume. These proposals were not entrusted to writing; the letter which was openly sent did not contain them. Having breakfasted with Isaac they hastened to the shore, crossed the Bosphorus, and reached the imperial palace early in the day. The assembly and the negotiations had taken place in the early morning. The

Emperor agreed to all the demands, and after the space of a day the ambassadors recrossed the straits. Komnênos appeared perfectly satisfied with the reply of the Emperor, promised to disband his troops and proceed to Constantinople. Psellos, Leichudês, and Alôpos congratulated themselves that they had contributed a service to their sovran by their prudent conduct of the embassy, and prepared to return on the morrow; Isaac was to move to Scutari the day after.

But before eventide they were surprised by the news that the Emperor had been deposed by a conspiracy of senators. At first both the ambassadors and apparently the Cæsar looked upon the report as an invention, but messenger after messenger arrived confirming the tidings, and doubt could be no longer entertained. A more reliable and accurately informed person soon appeared, who explained that certain dissatisfied and seditious members of the Senate had excited the inhabitants of the city, and, compelling the patriarch to act as their leader, inveighed against Michael and extolled Isaac; so far nothing more had happened. Before sunset, as Isaac and the ambassadors were conversing outside his tent, one arrived out of breath with the news that Michael had been forced to become a monk, and that the city was awaiting the arrival of Isaac to take his place. Ere he had finished speaking another came with the same news.

"How my fellow-ambassadors passed that night", says Psellos, "I know not, but I despaired of life, and expected that I should without delay be led to the sacrifice". But before daybreak the camp was in motion, and the philosopher's terror was dispelled. The Emperor called him to his side and addressed him as a counsellor, asking his advice as to the best mode of administration, and by what policy he might rival the greatest sovrans.

He treated Alôpos and Leichudês with the same kindness.

The whole city streamed forth to meet the new Emperor, and he, turning to Psellos, said, "This extreme good fortune, philosopher, seems to me slippery, and I know not if the end will turn out favourable". The philosopher reassured the Emperor with smooth and flattering words, and took the opportunity of begging him not to bear a grudge against himself. The eyes of Komnênos filled with tears, and he said, "I liked your tongue better the other day when it reviled me than now when it speaks smooth words". He then appointed Psellos president of the Senate.

This important revolution, which transferred the crown from the Macedonian to the Komnênian dynasty, possesses considerable interest. It was accomplished by the coalition of a party within the city with the army without, and in this respect reminds us of the unsuccessful revolt of Vitalian in the reign of Anastasios. But our historians represent this coalition as undesigned; they represent Isaac Komnênos as completely surprised by the news of the part taken by the patriarch and certain members of the Senate. Of course we cannot believe this; we must seek for something a little more mystic, μυστικώτερον—to use a phrase of Byzantine diplomacy. It is clear that Komnênos had a party in the city, which he and his friends, Katakalôn and the others, had time to organise before they departed to Asia after their rebuff by Michael. We are told expressly that they remained for some time in the capital. The cabinet ministers of Theodôra and Michael were very unpopular with others as well as with the soldiers, and Isaac would not fail to take advantage of this.

This faction consisted of members of the Senate, and

of party organisations or clubs, *hetaireiai*.[1] These clubs, which Zônaras has fortunately mentioned, had politically somewhat the same signification in the eleventh century as the *dêmoi* or factions of the hippodrome in the sixth; though doubtless they were much smaller and possessed far less influence than the blues and greens. Whether the patriarch had an understanding with this party beforehand, or whether he was forced into the action he took on the day of the insurrection by the threats of the disaffected, was a question on which Byzantine historians differed. From the position of Kêrularios as opposed to and overlooked by the existing administration, and from his character as a man of strong will and great ambition, we might judge that he had throughout been a prime mover in the political revolution. The weight of the opinion of the historian Attaleiatês inclines in the same direction. And I think we cannot hesitate to suppose that Kêrularios and Komnênos had a distinct understanding with one another. The remarkable honours and privileges which Isaac, when he ascended the throne, conferred upon the patriarch, can be best explained by supposing a secret compact; and the negotiation would have been all the more easy, as Constantine Dukas was an intimate friend of both the Emperor and the patriarch.[2] In his *Epitaphios* on Kêrularios, Psellos gives an account of the

[1] Zônaras, IV, 190: στασιώδεις τινὲς τῶν τῆς συγκλήτου βουλῆς...οἷς καὶ οἱ τῶν ἑταιρειῶν συνῄεσαν ἄρχοντες. Attaleiatês merely mentions some of the persons ἐν τέλει as conspirators.

[2] Attaleiatês, *Hist.* p. 56: εἴτε δὲ καὶ ὁ τῆς ἀρχιερωσύνης ἔξαρχος καὶ πατριάρχης ὁ Κηρουλάριος κεκοινώκει τούτοις τῆς σκέψεως εἴτε καὶ μή, ἄδηλον καὶ προφανὲς οὐδέν. ὅμως δ᾽ ἐκ προλήψεων καὶ τῶν μετὰ ταῦτα συνενεχθέντων τὰ τῆς ὑπονοίας εἰς ἀληθείας ἀμυδρὰν προκεχωρήκασι ἔμφασιν· καὶ γὰρ τῷ Κομνηνῷ τὰ πάντα συνδιαφέρων ἦν καὶ συμπράττων καὶ τῆς πρώτης βουλῆς γινωσκόμενος ὡς καὶ τῆς φιλίας καὶ τῆς ἀξίας καὶ τῆς ἀγχιστείας ἐγγύτατος ὁ βέσταρχος Κωνσταντῖνος ὁ Δοῦκας ἀδελφιδῆς τοῦ πατριάρχου σύνευνος καθιστάμενος καὶ πολλὴν εὔνοιαν διδοὺς καὶ λαμβάνων ἐκεῖθεν.

revolution, and represents the patriarch as acting the part of a conciliator between two foes, and attributes to his interference the fact that the revolution was effected with little violence or bloodshed.[1]

It took place in the following manner. On the fatal day the conspirators repaired to the church of St Sophia, and took oaths that bound them to carry out their purpose. The act was attended with commotion both within and without the sacred edifice, and the patriarch sent his nephews to discover the cause of the commotion. They were captured by the leaders of the insurrection and threatened with death if the patriarch did not consent to countenance the plot. "Moved with compassion for his nephews, who were as his sons, and deeming it necessary to prevent civil war", Kêrularios gave his consent. This was what apparently took place; but there can be little doubt that the whole affair was a preconcerted ruse.[2]

Some days before, Michael had induced all the senators and civil officers to sign a document, by which they engaged not to call Komnênos *Basileus*, nor to pay him imperial honour. The conspirators professed that their object was to cancel this document, which they had signed under compulsion, and the patriarch undertook to obtain it from Michael. But in a short time they waxed bolder, and openly proclaimed Komnênos Emperor. Kêrularios despatched one messenger to Isaac— one of those whose arrival in the camp we witnessed above—bidding him not tarry, and another to Michael

---

[1] P. 362 *sqq.*: δυεῖν τότε γεγονότων ἀντιπάλων τμημάτων μέσος ἐκεῖνος ἐφειστήκει καὶ ἄτμητος. He is compared to a pilot in the storm. He took the side of Komnênos because he saw Providence clearly leaning that way. Pp. 364–5: διαιτᾷ ὅπως ἂν τῷ μὲν περιλειφθείη τὸ ζῆν ἐκείνῳ δὲ ἀναιμωτὶ μνηστευθείη τὸ κράτος. Michael VI is praised for his ready compliance with the inevitable.

[2] Zônaras, IV, 190: λέγεται δὲ ταῦτα σκήψεις εἶναι καὶ προβουλεύματα ἵν' ἄκων δοκοίη συνελθεῖν ὁ πατριάρχης τοῖς στασιάζουσι.

bidding him leave the palace. Michael asked the clerical messengers of the patriarch, "What will ye give me instead of the kingdom?" and they answered, "The kingdom of heaven".[1] He then put off his imperial robes and retired to a religious retreat, which was under the special care of the patriarch, who received him with a kind and smiling face, and kissed him and bade him farewell. And Michael said, "God requite thee thy kiss worthily, patriarch".[2]

11. *The Patriarch Michael Kêrularios.* The head of the Church who took such a prominent part in the revolution of 1057 was a striking and important figure in the middle part of the eleventh century. We have already come across him on several occasions; but I passed over his name lightly, preferring to give a short connected account of his career. He attempted, as far as was possible under the completely different circumstances, to do for the patriarchate in the eastern Church what his younger contemporary Hildebrand did for the pontificate in western Christendom.

He was a man remarkable for physical beauty as well as for learning and intellect. His first appearance on the scene of history is in the reign of Michael IV (1040); he was involved in a serious conspiracy against the Emperor, and was banished along with Joannês Makrembolitês—the father of the Empress Eudokia and spiritual brother of Psellos—and many others. In the notice of Kedrênos, Kêrularios is mentioned as a leader,[3] but Psellos in his *Epitaphios* gives a very curious account of the affair. A large number of noble and able men, dis-

---

[1] See Zônaras, IV, 191.

[2] Attaleiatês, p. 59: ἀντασπάσαιτο, "may he kiss in return". Although Psellos (*M. Kêrularios*, p. 365) describes the cordial reception given by the patriarch to the deposed monarch, I am sure that Michael's words were ironical, and that he looked on the patriarchal salute as the kiss of Judas.

[3] Kedrênos, II, 540.

gusted with the government of the Paphlagonian family, formed the design of electing a new Emperor. They determined to select the man on whom heaven had conferred in most abundance excellences of mind and body —the best man in the Empire; each excluded from his thoughts all wish to reign. They unanimously voted for Michael Kêrularios; and the unanimity seemed equivalent to oracular certainty that he was the best man. They did not, however, inform the object of their choice, feeling that he would be reluctant to yield to their wishes; Kêrularios remained in ignorance that a large assembly of men of light and leading had chosen him to reign over them. But some of the conspirators misdoubted the chance of success and turned informers; and Michael was punished even more severely than the others for the tribute which without his knowledge they had paid to his excellence.

He returned from exile in 1042, at the time of the accession of Monomachos, who showed him marked favour—although he had never met him before—and is reported to have exclaimed when he first saw him, "He is just the man for the patriarchate". In the meantime, as the patriarchal chair was not vacant, he made him his most confidential adviser;[1] but in less than a year (Feb. 1043) Alexios died, and Kêrularios was elected to the high and influential position of head of the eastern Church.

There were two limits on the ecclesiastical power of the patriarch. One of these was theoretical rather than practical; in the organisation of universal Christendom he held a subordinate position.[2] It had been defined in

---

[1] *Epitaph.* p. 324: καὶ συνοικίζει τοῦτον εὐθὺς ἑαυτῷ τοῖς ἀδύτοις καὶ τὰ πρῶτα τῶν περὶ ἐκεῖνον ποιεῖται, κ.τ.λ.

[2] The claim of the patriarch of Constantinople to the title of "ecumenical" was first raised in the reign of Maurice, and was then resisted

the council of Constantinople (381) that the See of Constantinople was second in dignity to the See of Rome. The other limit was practical rather than theoretical; the patriarch was dependent on the Emperor. The eastern Emperors, like Constantine and like Justinian, continued to interfere in ecclesiastical matters, as was indeed inevitable.

From such subordination and dependence Michael Kêrularios made an attempt to deliver the Byzantine pontificate, and was to a certain extent not unsuccessful.

To break with Rome was not difficult; the eastern and western Churches were practically severed. Into the details of the schism we need not enter here; we need merely indicate that a general account of it is given by Psellos in his *Epitaphios* on the patriarch. He notes the difference as to the "theology of the holy Trinity" as the main point of the dissension, and tells us that others thought the matter of no consequence, while the patriarch deemed the heresy intolerable and exerted himself in the matter with unusually ardent activity.[1] On July

by Gregory I. The claim was of practical value in so far as it was connected with the subordination of the sees of Alexandria and Antioch to Constantinople; and thus Leo IX (in his sixth epistle) writes that it is intolerable *quod nova ambitione Alexandrinum et Antiochenum patriarchas antiquis suæ dignitatis privilegiis privare contendens contra fas et jus suo dominio subjugare conaretur.* An attempt was made in 1024 to bribe the pope into conceding the coveted title to the Byzantine bishop (see Lequien, *Or. Christ.* I, 89).

[1] τῷ δὲ τῆς εὐσεβείας προμάχῳ καὶ προθύμῳ καὶ τοῦ θείου λόγου ἀγωνιστῇ οὐκ ἀνεκτὸν ἐλογίζετο· ὅθεν προὔκαμέ τε τῆς μητροπόλεως καὶ ὑπὲρ ἐκείνης πρὸς ἐκείνην πολλάκις ἠκριβολογήσατο καὶ θερμότερον ἢ περὶ τἆλλα διηγωνίσατο νουθετῶν ἐπιστέλλων παρακαλῶν γραφικαῖς χρώμενος ἀποδείξεσι...ὡς δ' οὐκ ἔπειθε πάντα πράττων ἀλλ' ἐγεγόνεισαν οἱ παιδαγωγούμενοι θρασύτεροι καὶ ἀναισχύντεροι τηνικαῦτα καὶ αὐτὸς ἀναρρήγνυνται καὶ τῇ ἀναισχυντίᾳ τῆς ἀσεβείας τῆς εὐσεβείας ἀντιτίθησι τὴν ἀκρίβειαν. For the schism compare Leo Ostiensis, *Chronicle of Monte Casino*, bk. II, chap. LXXXV. See Hefele, *Conciliengeschichte*, IV, 725 sq., and the article on Cärularios by Gass in the *Realencyclopädie für protestantische Theologie*, edited by Herzog and Plitt (now by Hauck). Kêrularios threw down the gauntlet in a letter to the bishop of Trani.

16, 1054, the envoys of the pope deposited the act of excommunication on the altar of St Sophia.

That Kêrularios made some attempts to render his office independent of imperial interference during the reign of Constantine IX, I should infer from the incidental remark of Psellos that he owed many grudges to Monomachos.[1] He had a high ideal of the archieratic office. The patriarch was bound, he thought (for though Psellos speaks with his own words, he speaks in the spirit of Kêrularios), to speak "holy words" to secular powers, to resist *tyrannies*, to exalt the humble and pull down the self-willed, to superintend education:[2] it was the ideal of Ambrose and Chrysostom. The Emperor did not support Michael in his quarrel with the pope and did not approve of his unconciliatory attitude; he compelled Nikêtas Pectoratos, a partisan of Michael, to burn the book he had written against the false doctrines of the Latins.

We have seen how the patriarch was opposed to the governments of Theodôra and Michael VI, and how he assisted in the elevation of Isaac I. It seems extremely probable that he arranged beforehand with Isaac, as conditions of lending his support, those privileges which Isaac granted when he was seated on the throne. We are told that he honoured the patriarch as a father, and he granted to the Church a completer power in its own affairs than it had before possessed. The treasurer (σκευοφύλαξ) and the grand chancellor (ὁ μέγας οἰκονόμος) used to be appointed directly by the Emperor; Isaac transferred these appointments to the patriarch. He rendered the Church wholly independent of the

---

[1] *Epitaph.* p. 357: καίτοι πολλὰ μνησικακεῖν ἔχων τῷ ἀπελθόντι.

[2] *Ibid.* p. 354: τὸ πᾶσαν ἰδέαν παιδαγωγίας τοῖς πρὸς ἀρετὴν ἀπευθυνομένοις ἐπιδείκνυσθαι πρός τε δυναστείας παρρησιάζεσθαι καὶ τυραννίαις (usurpations) ἀνθίστασθαι καὶ τοὺς μὲν ταπεινοτέρους ὑψοῦν καθαιρεῖν δὲ τοὺς αὐθαδεστέρους καὶ θρασυτέρους.

palace; the entire ecclesiastical administration was to depend henceforward on the head of the Church.[1]

Kêrularios seems to have been popular with the clergy, and he tried to strengthen his position by the advancement of his nephews, who, as we saw, played a part in the revolt against Michael VI. Isaac conferred on them the highest honours and offices; and this is the nearest parallel to papal nepotism that we meet in Byzantine history—the advancement of the patriarch's nephews by the Emperor.

But Kêrularios presumed too far, and he fell. He took upon himself, in accordance with his idea of the duties or privileges of the patriarchal office, to admonish the Emperor like a father or censure him like a master, if he did or designed to do anything of which he did not approve. The ears of an Emperor are accustomed to praise, not to rebuke; and Isaac, however friendly his feelings to the patriarch were, could not long submit to the schooling of an ecclesiastic. Moreover, Kêrularios in mere external trivialities gave proof of a dangerously autocratic spirit; he wore red boots like the Emperor's, asserting that it was an ancient pontifical privilege. Things came to a crisis when on one occasion the Emperor exhibited his impatience and the indignant patriarch cried "It was I who gave you the Empire, I too can take it from you".[2] At the feast of the archangels it was necessary for the patriarch to officiate outside the city, and the Emperor seized the opportunity and caused Kêrularios to be arrested, as he feared that his arrest in the city might cause a disturbance. The Varangian soldiers who were employed for the purpose transported him to Prokonnêsos, where he died in a few days and relieved the Emperor from further trouble.

[1] See Attaleiatês, p. 60; Skylitzês, pp. 641–2; Zônaras, IV, 352.
[2] It is not easy to see the point of τὸ δημῶδες τοῦτο καὶ καθημαξωμένον, which Skylitzês (p. 643) puts into the mouth of the patriarch: ἐῶ σε ἔκτισα φοῦρνε· ἐῶ ἵνα σε χαλάσω.

10. A SURVEY OF BYZANTINE HISTORY*

The present volume carries on the fortunes of a portion of Europe to the end of the Middle Ages. This exception to the general chronological plan of the work seemed both convenient and desirable. The orbit of Byzantium, the history of the peoples and states which moved within that orbit and always looked to it as the central body, giver of light and heat, did indeed at some points touch or traverse the orbits of western European states, but the development of these on the whole was not deeply affected or sensibly perturbed by what happened east of Italy or south of the Danube, and it was only in the time of the Crusades that some of their rulers came into close contact with the Eastern Empire or that it counted to any considerable extent in their policies. England, the remotest state of the West, was a legendary country to the people of Constantinople, and that imperial capital was no more than a dream-name of wealth and splendour to Englishmen, except to the few adventurers who travelled thither to make their fortunes in the Varangian guards. It is thus possible to follow the history of the Eastern Roman Empire from the eighth century to its fall, along with those of its neighbours and clients, independently of the rest of Europe, and this is obviously more satisfactory than to interpolate in the main history of Western

[* This is the Introduction from the *Cambridge Medieval History* (1923), vol. IV, *The Eastern Roman Empire*, pp. vii–xiv. The references are to chapters in the volume. It has been thought better to leave these just as they stand.]

Europe chapters having no connexion with those which precede and follow.

Besides being convenient, this plan is desirable. For it enables us to emphasise the capital fact that throughout the Middle Ages the same Empire which was founded by Augustus continued to exist and function and occupy even in its final weakness a unique position in Europe—a fact which would otherwise be dissipated, as it were, and obscured amid the records of another system of states with which it was not in close or constant contact. It was one of Gibbon's services to history that the title of his book asserted clearly and unambiguously this continuity.

We have, however, tampered with the correct name, which is simply *Roman Empire*, by adding *Eastern*, a qualification which, although it has no official basis, is justifiable as a convenient mark of distinction from the Empire which Charlemagne founded and which lasted till the beginning of the nineteenth century. This Western Empire had no good claim to the name of Roman. Charlemagne and those who followed him were not legitimate successors of Augustus, Constantine, Justinian, and the Isaurians, and this was tacitly acknowledged in their endeavours to obtain recognition of the imperial title they assumed from the sovrans of Constantinople whose legitimacy was unquestionable.

Much as the Empire changed after the age of Justinian, as its population became more and more predominantly Greek in speech, its descent from Rome was always unmistakably preserved in the designation of its subjects as Romans ('Ρωμαῖοι). Its eastern neighbours knew it as Rūm. Till the very end the names of most of the titles of its ministers, officials, and institutions were either Latin or the Greek translations of Latin terms that had become current in the earliest days of the Empire.[1] Words of Latin derivation form a large class in medieval Greek. The modern Greek language was commonly called *Romaic* till the middle of the nineteenth century. It is only quite recently that *Roumelia* has been falling out of use to designate territories in the Balkan peninsula. Contrast with the persistence of the Roman name in the East the fact that the subjects of the Western Empire were never called Romans and indeed had no common name as a whole; the only "Romans" among them were the inhabitants of the city of Rome. There is indeed one district in Italy whose name still commemorates the Roman Empire—*Romagna*; but this exception only reinforces the contrast. For the district corresponds to the Exarchate of Ravenna, and was called Romania by its Lombard neighbours because it belonged to the Roman Emperor of Constantinople. It was at the New Rome, not at the Old, that the political tradition of the Empire was preserved. It is worth remembering too that the greatest public buildings of Constantinople were originally built, however they may have been afterwards changed or extended—the Hippodrome, the Great Palace, the Senatehouses, the churches of St Sophia and the Holy Apostles—by Emperors of Latin speech, Severus, Constantine, Justinian.

On the other hand, the civilisation of the later Roman Empire was the continuation of that of ancient Greece. Hellenism entered upon its second phase when Alexander of Macedon expanded the Greek world into the

---

[1] Examples: (1) ἀσηκρῆτις (*a secretis*), δούξ, κόμης, μάγιστρος, πατρίκιος, δομέστικος, πραιπόσιτος, πραίτωρ, κουαίστωρ, κουράτωρ; ἰδίκτον, πάκτον; κάστρον, φοσσάτον, παλάτιον, βῆλον (*velum*); ἀπληκεύειν = (*castra*) *applicare*, πραιδεύειν, δηριγεύειν; μοῦλτος=(*tu*)*multus*; (2) (ancient equivalents of Latin terms) βασιλεύς, αὐτοκράτωρ (*imperator*), σύγκλητος (*senatus*), ὕπατος (*consul*), ἀνθύπατος (*proconsul*), ὕπαρχος (*praefectus*), δρόμος (*cursus publicus*).

east, and on its third with the foundation of Constantine by the waters where Asia and Europe meet. Christianity, with its dogmatic theology and its monasticism, gave to this third phase its distinctive character and flavour, and *Byzantine* civilisation, as we have learned to call it, is an appropriate and happy name. Its features are very fully delineated in this volume by Professor Diehl (Chapter xxiv) * The continuity which links the fifteenth century A.D. with the fifth B.C. is notably expressed in the long series of Greek historians, who maintained, it may be said, a continuous tradition of historiography. From Critobulus, the imitator of Thucydides, and Chalcocondyles, who told the story of the last days of the Empire, we can go back, in a line broken only by a dark interval in the seventh and eighth centuries, to the first great masters, Thucydides and Herodotus.

The development of "Byzantinism" really began in the fourth century. The historian Finlay put the question in a rather awkward way by asking, When did the Roman Empire change into the Byzantine? The answer is that it did not change into any other Empire than itself, but that some of the characteristic features of Byzantinism began to appear immediately after Constantinople was founded. There is, however, a real truth in Finlay's own answer to his question. He drew the dividing line at the accession of Leo the Isaurian, at the beginning of the eighth century. And, in fact, Leo's reign marked the consummation of a rapid change which had been going on during the past hundred years. Rapid: for I believe anyone who has studied the history of those centuries will agree that in the age of the Isaurians we feel much further away from the age of Justinian than we feel in the age of Justinian from

[* Chap. xxiv, *Byzantine Civilisation*.]

the age of Theodosius the Great. Finlay's date has been taken as the starting point of this volume; it marks, so far as a date can, the transition to a new era.

The chief function which *as a political power* the Eastern Empire performed throughout the Middle Ages was to act as a bulwark for Europe, and for that civilisation which Greece had created and Rome had inherited and diffused, against Asiatic aggression. Since the rise of the Sasanid power in the third century, Asia had been attempting, with varying success, to resume the rôle which it had played under the Achaemenids. The arms of Alexander had delivered for hundreds of years the Eastern coasts and waters of the Mediterranean from all danger from an Asiatic power. The Sasanids finally succeeded in reaching the Mediterranean shores and the Bosphorus. The rôles of Europe and Asia were again reversed, and it was now for Byzantium to play on a larger stage the part formerly played by Athens and Sparta in a struggle for life and death. Heraclius proved himself not only a Themistocles but in some measure an Alexander. He not only checked the victorious advance of the enemy; he completely destroyed the power of the Great King and made him his vassal. But within ten years the rôles were reversed once more in that amazing transformation scene in which an obscure Asiatic people which had always seemed destined to play a minor part became suddenly one of the strongest powers in the world. Constantinople had again to fight for her life, and the danger was imminent and the strain unrelaxed for eighty years. Though the Empire did not succeed in barring the road to Spain and Sicily, its rulers held the gates of Europe at the Propontis and made it impossible for them to sweep over Europe as they had swept over Syria and Egypt. Centuries passed, and the Comnenians guarded Europe from the Seljūqs.

The Ottomans were the latest bearers of the Asiatic menace. If the Eastern Empire had not been mortally wounded and reduced to the dimensions of a petty state by the greed and brutality of the Western brigands who called themselves Crusaders, it is possible that the Turks might never have gained a footing in Europe. Even as it was, the impetus of their first victorious advance was broken by the tenacity of the Palaeologi—assisted it is true by the arms of Tīmūr. They had reached the Danube sixty years before Constantinople fell. When this at length happened, the first force and fury of their attack had been spent, and it is perhaps due to this delay that the Danube and the Carpathians were to mark the limit of Asiatic rule in Europe and that St Peter's was not to suffer the fate of St Sophia. Even in the last hours of its life, the Empire was still true to its traditional rôle of bulwark of Europe.

As a civilised state, we may say that the Eastern Empire performed three principal functions. As in its early years the Roman Empire laid the foundations of civilisation in the West and educated Celtic and German peoples, so in its later period it educated the Slavs of eastern Europe. Russia, Bulgaria, and Serbia owed it everything and bore its stamp. Secondly, it exercised a silent but constant and considerable influence on western Europe by sending its own manufactures and the products of the East to Italy, France, and Germany. Many examples of its embroidered textile fabrics and its jewellery have been preserved in the West. In the third place, it guarded safely the heritage of classical Greek literature which has had on the modern world a penetrating influence difficult to estimate. That we owe our possession of the masterpieces of Hellenic thought and imagination to the Byzantines everyone knows, but everyone does not remember that those books would not have travelled to Italy in the fourteenth and fifteenth centuries, because they would not have existed, if the Greek classics had not been read habitually by the educated subjects of the Eastern Empire and therefore continued to be copied.

Here we touch on a most fundamental contrast between the Eastern Empire and the western European states of the Middle Ages. The well-to-do classes in the West were as a rule illiterate, with the exception of ecclesiastics; among the well-to-do classes in the Byzantine world education was the rule, and education meant not merely reading, writing, and arithmetic, but the study of ancient Greek grammar and the reading of classical authors. The old traditions of Greek education had never died out. In court circles at Constantinople everyone who was not an utter parvenu would recognise and understand a quotation from Homer. In consequence of this difference, the intellectual standards in the West where book-learning was reserved for a particular class, and in the East where every boy and girl whose parents could afford to pay was educated, were entirely different. The advantages of science and training and system were understood in Byzantine society.

The appreciation of method and system which the Byzantines inherited both from the Greeks and from the Romans is conspicuously shewn in their military establishment and their conduct of war. Here their intellectuality stands out in vivid contrast with the rude dullness displayed in the modes of warfare practised in the West. Tactics were carefully studied, and the treatises on war which the officers used were kept up to date. The tacticians apprehended that it was stupid to employ uniform methods in campaigns against different foes. They observed carefully the military habits

of the various peoples with whom they had to fight—
Saracens, Lombards, Franks, Slavs, Hungarians—and
thought out different rules for dealing with each. The
soldiers were most carefully and efficiently drilled. They
understood organisation and the importance of not
leaving details to chance, of not neglecting small points
in equipment. Their armies were accompanied by am-
bulances and surgeons. Contrast the feudal armies of
the West, ill-disciplined, with no organisation, under
leaders who had not the most rudimentary idea of
tactics, who put their faith in sheer strength and courage,
and attacked all antagonists in exactly the same way.
More formidable the Western knights might be than
Slavs or Magyars, but in the eyes of a Byzantine officer
they were equally rude barbarians who had not yet
learned that war is an art which requires intelligence as
well as valour. In the period in which the Empire was
strong, before it lost the provinces which provided its
best recruits, its army was beyond comparison the best
fighting machine in Europe. When a Byzantine army was
defeated, it was always the incompetence of the general
or some indiscretion on his part, never inefficiency or
cowardice of the troops, that was to blame. The great
disaster of Manzikert (1071), from which perhaps the
decline of the Eastern Empire may be dated, was caused
by the imbecility of the brave Emperor who was in
command. A distinguished student of the art of war has
observed that Gibbon's dictum, "the vices of Byzantine
armies were inherent, their victories accidental",* is

[* v. Bury's *Gibbon* [1898], vol. v, pp. 59–60, "The genius of Belisarius
and Narses had been formed without a master, and expired without
a disciple. Neither honour, nor patriotism, nor generous superstition,
could animate the lifeless bodies of slaves and strangers, who had
succeeded to the honours of the legions—their vices were inherent, their
victories were accidental, and their costly maintenance exhausted the
substance of a state which they were unable to defend".]

precisely the reverse of the truth. He is perfectly right.

Military science enabled the Roman Empire to hold its own for many centuries against the foes around it, east and west and north. Internally, its permanence and stability depended above all on the rule of Roman law. Its subjects had always "the advantage of possessing a systematic administration of justice enforced by fixed legal procedure"; they were not at the mercy of caprice. They could contrast their courts in which justice was administered with a systematic observance of rules, with those in which Mohammedan lawyers dispensed justice. The feeling that they were much better off under the government of Constantinople than their Eastern neighbours engendered a loyal attachment to the Empire, notwithstanding what they might suffer under an oppressive fiscal system.[1]

The influence of lawyers on the administration was always great, and may have been one of the facts which account for the proverbial conservatism of Byzantine civilisation. But that conservatism has generally been exaggerated, and even in the domain of law there was a development, though the foundations and principles remained those which were embodied in the legislation of Justinian.

The old Roman law, as expounded by the classical jurists, was in the East considerably modified in practice here and there by Greek and oriental custom, and there are traces of this influence in the laws of Justinian. But Justinianean law shews very few marks of ecclesiastical influence which in the seventh and following centuries led to various changes, particularly in laws relating to marriage. The law-book of the Isaurian Emperor, Leo III, was in some respects revolutionary, and

[1] Compare Finlay, *History of Greece*, II, 22–4; I, 411–12.

although at the end of the ninth century the Macedonian Emperors, eager to renounce all the works of the heretical Isaurians, professed to return to the pure principles of Justinian, they retained many of the innovations and compromised with others. The principal reforms of Leo were too much in accordance with public opinion to be undone. The legal status of concubinate for instance was definitely abolished. Only marriages between Christians were recognised as valid. Marriages between first and second cousins were forbidden. Fourth marriages were declared illegal and even third were discountenanced. It is remarkable however that in the matter of divorce, where the differences between the views of State and Church had been sharpest and where the Isaurians had given effect to the un-Roman ecclesiastical doctrine that marriage is indissoluble, the Macedonians returned to the common-sense view of Justinian and Roman lawyers that marriage like other contracts between human beings may be dissolved. We can see new tendencies too in the history of the *patria potestas*. The Iconoclasts substituted for it a parental *potestas*, assigning to the mother rights similar to those of the father. Other changes are mentioned below in Chapter xxii, pp. 709–10.[1]

In criminal law there was a marked change in tendency. From Augustus to Justinian penalties were ever becoming severer and new crimes being invented. After Justinian the movement was in the direction of mildness. In the eighth century only two or three crimes were punishable by death. One of these was murder and in

[1] It has been commonly held that the codes known as the Rhodian (Maritime) Law, the Farmer's (Rural) Law, and the Military Law were the work of the Isaurian Emperors, and this view is taken below in Chapter i (pp. 4–5) and Chapter xxii (pp. 708, 710). In the opinion of the present writer the investigations of Mr Ashburner have rendered it quite untenable, at least in regard to the two first.

this case the extreme penalty might be avoided if the murderer sought refuge in a church. On the other hand penalties of mutilation were extended and systematised. This kind of punishment had been inflicted in much earlier times and authorised in one or two cases by Justinian. In the eighth century we find amputations of the tongue, hand, and nose part of the criminal system, and particularly applied in dealing with sexual offences. If such punishments strike us to-day as barbaric (though in England, for instance, mutilation was inflicted little more than two centuries ago), they were then considered as a humane substitute for death, and the Church approved them because a tongueless or nose-less sinner had time to repent.* In the same way, it was a common practice to blind, instead of killing, rebels or unsuccessful candidates for the throne. The tendency to avoid capital punishment is illustrated by the credible record that during the reign of John Comnenus there were no executions.

The fact that in domestic policy the Eastern Empire was far from being obstinately conservative is also illustrated by the reform of legal education in the eleventh century, when it was realised that a system which had been in practice for a long time did not work well and another was substituted (as is explained in Chapter XXII, p. 719).** That conception of the later Empire which has made the word Byzantine almost equivalent to Chinese was based on ignorance, and is now discredited. It is obvious that no State could have lasted so long in a changing world, if it had not had the capacity of adapting itself to new conditions. Its administrative machinery was being constantly modified

[* This subject is carried further by Bury in *R.P.A. Annual*, 1918, "The influence of Christianity on Roman Criminal Law".]

[** Chap. XXII, *Byzantine Legislation* 565–1453, by Professor Paul Collinet.]

by capable and hardworking rulers of whom there were many; the details of the system at the end of the tenth century differed at ever so many points from those of the eighth. As for art and literature, there were ups and downs, declines and renascences, throughout the whole duration of the Empire. It is only in quite recent years that Byzantine literature and Byzantine art have been methodically studied; in these wide fields of research Krumbacher's *Byzantine Literature* and Strzygowski's *Orient oder Rom* were pioneer works marking a new age. Now that we are getting to know the facts better and the darkness is gradually lifting, we have come to see that the history of the Empire is far from being a monotonous chronicle of palace revolutions, circus riots, theological disputes, tedious ceremonies in a servile court, and to realise that, as in any other political society, conditions were continually changing and in each succeeding age new political and social problems presented themselves for which some solution had to be found. If the chief interest in history lies in observing such changes, watching new problems shape themselves and the attempts of rulers or peoples to solve them, and seeing how the characters of individuals and the accidents which befall them determine the course of events, the story of the Eastern Empire is at least as interesting as that of any medieval State, or perhaps more interesting because its people were more civilised and intellectual than other Europeans and had a longer political experience behind them. On the ecclesiastical side it offers the longest and most considerable experiment of a State-Church that Christendom has ever seen.

The Crusades were, for the Eastern Empire, simply a series of barbarian invasions of a particularly embarrassing kind, and in the present volume they are treated merely from this point of view and their general significance in universal history is not considered. The full treatment of their causes and psychology and the consecutive story of the movement are reserved for Vol. v.

But the earlier history of Venice has been included in this volume. The character of Venice and her career were decided by the circumstance that she was subject to the Eastern Emperors before she became independent. She was extra-Italian throughout the Middle Ages; she never belonged to the Carolingian Kingdom of Italy. And after she had slipped into independence almost without knowing it—there was never a violent breaking away from her allegiance to the sovrans oᴌ Constantinople—she moved still in the orbit of the Empire; and it was on the ruins of the Empire, dismembered by the criminal enterprise of her Duke Dandolo, that she reached the summit of her power as mistress in the Aegean and in Greece. She was the meeting-place of two civilisations, but it was eastern not western Europe that controlled her history and lured her ambitions. Her citizens spoke a Latin tongue and in spiritual matters acknowledged the supremacy of the elder Rome, but the influence from new Rome had penetrated deep, and their great Byzantine basilica is a visible reminder of their long political connexion with the Eastern Empire.

APPENDIX

Causes of the Survival of the
Roman Empire in the East

CAUSES OF THE SURVIVAL OF THE ROMAN EMPIRE IN THE EAST*

THE causes of decline did not operate equally in all parts of the Empire. Thus Egypt did not share in the general depopulation; and the Asiatic provinces seem not to have been affected to the same extent by the evils which led, in the West, to the destruction of the middle class and the growth of vast estates. In the fourth century, the commerce of the Mediterranean and the carrying trade of Western Europe were mainly in the hands of the Greeks; and, in general, the Eastern half of the Roman world was more prosperous and wealthy than the Western. Moreover—

the numbers of the Greek population in the Eastern Empire gave a unity of feeling to the inhabitants, a nationality of character to the government, and a degree of power to the Christian church, which were completely wanting in the ill-cemented structure of the West.[1]

This unity and quasi-nationality assumed some shape and substance when the Empire was finally divided after the death of Theodosius.

In the Western Empire, the people, the Roman aristocracy, and the imperial administration, formed three separate sections of society, unconnected either by religious opinion or national feelings; and each was ready to enter into alliances with armed bands of foreigners in the Empire in order to serve their respective interests or gratify their prejudices or passions.[2]

It is an essential moment in the situation that in the East there was no powerful pagan aristocracy. "The popular

[* This extract is given from the *Quarterly Review*, vol. cxcii, No. 383, pp. 146–55, by permission of the Editor. The article was written in 1900 and the theory of causation plays a large part in it. As has been indicated elsewhere, Bury's views as regards the fall of the Empire in the West were subsequently revised. There is however no such evidence that he altered his views about the survival of the Empire in the East, and they are given here as being an interesting pendant to his Byzantine studies.]

[1] Finlay, i, p. 147.   [2] *Ibid.*, p. 138.

element in the social organisation of the Greek people, by its alliance with Christianity, infused into society the energy which saved the Eastern Empire";[1] and the clergy in the East seem to have possessed more influence, and to have been able to protect the people to some extent against the oppression of the Government officials.

If we examine the resistance which the Illyrian peninsula presented to the barbarians, we are struck by the following points. European Greece, which had declined under the early Empire, had recovered in some measure its well-being and populousness, and though an invader might plunder it easily enough, it was so populous and homogeneous that a permanent occupation would not have been an easy matter. The task which faced an invader who aimed at permanent conquest was vastly increased by the number of strongly walled towns in the Illyrian peninsula. The cases in which even a small fortress successfully defied Goth or Hun illustrate this difficulty. Moreover, geographical configuration defended the Eastern Empire.

> The sea which separated the European and Asiatic provinces opposed physical difficulties to invaders, while it afforded great facilities for defence, retreat, and renewed attack to the Roman forces, as long as they could maintain a naval superiority.[2]

The mountain ranges in the Balkan peninsula and in the Asiatic provinces, though not a safeguard against invasion, afforded the inhabitants a bulwark which rendered them more active and daring in resisting the invaders. It may be added that while the wealth of the Eastern Empire[3] invited the barbarians, "it furnished the means of repulsing their attacks or of bribing their forbearance".

In short, the East was more united and vigorous than the West, more populous, richer, and physically less easy for an invader to occupy. But with all these advantages it might not have escaped dismemberment if Constantine had not had the inspiration to plant a new capital of the Empire on the shores of the Bosporus. The advantages of its site

[1] Finlay, i, p. 138.　　　　[2] Ibid., i, p. 163.
[3] Due especially to its commerce, and the gold and silver mines of Thrace and Pontus. Cp. Finlay, i, p. 167.

have been so often described that they are almost a common-place, but they have been put so strikingly and freshly by Mr A. van Millingen, in his recent scientific work on the walls and gates of Constantinople, that we need not hesitate to quote a part of his description (*Byzantine Constantinople*, p. 4).

No city owes so much to its site....Nowhere is the influence of geography upon history more strikingly marked. Here, to a degree that is marvellous, the possibilities of the freest and widest inter-course blend with the possibilities of complete isolation. No city can be more in the world and out of the world. It is the meeting point of some of the most important highways on the globe, whether by sea or land; the centre around which diverse, vast, and wealthy countries lie within easy reach, inviting intimate com-mercial relations, and permitting extended political control. Here the peninsula of Asia Minor, stretching like a bridge across the seas that sunder Asia and Europe, narrows the waters between the two great continents to a stream only half a mile across. Hither the Mediterranean ascends, through the avenues of the Ægean and the Marmora, from the regions of the south; while the Euxine and the Azoff spread a pathway to the regions of the north. Here is a harbour within which the largest and richest fleets can find a perfect shelter.

But no less remarkable is the facility with which the great world, so near at hand, can be excluded. Access to this point by sea is possible only through the straits of the Hellespont on the one side, and through the straits of the Bosporus on the other—defiles which, when properly guarded, no hostile navy could penetrate. These channels, with the Sea of Marmora between them, formed, moreover, a natural moat which prevented an Asiatic foe from coming within striking distance of the city; while the narrow breadth of the promontory on which the city stands allowed the erection of fortifications along the west, which could be held against immense armies by a comparatively small force.

This impregnable fortress was the palladium of the Balkan peninsula. We believe that its proximity was, above all others, the consideration which drove Alaric, Attila, and Theodoric to turn away from the Illyrian provinces. There was no city to do for the West what Constantinople did for the East. If Honorius had decided, like Valentinian I and Gratian, to make Trier the seat of empire, he might have saved Gaul, but he would have sacrificed Italy; by choosing Ravenna, he saved Italy and lost Gaul. If he had established his government at Rome he might have saved her from the humiliation of Alaric's sieges; but from a geographical point of view no city was less fitted to be the centre of her Empire, or even of the Western half of her Empire, than Rome herself. At this time she was equally unfitted from a political point of view; and this is the secret of the choice of Ravenna by Honorius. There was a distinct lack of sympathy between the Roman senators, most of whom were still devotedly attached to paganism, and the Christian court of the Emperor. This antagonism is in marked contrast with the state of things at Constantinople. There might be a pagan party there, but it was not an influential order, it was merely a handful of individuals. Arcadius was enveloped by a congenial atmosphere in Byzantium; at Rome Honorius could never have felt himself at home.

The population of Constantinople had increased so enormously since its foundation that it became necessary to extend its area by taking in the suburbs and erecting new fortifications. The enlargement had been foreseen in the reign of Theodosius the Great,[1] but was not carried out till the reign of Theodosius II. The able and experienced prefect Anthemius, who guided the helm of the Eastern Empire in the infancy of Theodosius, undertook this task and determined the future shape of the city. Anthemius did as much for the East as Stilicho did for the West, though the world has remembered Stilicho and forgotten Anthemius.[2] He had to face the Huns, who were now, under their chieftain Uldin, beginning to attack the Illyrian provinces. Anthemius beat them back beyond the Danube, and established upon that river a flotilla of two hundred and fifty vessels; he took care that the walls of the Illyrian cities, which had suffered through the Visigothic devastations, were rebuilt; and in planning the new walls of the capital he was preparing con-

---

[1] This is clear from a passage in an oration of Themistius quoted by Mr van Millingen, p. 42.

[2] Anthemius too was celebrated by a poet, named Theotimus; but the work of Theotimus is lost, and we may be sure that it did not approach the level of Claudian.

sciously for the Hunnic war which he foresaw, unconsciously for the assaults of successive hordes of barbarians, still beyond the Roman horizon, but destined to arrive one after another and vainly knock at the mighty gates for more than a thousand years. The inner of the two western walls is the wall of Anthemius, and it probably saved the city a siege by Attila. But violent earthquakes—Constantinople had no deadlier enemy—destroyed portions of this wall before the end of the same reign, and we may wonder that Attila did not seize the opportunity. The prefect Constantine met the crisis with an energy worthy of Anthemius, and his name, in Greek and in Latin, may still be read on one of the gates. He not only restored the Anthemian wall but he erected a second wall in front of it, outside of which was constructed a broad and deep moat. Thus the city was placed behind a triple line of defence.

The walls were flanked by 192 towers, while the ground between the two walls and that between the outer wall and the moat provided room for the action of large bodies of troops. These five portions of the fortifications rose tier above tier, and combined to form a barricade 190–207 feet thick, and over 100 feet high.[1]

The reign of Theodosius II was thus of the highest importance in the history of Constantinople, and thereby in that of the Eastern Empire. But the military fortification of the great citadel does not exhaust its importance. A university was founded at Constantinople, and the Theodosian code of laws was issued.

The Theodosian Code (says Finlay) afforded the people the means of arraigning the conduct of their rulers before fixed principles of law, and the University of Constantinople established the influence of Greek literature and gave the Greek language an official position in the Eastern Empire.[2]

The point which it here concerns us to insist upon is that these measures are significant of a steady desire for solid reform and the good of the people, a desire which is also shown in the alleviation which was afforded by two large remissions of arrears of taxation, wiping out the claims for unpaid taxes over a period of sixty years. Fortunately the

[1] van Millingen, p. 46.   [2] Finlay, i, p. 173.

reign of Theodosius did not stand alone. He was followed by a series of able sovereigns—Marcian, Leo, Zeno, Anastasius—who, whatever their faults may have been, were steadily bent on reform. They were "men born in the middle or lower ranks of society", and "appear to have participated in popular sympathies to a degree natural only to men who had long lived without courtly honours". It is certain that these strong intelligent men, who form such a striking contrast to the later Emperors of the West, contributed incalculably to the conservation of the Eastern Empire. They had no brilliant or showy qualities, and they are now well-nigh forgotten; but Leo, Zeno, and Anastasius were exceptionally able statesmen.

In the fifth century, then, a healthy spirit of reform, due to the fact that the Government was in touch with the people, manifested itself in the East, while in the West the pathetic and forlorn appeals of such Emperors as Majorian, seeking to arrest decay and suppress intolerable abuses, evoked no response. But there was another moment in the situation which, if we mistake not, had considerable significance. We have already referred to the fact that the chief ministers of Honorius and his successors were men of German race. We would not detract from the great services of Stilicho, or from the greater services of Aetius, but we would point out that these statesmen were sources of weakness, as well as strength. This will be readily admitted in the case of Count Ricimer, whose policy clearly paved the way for Odovacar; but it is also true of Stilicho and Aetius. If Honorius had been a strong ruler and had not consigned his power to Stilicho, or if Stilicho had not been a German, it is highly probable that the Empire would not have been divided by the revolt of Constantine, whose tyranny helped the successes of the barbarians. It has been said that the Vandals would never have occupied Africa if they had not been invited by Count Boniface; and though this statement is an exaggeration, the fact remains that the disasters of the reign of Valentinian III were partly due to the jealousy and antagonism which existed between Aetius, a minister of German stock, and Romans like Boniface. Now the Eastern Empire was also threatened by the ascendency of men of foreign extraction, first in the reign of Arcadius, and again in the reign of Leo. Each time the danger was averted. On the first occasion it took the form of an actual rebellion of Gothic troops under an ambitious leader named Gainas, whose programme was to revive the lost cause of Arianism. After the death of Marcian (A.D. 457) a powerful general of Alan race, named Aspar—an Arian, like most of the barbarians who embraced Christianity—assisted Leo to ascend the throne, and it might have seemed that he was destined to play in the East the same part, and to exercise the same authority, which had fallen to Stilicho, Aetius, and Ricimer in the West. But Leo apprehended the situation; he averted the immediate peril by assassinating Aspar, and he forestalled future dangers of the same kind by a reform of the military system. He began to recruit the army out of native troops, and ceased to rely, as his predecessors had relied, on foreign mercenaries. What Leo thus began, Zeno carried out. The great work of Zeno's reign, as Finlay observes, "was the formation of an army of native troops to serve as a counterpoise to the barbarian mercenaries who threatened the Eastern Empire with the same fate as the Western".

Within the limits of an article we have been unable to do more than indicate the various causes which determined the dismemberment of the Empire in the fifth century. Each, if it were to be illustrated fully, would almost demand an article to itself; but it may be of service to bring them together thus into a connected statement. We are now in a position to give a summary answer to the enquiry which we have attempted—an answer, however, which cannot be so briefly expressed as Professor Seeley's "depopulation". The Roman Empire as a whole was weakened by depopulation; Italy suffered eminently; and the original causes of this evil are not clear, though we can observe the forces—fiscal oppression, economic ignorance, the institution of slavery, and a new spirit of asceticism—which hindered the population from recovering itself. Like other ancient States, the Roman Empire suffered through ignorance of sound principles of economy; but to this universally prevailing evil it added a limitation of its own, which it inherited from the Republic, a certain antipathy or indifference to commerce. If an Adam Smith had arisen, the Empire might have been rescued from decline; but the only means which its rulers found to strengthen it was the settlement of barbarians in the provinces and the admission of barbarians into the legions.

This Germanising of the Empire (which was accompanied by a reciprocal process of Romanising the Germans) chiefly affected the European, Latin-speaking provinces; and it smoothed the way there for the ultimate ascendency of the German race. One of its immediate effects was a relaxation of military discipline, the upgrowth of a free spirit in the army; and without this the rebellions, revolutions, and usurpations of the third century would hardly have been possible. The disunion within the State at this period would have soon made it a prey for its enemies unless Diocletian had reorganised it and Constantine consolidated and completed the work of Diocletian. But though these statesmen restored the unity and defended the frontiers of the State, their new system aggravated, instead of removing, some essential weaknesses. The municipal classes declined in prosperity and were ultimately ruined; and this process was hastened by the incredible corruption of the collectors of revenue under the Constantinian system. Here again, however, the West suffered more severely than the more populous East. Neither Government did much for commerce and industries, but the industries and commerce which existed were mainly in the hands of the inhabitants of the Greek and Asiatic provinces. In these parts of the Empire men were better able to bear the fiscal burdens. Moreover Constantine, by his greatest work, the foundation of Constantinople, did for the East what he was unable to do for the West, and not only gave it a citadel but supplied a rallying-point for a sort of national unity. Christianity and the influence of the Church acted as a cement of such a unity, whereas in the West the members of the wealthy senatorial class were largely pagans and were out of touch both with their humbler fellow-subjects and with the Government.

In the same connexion it may be observed that there

existed in the Eastern Empire a public opinion which was able more easily to make itself felt than in the West. The Eastern provinces were also more favourably situated in point of geographical configuration. Accordingly it came about that, though the East had to bear the first brunt of the northern barbarians pressing in upon the Empire in the fourth century, and though it suffered severely from their devastations, yet the invaders saw that they would be unable to make good a permanently satisfactory lodgment in the East, and decided to divert their efforts to the feebler and distracted West, where men of their own race were influential in the State. Delivered of the presence of Alaric and his Visigoths, the Eastern Empire had escaped from its first great danger; and its future safety was confirmed and assured by a succession of able statesmen, from Anthemius to Anastasius I. It may be said that the strength of the East was a cause of calamity to the West, since Visigoth, Hun, and Ostrogoth turned successively from the Balkan lands to seek conquest in Italy, Gaul, or Spain; but this is no reproach to the rulers of Byzantium, who could reply that if the realm of Arcadius and Theodosius had been weaker, such weakness would assuredly not have saved the realm of Honorius and Valentinian. In the West all the causes of decline operated without check, and the ascendency of Germans at court was a source of division and discontent which led to rebellions. With the help of all these considerations we may be able to understand how the Latin half of the Empire was dismembered, while the Greek half held together and perpetuated the Empire of Rome.

Our enquiry, finished here, might naturally lead us on to meditate on the causes which brought about the subsequent dismemberment of the Eastern Empire by Persians, Saracens, and Bulgarians in the seventh century. Professor Seeley bracketed this later series of events with the events known as the fall of the Western Empire, and sought to embrace both under the same solution. We regard this view as completely erroneous. The causes which led to the success of the Saracens were wholly distinct from the causes which led to the success of the Germans. In one, but only in one, respect was there a continuity in the process. The ravages of Goths, Huns, and other barbarian hordes in the fifth century in the Illyrian provinces caused anew a decline in the population which facilitated the gradual infiltration of a new set of strangers, the Slavs. This influx began actively in the sixth century, and smoothed the way for the Slavonic and Bulgarian conquests in the seventh century—a repetition of the same process which we witnessed in the case of the German conquests. The Slavonic settlements were one cause of disintegration. A second, and perhaps the most vital and far-reaching, was the religious disunion of the Empire. The political importance of the theological controversies which raged in the fifth century as to the nature or natures of Christ can hardly be too highly estimated. In Egypt and Syria men's intellects did not move on the same lines as in the Greek provinces; and this fundamental divergence in spirit and modes of thought expressed itself in rival doctrines touching Christ's nature and personality. Never was the decree of an ecclesiastical council more fatal to the State than the wire-drawn formula issued by the Churchmen who met at Chalcedon. Egypt and Syria were alienated, and the tendency towards a quasi-national unity, which had been perceptible, was checked by this religious division. The mistake of Chalcedon must be largely imputed to the un- fortunate influence of the Bishop of Rome; and when it had been committed, no more urgent problem faced the Govern- ment of Constantinople than to discover some means of rectifying it. Zeno and the able Patriarch Acacius, a Church- man exceptionally free from bigotry, grappled with the difficulty, and an Act of Union (Henotikon) was proclaimed, which recognised the doctrines of Nicæa and Ephesus and ignored the decision of Chalcedon. On this basis the Churches of Alexandria and Antioch were reunited in communion with Constantinople, and the religious peace of the East was restored. Statesmanship and tact could have maintained this union, but the disastrous policy of Justinian undid the work of Zeno and revived the political error of Chalcedon.

If any man can be regarded as distinctly, if partially, responsible for such a vast event as the dismemberment of the Eastern Empire, first by the Persians and then by the

Saracens, we say deliberately that it is the Emperor Justinian. We fear that this statement will appear startling and paradoxical; for we are accustomed to look upon Justinian's reign as an epoch of singular glory and brilliance. Two glorious achievements, beyond all blame or cavil, were accomplished under his auspices. Lawyers of unrivalled learning enriched the world with the *Digest*, the *Institutes*, and the *Code*; architects of matchless skill and soaring imagination built the church of St Sophia. But the famous conquests of the ambitious ruler were purchased at an exorbitant price. In the first place, seeing that in order to carry out his scheme of recovering Italy and the Western provinces from their German lords it would be of the highest importance to reconcile the Roman Church, which had been alienated by the policy of Zeno, he revived the doctrine of Chalcedon. Thus Rome was conciliated at the expense of the unity of the East, and the attempts which Justinian subsequently made to alleviate the consequences of his act only served to make the evil worse. The East was irrevocably disunited; Egypt and Syria were alienated from Constantinople. In the second place, Justinian's conquests were an enormous strain on the treasury. The grave struggle in which the Empire was then involved with the great Persian king Chosroes imposed such a heavy burden on the revenue that a ruler in Justinian's position was not justified in gratuitously undertaking other wars. If Justinian had merely spent the fund which had been accumulated by the economies of his predecessors, it might have been well; but in order to meet the expenses of his policy he overtaxed his subjects and revived financial oppression in its worst form.[1]* Alleviation of fiscal burdens had been one of the best features of the reigns of the Emperors who preceded him; and Anastasius had even reformed the curial system by doing away with the principle of joint responsibility. But the progress which their discreet policy inaugurated was undone by Justinian; the merciless system of impositions, associated with the abominable name of John the Cappa-

---

[1] The evidence for this is treated in Panchenko's full and important study on the *Historia Arcana* of Procopius; [* published at St Petersburg: Press of Imperial Academy of Sciences].

docian, impoverished and ruined the people, and precipi-
tated the Empire down that path of decline which ended in
the disasters of the next century.

It would exceed the space and scope of this article to go
on to show how within its diminished borders the Eastern
Empire recovered its strength, so that during the eighth,
ninth, and tenth centuries, as Mr Frederic Harrison observes
in his eloquent Rede lecture, "the Emperors of New Rome
ruled over a settled State which, if not as powerful in arms,
was far more rich in various resources, more cultured, more
truly modern, than any in Western Europe".* In the second
decline, if we may so speak, which began in the eleventh
century and culminated in the Latin capture of Constantinople (A.D. 1204), we see repeated some of those
economic causes which induced the decay of the early
Empire. We can mark especially the fatal growth of vast
estates and the ruin of the small proprietors—a process
against which the Emperors had legislated and struggled
in vain. The day of doom came for the Younger as it had
come for the Elder Rome. It is perhaps seldom realised how
much longer the sway of Constantinople as an Imperial city
endured than the rule of Rome herself. Even if we date the
Empire of Rome from the conquest of Sicily, her first
province, in the third century before our era, and extend
the duration of her power to the subjugation of Italy by
Odovacar (A.D. 476), her period amounts to little more than
seven centuries. On the other hand, even if we omit to
count the two hundred years of the restored Empire of the
Palæologi, Constantinople, from her foundation to her capture by the Crusaders, reigned for little less than nine
centuries. We are satisfied that this advantage which the
daughter city enjoyed was due, above all, to the incomparable
strength of her situation and her walls.

[* *Byzantine History in the Early Middle Ages*. The Rede Lecture,
June 12, 1900, by Frederic Harrison, Macmillan & Co. (1900), p. 8.]

INDEX

INDEX

I. GENERAL

II. CLASSICAL AND BYZANTINE

CAMBRIDGE : PRINTED BY
W. LEWIS, M.A.
AT THE UNIVERSITY PRESS